T0326718

121:1 · January 2022

Black Temporality in Times of Crisis
Badia Ahad and Habiba Ibrahim, Special Issue Editors

AGAINST the DAY

Universities as New Battlegrounds
Zeynep Gambetti and Saygun Gökarıksel, Editors

Habiba Ibrahim and Badia Ahad

Introduction:
Black Temporality in Times of Crisis

This special issue of the *South Atlantic Quarterly* explores how experiences of times of crisis at any historical period are formative of Black life. Black temporality of crisis is an analytical framework that uncovers how history is constituted through experiences that often escape the brush of serious historical consideration, in addition to clearly discernible and momentous events. In this special issue we focus on *crisis* as a critical term in our considerations of Black culture, feeling, being, and life in order to pinpoint temporalities of transformation and times of action. How might various aspects of temporality contribute to what is knowable about Black life and moments of crisis? How does focusing on crisis reveal the constructedness of what is frequently taken to be natural and inevitable? How does crisis draw us toward the precarities, but also the possibilities, of Black life?

The previous century opened in a time of crisis. W. E. B. Du Bois described it as the potential of a horrifying return. As he asks in *The Souls of Black Folk*, "The power of the ballot we need in sheer self-defence—else what shall save us from a second slavery?" ([1903] 1999: 15). In other words, if we fail to wrest political power *now*, what will prevent slavery from returning? A few years later,

The South Atlantic Quarterly 121:1, January 2022
DOI 10.1215/00382876-9561489 © 2022 Duke University Press

in the inaugural editorial for the *Crisis* in 1910, Du Bois explains why *crisis* was the chosen term for the periodical: "It takes its name from the fact that the editors believe that this is a critical time in the history of the advancement of men" (10). The "critical time" of the twentieth century's second decade was a decisive moment at which either the "world-old dream of human brotherhood" or the repetition of racialization's "awful history" would prevail. For Du Bois and a wide sphere of colleagues, cultural producers, activists, and intellectuals, *crisis* expressed urgency. In the shadow of the reactionary post-Reconstruction era, one had to act in order to stave off the reenchantment of the past.

In the twenty-first century, the temporality of crisis—the critical time of action—pulses like a heartbeat of Black life: Hurricane Katrina, the subprime mortgage crisis, deadly acts of police brutality, one after the other. Just as the power of the ballot was a critical concern in Du Bois's time, so too are voting rights imperiled in ours. Contemporary Black life periodically reveals the hidden outcomes of long historical processes in the form of environmental, financial, social, and political crises. Thus, while a crisis is generally considered a moment that necessitates urgent action, the constancy of crisis manifests in the experience of an enduring, unending, and unfinished past. To the degree that the crisis of Black life feels constant, it has a more quotidian quality. Constant, quotidian experiences of crisis in the lives of the African descended that can be distinguished from conceptions of trauma. The traumatic suggests that devastation has already happened, that it exists in the past tense. Yet, the prolonged state of crisis creates a sense of liminality that is neither past nor present; instead, the time of crisis feels more like flight rather than arrival. Margo Crawford, following Jose Muñoz, describes this sensation as the "not yet here" (3). As the essays in this issue demonstrate, the time of Black crisis takes the form of "proposition," "anticipation," and "finna"—the Black vernacular future perfect tense, or, a projection of a future that is certain to come.

In this brief introduction, we consider such non-arrival through concepts of "quotidian time" and "times of return," which expand the framework of crisis beyond the immediacy and swiftness of urgency. To this end, we posit that 2020 will forever exist for us not only as a moment of crisis but also as a time of visceral temporality, consisting of both quotidian and repetitive experience. "Pandemic time" has emerged as the experience of time's (simultaneous) expansion and compression, felt through the slow time of monotony, the racing time of anxiety, the cyclical time of mourning. Our framework of crisis, which we use to explore the general and present-day conditions of Black temporality, draws from paradoxical registers of time felt in 2020 and its aftereffects. A time of crisis demands action and makes no clear demands at all; it confronts us with new dangers and returns us to the past; it holds us in forms of suspension and expectation. Ultimately, we consider Black modes of emergence—the ordinary and radical possibilities of Black life now—in times of emergency.

Quotidian time is surprisingly conspicuous: feelings of everyday time are attached to the uneven distribution of labor and economic vulnerability; compression of time has implications for wellness and care—yet another denial of humanity. By definition, a crisis connotes a sense of urgency, of chaos. However, as the recent COVID-19 pandemic has taught us, living in a crisis-state over a prolonged and indefinite period of time ceases to *feel* like a crisis. Instead, it begins to feel like . . . life, like affects "rooted not in fixed conditions of possibility but in the actual lines of potential that a something coming together calls to mind and sets in motion, they can be seen as both the pressure points of events or banalities suffered and the trajectories that forces might take if they were to go unchecked" (Stewart 2007: 2). There are implications when times of crisis become quotidian. We become desensitized to unwellness, death, grieving, mourning as they emerge as part of the everyday. Time is at once drawn out and compressed. Living in a steady state of crisis is now a globally familiar dread, and yet a doubled doom for folks who have managed to exist—even thrived—under the crisis of Blackness for lifetimes. To persist in an ongoing state of crisis is to be made vulnerable by time's indefatigability.

In addition to time's affective registers, the pandemic and national racial unrest evoked an awareness of time's structural dimensions. The year 2020's singular moment of crisis split into two crises or, as it was frequently described, "two pandemics." Through the Du Boisian twoness of crisis, one ever feels the repetition of time and the novelty of the present. State-sanctioned brutality that killed George Floyd, Breonna Taylor, Philando Castile, and millions more is recursive, and repetition is a reminder of the interminable past. At the same time, the COVID-19 pandemic impacted all lives as a distinctive once-in-a-lifetime event. But underlying the universality of shared infection was a historically constituted structure of racism, which Ruth Wilson Gilmore (2007: 28) defines as "the state-sanctioned or extralegal production and exploitation of group-differentiated vulnerability to premature death." As a concept that captured both the repetitive and the new, "two pandemics" expressed the uneven effects of historical violence, compounded by the problems of the present. It also conveyed the quickness and slowness of such an intensified time of crisis. The quick death that police officer Derek Chauvin caused by fatally kneeling on George Floyd's neck shared the same framework of crisis as the slow death of inadequate health care and exposure to environmental harm.

The perpetual crisis of Black life has inaugurated a wealth of aesthetic and critical ideations that seek to contend with what Saidiya Hartman (2007: 6) influentially has called "the afterlife of slavery." For Black cultural studies—the field to which the essays in this special issue belong—what marks this moment of time? While time has always served as a key in the rhythm of Black life, Black temporality now appears to be a defining feature of contemporary Black culture. The return to the Black historical past (literature, film, visual art), Black feminist imperatives of self-care (pause, rest, nap), and Afro-futurist imaginings of r(evolution) denote an overwhelming imperative in the field of Black cultural studies not only to make sense of time but to shift, shape, and wield temporality. Black culture, Black literature in particular, has challenged linear conceptions of temporality by demonstrating how Blackness operates on an alternative temporal register. Michelle Wright (2015: 172), for example, has persuasively argued that Blackness best achieves its meaning through the "continual updating of intersecting interpellations in the 'now.'"

So, what is the "now"? Specifically, how does contemporary Black cultural studies contend with Black crises, that is, the spectacle of Black death, environmental crises, pandemic disparities? If we attend to Black cultural productions of the past decade, the answer appears to point in two distinct directions: by returning to the Black historical past, and through the quotidian imperative to "reclaim time." Though Wright cautions against the reflexive return to the Middle Passage as the origin story of Black diasporic life, the preoccupation with slavery and its afterlife serves as the unifying theme of contemporary Black studies. However, such retreats are more than traumatic or melancholic time-traveling; they are attempts to reclaim time in ways that are restorative and reparative. A crisis can lead to more generative ways of imagining the future, possibility, and alternative ways of being. A key moment of crisis, 2020 revitalized our understanding of care, abolition, mutual aid, and other approaches to repairing and reenvisioning the present. It is not that an idea such as abolition is new. Rather, the possibilities that abolition, mutual aid, and another not-new idea, reparations, suggest are revitalized. These ideas of repair or restoration return in new generations as the means of revitalization. In a moment of crisis, a response transforms what we believe is suddenly possible, and it transforms the experience and potentials of time.

Just as abolitionism isn't new, neither is the current impetus in Black cultural studies to explore the counter-hegemonic dimensions of Black temporality. Daylanne English (2013: 3) has argued that "black people in the United States live within a distinct temporality produced by both race and injustice." The decisive return to the history of slavery since the 1980s indicates that the question Black scholars and artists have been tacitly asking, What time is now? is closely related to developments of the post–civil rights era. The era frequently referred to as "post–civil rights" is actually a time of numerous "posts": post–rise and suppression of Black liberationist movements of the 1960s and 1970s, post–philanthropic support for Black arts institutions, post–"soul" as an aesthetic related to what Kevin Quashie (2021) more recently calls Black "aliveness," post–devastation wrought by Reagan-era neoliberalism on poor Black communities, post–intensive commodification of Black culture. The return to slavery occurs amid the endings.

As literary scholar Aida Levy-Hussen (2016) contends, the return to slavery in contemporary Black literature has elicited either a strong desire for a "therapeutic," reparative encounter with a painful historical past, or a staunch refusal of historical return-as-presentism. Yet, Levy-Hussen finds that neither approach speaks to the complicated temporal structure of the contemporary moment, in which ambivalence toward the past and present is worked out through a disorderly interplay of multiple desires and melancholia. Stephen Best (2018) also addresses the return to slavery through contemporary loss, which he names "melancholy historicism." If accounts of contemporary melancholia and negation signal a "crisis" of the present, then it's a crisis that demands a choice between our holding onto or letting go of our attachments to what has been lost. The crisis pertains to how we return to history.

Tropes of return that are so prevalent in Black expressive culture indicate an ongoing, collective desire to actively engage the past. Crises and returns are entangled with each other, although not necessarily as trauma or melancholia. Crises and returns compel us to take up the unfinished work of resolving historical harm, dispossession, injustice in the present. The entanglement between crises and returns may explain why recent cultural representations of return also represent crises.

In real time and in fiction, we recently have experienced and borne witness to returns to earlier periods: the 1918 flu pandemic (COVID-19) and the 1921 Tulsa Race Massacre (*The Watchmen*) emerge as the starkest exemplars of the conspicuousness of historical repetition (with a difference). This includes historical novels of slavery (*The Underground Railroad*, *The Good Lord Bird*), film and television media (*Antebellum*, *Lovecraft Country*), and visual art and culture (Glenn Ligon, Lorna Simpson), as well as Black culinary culture (Michael W. Twitty, Thérèse Nelson). We might consider Black crises in light of the Nietzschean concept of "eternal recurrence": that events are repeated sequentially at different moments in a cyclical fashion. In this conception, the passage of time does not signal progress but a futurity that is shaped by past events. What might this mean for Black lives as experienced through a perpetuality of crisis, an infinite catastrophic loop? Afro-pessimism would tell us that Black crisis is formative, that Blackness is not *in* crisis but *a* crisis.

The ever-present nature of Black crisis emerges most explicitly in the historical novel of slavery, which may be argued as the defining genre of contemporary Black fiction. Novels like *Beloved, Dessa Rose,* and *The Known World* resonate among contemporary audiences precisely because the crises they narrate are enduring. This resonance with contemporary Black crises is made even more evident by virtue of the fact that many recent novels of slavery have been translated into other media, particularly film and television. Edward P. Jones's *The Known World,* by way of example, plays with the alternative registers of time through the use of prolepsis as a structural device meant to signify the palimpsestic quality of Black temporal crisis. In the case of *The Known World,* the "return" to the past is set against a glimpse of the future. And in this future lies a kind of reparation, some justice for the formerly enslaved. As Hartman (2008: 6) puts it, "Loss gives rise to longing . . . it would not be far-fetched to consider stories as a form of compensation or even as reparations, perhaps the only kind we will ever receive."

In addition to the novel of slavery, other genres structure temporality and determine how crises are intelligible. Horror, as the thick genre that combines fantasy and realism, has been most salient in recent television and film. Cinematic representations of crisis are often visually illustrated as slow-motion, artificially suspending the moment of chaos to create what is called an "aesthetic of violence." Aesthetic representations of crisis emerge in horror, particularly in the illustration of ordinary Black life as persistently endangered in white America. Recent films and television series—*Get Out* (2017), *Us* (2019), *Watchmen* (2019), *Candyman* (2020), *Lovecraft Country* (2020), *Antebellum* (2020), *Them* (2021)—signal both the prominence and circularity of historical time in contemporary Black life. These narratives harken to Black pasts to point to reverberations of white violence as an ongoing, circular trope. *Lovecraft Country, Watchmen, Candyman,* and *Antebellum* invoke Black temporal horror through the mere act of periodization. Recent Black popular culture tells us that there is nothing more terrifying for Black folks than the historical past.

Horror also expresses the return of the repressed: the moment of crisis is simultaneously unanticipated and dreadfully familiar. To anticipate a future in the present time of horror is to experience intense apprehension of the disaster, which could be what we had coming, what has long been awaiting us, what finally confronts us, what we never escaped in the course of living our quotidian, crisis-free lives. The present is a moment of reckoning with what has been disavowed but not left behind. And yet, to anticipate a future in the present time of horror is also to expect survival and resolution—the defeat of destructive forces, the final escape, the long-awaited end of catastrophe. Horror's emplotment of crisis entails present-day anticipation of both disaster and survival.

As the example of horror illustrates, returns to history invite us to reexamine what has been rendered unthinkable through periodizing practices. Crawford's (2017: 3) return to the very specific period of the Black Arts Movement reveals how the Black aesthetics of the 1960s and 1970s, far from evincing an essential Black presence, shares with twenty-first-century Black aesthetics a temporality of anticipation, a time of the "not yet here." On a broader scale, the Middle Passage evokes a mode of suspension in which Black bodies were held and, simultaneously, a mode of transition from one place to another, from one—or many—modes of being in time. John Ernest characterizes the history of African American literature as "chaotic"—a spatiality and temporality that defies a linear framework. And Wright's notion of "epiphenomenal time" suggests that Blackness is best understood in the "now," which encompasses both the past and the future. Inherent in all these conceptions of Black time is the belief that Blackness "disorders" temporality through its refusal to be contained and constricted within dominant Western ontologies.

In the racial logic of neoliberalism, such disordered temporality is itself a crisis, rather than a response to one. Disordered, counter-hegemonic time potentially defies the laws and schedules of contingent labor, unending debt, and carcerality that structures the lives of children and adults alike. From the early modern past of conquest to present-day global capitalism, dispossession has entailed the deprivation of time. As a resource in the senses of both material accumulation and the means of simply living and surviving, time is key to ongoing struggles over who has the legal and social capacity to be human. From this vantage point, Black temporality—conscientious, experiential, and sensory relations to time—names a strategy for living and a radical reclamation of humanity.

Congresswoman Maxine Waters's fervent reclamation of time during the House Financial Services hearing in 2017 quickly became a contemporary

Black feminist battle cry that called attention to the demands of labor that Black women in particular have endured under the guise of "black girl magic" and "black excellence." As Tressie McMillan Cottom (2019: 207) puts it, "I love black women too much to ever wish for us another part-time job." Tricia Hersey, the Nap Bishop of the Nap Ministry, an organization founded in 2016 to call for the "liberating power of naps," has long proclaimed that— for Black folks—"rest is resistance." These recent calls to reclaim time are, in part, in response to the crisis of the nation. Black women have been heralded as "saviors" of American democracy with little attention to the deleterious physical and psychological effects of their activist efforts. Yet, the emphasis to reclaim time isn't altogether new but harkens to the 1970s Black feminist imperatives of "self-care" most famously realized in Audre Lorde's ([1988] 1996) proclamation, "Caring for myself is not self-indulgence, it is self-preservation, and that is an act of political warfare" (332). The return to Black feminism of the 1970s and early 1980s is to reclaim a radical, anticolonial temporal embodiment of care.

Aligned with the 1970s Black radical rejection of Western ontologies and temporalities, Toni Morrison's heroine, Pilate, in her 1977 (2004) novel *Song of Solomon*, serves as an exemplar of the emancipatory potential inherent in reclaiming Black time in the midst of crises through subverting the logic of linearity and choosing to begin anew.

> Although she was hampered by huge ignorances, but not in any way unintelligent, when she realized what her situation in the world was and would probably always be she threw away every assumption she had learned and began at zero. . . . Her mind traveled crooked streets and aimless goat paths, arriving sometimes at profundity, other times at the revelations of a three-year-old. Throughout this fresh, if common, pursuit of knowledge, one conviction crowned her efforts: since death held no terrors for her (she often spoke to the dead), she knew there was nothing to fear. (149)

Beginning "at zero," Pilate embarks on the path toward self-actualization, and it is here that her process of emancipation begins. When Milkman and his friend, Guitar, plot to steal what they believe to be gold from Pilate's home, Milkman tells him, "They're not regular. They don't have regular habits. . . . They're not clock people, Guitar. I don't believe Pilate knows how to tell time except by the sun." Milkman's description of them as "not regular" points to the extent to which they stand outside of the norms of Western temporality and mechanical time. Pilate's decision to disengage from "clock time" to become a "not clock person" proffers a lens through which we might better understand recent Black feminist imperatives of temporality that contend with crisis through the reclamation of time.

Disengagement from "clock time" is a counter-nationalist (feminist) temporality that reemerges in the present as newly imagined Black futures. As Hersey puts it, "May you realize the power of taking rest since no one will give it to you. This is why rest is a resistance and a slow meticulous love practice. We must continue deprogramming from grind culture. . . . We must deconstruct around the ways we uphold grind culture, capitalism and white supremacy. We must wake up. We will rest." Rest, as a condition that resolves the contradiction between sleep and wakefulness, is not a retreat from consciousness. Rather, it becomes the engine of human evolution. It names the imperative to bring the unceasing, inhuman time of global capitalism to a grinding halt by (re)claiming the capacity to be more fully human. The notion of bodily, cognitive, and social reparation as a response to the global crisis of capitalism entails a refusal to exist in a state of constant emergency/urgency. Reparation, as a response to racialized, political-economic systems that separate humans from their humanity, brings about a new way of being, and of being in time.

The Black feminist imagination has often dreamed of forms of reclamation. In the twenty-first century, Hersey proposes that we take our time. Such a proposal reminds us that time is a site of constant struggle, and Black temporality is the sensory route to what is not yet here but could possibly be. As the events of 2020 have shown, times of crisis prompt urgent action; and yet, crisis simultaneously draws us closer to the quotidian constancy of struggle, which is, by definition, an unabated, round-the-clock condition. As Walter Benjamin (1968: 257) states, "The tradition of the oppressed teaches us that the 'state of emergency' in which we live is not the exception but the rule." Black feminist scholars and artists have returned to history with this view and have revealed how the everyday life of power wages its violence in routinized, ordinary ways. A "crisis" is simply when ordinary violence becomes extraordinary. Ordinary or not, Black feminism rejects the rule of violence by proposing that we do not succumb to its demands, but rather craft technologies of temporality for resisting the impulse to exist in a persistent state of emergency. Claudia Rankine (2014: 126) evokes the liberatory potential of temporality when she writes, "The state of emergency is also always the state of emergence." To distinguish Black temporality from times of crisis is to reclaim the freedom to imagine the arrival of something new.

References

Benjamin, Walter. 1968. "Theses on a Philosophy of History." In *Illuminations*, edited by Hannah Arendt, 253–64. New York: Harcourt Brace.

Best, Stephen. 2018. *None Like Us: Blackness, Belonging, Aesthetic Life*. Durham, NC: Duke University Press.

Crawford, Margo. 2017. *Black Post-Blackness: The Black Arts Movement and Twenty-First-Century Aesthetics*. Urbana: University of Illinois Press.

Du Bois, W. E. B. (1903) 1999. *The Souls of Black Folk*. New York: W. W. Norton.

English, Daylanne K. 2013. *Each Hour Redeem: Time and Justice in African American Literature*. Minneapolis: University of Minnesota Press.

Hartman, Saidiya. 2007. *Lose Your Mother*. New York: Farrar, Straus and Giroux.

Hartman, Saidiya. 2008. "Venus in Two Acts." *Small Axe* 26, no. 2. doi.org/10.1215/-12-2-1.

Levy-Hussen, Aida. 2016. *How to Read African American Literature: Post Civil Rights Fiction and the Task of Interpretation*. New York: New York University Press.

Lorde, Audre. (1988) 1996. "A Burst of Light." *The Audre Lorde Compendium: Essays, Speeches, and Journals*. London: Pandora.

McMillan Cottom, Tressie. 2019. *Thick and Other Essays*. New York: New Press.

Morrison, Toni. (1977) 2004. *Song of Solomon*. 1st Vintage International ed. New York: Vintage International.

Quashie, Kevin. 2021. *Black Aliveness, or A Poetics of Being*. Durham, NC: Duke University Press.

Rankine, Claudia. 2014. *Citizen: An American Lyric*. Minneapolis, MN: Graywolf Press.

Stewart, Kathleen. 2007. *Ordinary Affects*. Durham, NC: Duke University Press.

Wilson Gilmore, Ruth. 2007. *Golden Gulag: Prisons, Surplus, Crisis, and Opposition in Globalizing California*. Berkeley: University of California Press.

Wright, Michelle. 2015. *The Physics of Blackness: Beyond the Middle Passage Epistemology*. Minneapolis: University of Minnesota Press.

Sarah Stefana Smith

Keeping Time:
Maroon Assemblages and
Black Life in Crisis

In August 2020, I traveled to the Great Dismal
Swamp (see fig. 1) on the border between Virginia
and North Carolina. It was for vacation; a moment
away from the perils of a pandemic, the everyday
banality of death and disease, that framed the day to
day, and the passing of time. As I write this now, I
am struck by the sheer weight of everyday grief,
everyday beauty, and that it could be another year,
another six months, another nine months, since
that visit, since that time, since that place. Over the
course of these months, I would sit down, in another
state of the Americas, having moved to another city,
apart from my loved one, to begin another beginning, and to write on Black people and time; Black
people, temporality, and crisis.

The Great Dismal Swamp, in addition to the
weight of its landscape, has considerable historical resonance.[1] The swamp is said to gets its name
from William Byrd II, who in 1728 surveyed the
land between the colonies of Virginia and North
Carolina and offered unfavorable reviews of
the site (Nevius 2020: 5). The hope was to drain
the swamp, harvest the trees, and use the land for
farming. By the mid-eighteenth century, settler-
colonialists from Virginia were interested in expanding plantation enterprises into the swamp. Efforts

The South Atlantic Quarterly 121:1, January 2022
DOI 10.1215/00382876-9561503 © 2022 Duke University Press

Figure 1. Photographs of Lake Drummond, Great Dismal Swamp, August 2020. Courtesy of Author.

for expansion began with the Dismal Swamp Company of 1736 and the construction of a plantation and town near the northwestern fringe of the swamp, two years later (5, 16).[2] We know the complication of language, of naming, of the name and how it brings with it so much of the violence of racial slavery and settler colonialism.

My primary interest in the history of the Great Dismal Swamp is the petit-maroon communities that resided in the marshy region during the period of 1763 up through 1856. Many enslaved Africans came to the region through the Dismal Swamp Land Company, which hired local enslaved people (Kars 2013). However, with challenges of labor, company agents tapped maroon communities to build and expand (Nevius 2020: 6). There were maroon populations living in concert with the swamp as early as William Byrd's account in 1728 and up through the Civil War. Maroon communities consisted of runaway slaves and freed people. Furthermore, the Dismal Swamp Company for a time relied on a biracial labor system alternative to slavery, often hiring maroons as key sources of labor alongside hundreds of enslaved peoples, whom the company dispatched onto timber plantations (6). Historian Marcus Nevius (2020) notes that Dismal communities were less a permanent fixture and more multiple and semipermanent settlements. Unlike more readily known communities in parts of the Caribbean, including Cuba and Jamaica, the maroon communities of Virginia and North Carolina were less known and more likely to practice petit-marronage.[3] Maroons, in this configuration, also attained some connection to the slave-labor camp and slave societies surround the swamp. Nevius notes, "Far more common were the conditions under which enslaved Africans and African Americans engaged in petit marronage, resisting enslavement in small-er-scale, highly mobile camps. These camps, too, provide an important lens through which the extent of the black freedom struggle is brought into sharper focus" (10). Many of these maroon communities were distinct from the freed-people communities that lived along the rim of the swamp and worked on timber plantations and with competing land companies (12).[4]

The environment of the Great Dismal Swamp was harsh at best. For millennia before the 1860s, it was a vast natural wetland that covered several thousand square miles along the border of Virginia and North Carolina, comparable in size to the modern state of Delaware. Various enterprises drained the swamp to a tenth of its original land area after the American Civil War, as growing postbellum industrial enterprises targeted forests in the US Southeast. Currently the Great Dismal Swamp is comprised of two wildlife preserves. The larger swamp sector, overseen by the US Fish and Wildlife Service as the Great Dismal Swamp National Wildlife Refuge, is an area of roughly 175 square miles. A smaller sector along the Great Dismal Swamp Canal in Camden County, North Carolina, comprises almost 14,500 acres and is maintained by the state as the Dismal Swamp State Park. Near the swamp's center is Lake Drummond, a circular natural body of freshwater that covers more than 3,000 acres and is no more than six feet deep (Nevius 2020: 3–4; Dismal Swamp Canal Welcome Center, n.d.).

═══

Throughout the present-day swamp, old canals and drainage ditches carry still waters covered in algae, most clogged with swamp undergrowth after years of lying fallow. The Dismal's low-hanging tree limbs and dense under-brush frame the swamp's fringes, verdant in the warmer months of the year, dry and foreboding in the colder months. In some swamp sectors, a range of tree species—Atlantic white cypress, bald cypress, maple, and pine—rise from the swamp floor, spreading their branches and leaves high above. In other swamp sectors, the trees have been burned away by the regular natural fires sparked by lightning during frequent spring and summer storms. The swamp's interior features a damp floor of vegetation covered in leaf litter and fallen branches in some places, muddy under foot and covered with layers of peat in other places, and with shallow, dark-amber-colored standing water in still other places. Small islands of dry landscape, known locally as hum-mocks, rise above the water table to heights of no more than ten feet. The hummocks are home to black bears, bobcats, otters, beavers, and squirrels. Colorful skinks and venomous snakes lie camouflaged on hummock floors where the sun's rays break through the forest canopy. The hummocks are also home to mosquitoes and yellow flies, voracious in their appetites for host animals and people. This brief description offers a bit of a sense of the conditions of living and surviving, of inhabiting, made possible by maroon communities in early American history. And perhaps it suggests some of the ways the weather, the environment, and the temperature made possible acts of fugitivity and refusal in the midst of slavery.

What follows is a set of ruminations on Black life, temporality and space in crisis. I use the current conjuncture of the COVID-19 pandemic and racial unrest as a backdrop to think through some of the tensions of survival, sociality, and communality in crisis. The experiences that I draw from are meant to be neither exemplary nor exceptional. I am aware, acutely aware, that multiple time-space pathways occur simultaneously in a variety of lives as they are lived through (and some perish) in the midst of COVID-19 and the ongoing crisis of racial unrest. In that purview I see this writing as an act of love, deep love, for those I know and those I do not know, and for our dead.

Maroon Assemblages: Lurking in Swamps, Woods, and Other Obscure Spaces[5]

Oh, those long, gloomy days, with no object for my eye to rest upon, and no thoughts to occupy my mind, except the dreary past and the uncertain future! I was thankful when there came a day sufficiently mild for me to wrap myself up and sit at the loophole to watch the passersby.
—Harriet Jacobs, *Incidents in the Life of a Slave Girl* (2001)

There we came upon a family of mulattoes that called themselves free, though by the shyness of the master of the house, who took care to keep least in sight, their freedom seemed a little doubtful.
—William Byrd, "The Westover Manuscripts: Containing the History of the Dividing Line Betwixt Virginia and North Carolina" (1841)

Time is awful to us because it makes us characters in a story that is not or was not always ours. Time is as wicked as my much-frazzled memory during the pandemic—which is to say mostly filled with instances of ongoing unrest, fits and starts, exhaustion and limited energy, wide open space, vulnerable. A memory can change what time does to us by framing us in its own time—the time the memory was conjured, the subject's time. But often we need such an account (the personal) of that time. The neo–slave narrative offers a personal account of Black life in crisis, within the conventions of a particular genre of writing—the abolitionist text. The personal narrative is a less readily available account of marronage. Especially less the case, in the Americas, specifically Virginia and North Carolina, as accounts of marronage are often visible through the colonial and plantation state. These accounts take the form of the outlawed, the insurgent, the unruly, and the runaway, who steals from the plantation. How then might one conjoin the plantation, the neo–slave novel, and maroon assemblages with contemporary Black life and death in the dual pandemics of racial unrest and COVID-19?

The quotations that open this section consider Black life and death in crisis. The first epigraph highlights a well-rehearsed passage from Harriet Jacobs's *Incidents in the Life of a Slave Girl*. In the book, first printed in 1861 under the pseudonym of Linda Brent, we come to find the actual author, Harriet Jacobs, retreat to fugitivity in the garret of her grandmother's attic in response to time and the crisis of plantation slavery. Given the circumstances of her enslavement, Jacobs hides in the garret and remains there for seven years. The garret sits among overlapping spatial and temporal geographies of the plantation from which she sought to escape. This not-quite space, to use Hortense Spillers's term, is where the implausible, but real, acts of seeing and overhearing take place (McKittrick 2006: 61; Spillers 1987: 77). It is through the loophole of retreat, the small holes in the walls of the garret, that Jacobs is able to view her children, overhear conversations of Dr. Flint (master of the plantation) as he seeks out his fugitive slave—Jacobs. Katherine McKittrick makes into a verb Jacobs's retreat to the garret, and it is informative to our discussion of temporality. For McKittrick, *garreting*, as verb, signals unresolved impacts that Black women's bodies have and do not have on traditional framings of geographical landscape. In this way, space as we might understand it is reshaped, particularly as Black women's stories rest on the not-quite spaces of displacement (McKittrick 2006: 61). Thus the importance of Jacobs's story in the pantheon of the neo–slave narrative and Black study—we are made privy to a moment of not-quite space and not-quite temporality, the loophole of retreat, whereby a life, Black life, exists in extreme violence and power.

Some one hundred and thirty years prior to Harriet Jacobs's account, and upon his excavation of the interior of the Great Dismal Swamp, William Byrd writes of contact with a mulatto family. Byrd notes, "There we came upon a family of mulattoes that called themselves free, though by the shyness of the master of the house, who took care to keep least in sight, their freedom seemed a little doubtful." Byrd is skeptical of the freedom of this mulatto family, though the passage in which the reader encounters Byrd's description of the lands suggests the excavators have yet to come in contact with anyone else (Nevius 2020). Byrd continues,

> It is certain many slaves shelter themselves in this obscure part of the world, nor will any of their righteous neighbors discover them. On the contrary, they find their account in settling such fugitives on some out-of-the-way corner of their land, to raise stocks for a mean and inconsiderable share, well knowing their condition makes it necessary for them to submit to any terms. Nor were these worthy borderers content to shelter runaway slaves, but debtors and criminals have often met with the like indulgence. (Byrd and Ruffin 1841)

Histographies of the region note this encounter as one of few instances of reference to petit-marronage in the Swamp lands and, in particular, where some recollection of a family living on site exists. Most other instances are gathered through slave revolts, broadsides, and advertisements in newspapers inquiring on the whereabouts of runaways. Take for example the 1795 advertisement run by the *Wilmington City Gazette* in North Carolina that a band of runaway slaves "in the daytime secreted themselves in the swamps and woods and at night committed various depredations on the neighboring plantations." After their capture by the local militia, local officials learned the group was led by an individual that named themselves the "General of the Swamps."[6] Tom Copper, the general of the swamps, led raids on surrounding plantations, utilizing a network of rivermen to coordinate networks of men (Nevius 2020: 52). The above examples highlight the tensions of the archive, but also account for the myriad ways Black subjects navigated crisis during this period of time.

The mulatto family, the general of the swamp, and Harriet Jacobs's narrative are significant to Black life in crisis and this not-quite space of displacement, particularly as it spatializes repeated acts of flight and insecurity. These instances of Black life occur in the cramped, in-plain-sight geographies of small spaces, cracks and fissures, and enact a disarray of temporality. I have previously written about a temporality that conjoins genealogies of Black studies and queer of color critique. Through an orientation to what I call the *elsewhere/when* of Black life I have sought to grapple with the ways in which biologically determined and linear temporality actually function to inhibit legible modes of engagement with Black life. In this context, I have used *elsewhere/when* as a moniker to move beyond the *what* of spatial and temporal forms of existence of Black life, and toward *where* and *when* it takes place (Smith 2019: 18). In the context of this article, I want to conjoin a consideration of the maroon (mulatto family and refuge in the swamp) and the fugitive slave (Jacobs) as co-constituted temporalities of flight and precarity, fugitivity and insecurity, that are significant to contemporary iterations of Black life in crisis, in pandemic, in racial unrest.

Marronage often has its uses as a broad term describing acts of flight from plantation slavery, alongside historical processes of negotiating communal dwelling away from the sphere of the plantation. In this way, maroon communities at times are positioned in stark contrast with the plantation. To use Neil Robert's (2015) term, "freedom as maroonage" equates freedom with maroon sensibilities while the conditions of the plantation account for absolute sites of surveillance, power, and captivity. Maroon studies scholar Ronald Cummings (2018) notes a hesitancy in collapsing freedom and not freedom to marronage and the plantation, respectively, and offers marronage as assemblage as a necessary configuration. Marronage as assemblage can account for insistent sites of insecurity and precarity. Cummings notes, "Marronage as assemblage, marked by repeated practices of flight, and as a remaking of structures of possibilities of communities and renegotiation of relationships to space, land and territoriality in response to ongoing structures of colonial violence" (49).[7] I am interested in Cummings's use of marronage as assemblage, particularly as it accounts for time and its space making practice. The use of assemblage accounts for a movement among processes of precarity and flight, rather than a dialectical opposition between fugitivity and precarity, marronage and plantation surveillance. Assemblage also invites a revisioning of grand narratives of heroism and resistance, while paying attention to sites of insecurity that warrant a recalibration between new strategies of response. Furthermore, assemblage and marronage bring to the fore the unknowability of the maroon, which is linked to the ocular surveillance of the plantation/ surveillance state.[8] Virginia and North Carolina, in their practice of petit-marronage, highlight how small acts are enacted alongside varying instances of precarity, collusion, and insecurity. Tom Copper (general of the swamp), for example, manages several raids on neighboring plantations (while simultaneously some maroons work with excavation companies) and evades capture for quite some time. While Jacobs's narrative in its most explicit way accounted for time as a convention of the genre of the neo–slave narrative, *Incidents in the Life of a Slave Girl* also provides a frame to think through Black life, time, and crisis through marronage as assemblage.[9] *Incidents in the Life of a Slave Girl* begins with Jacobs's recounting of a series of events that put into motion her decision to escape the Flint plantation.[10] These events lead to Jacobs's garretting. In an effort to think marronage and plantation as relational practices to the colonial and slavery state, is it possible to think of Jacobs's practice of garretting as a practice of petit-marronage as assemblage? It is undisputable that Jacobs is in a space of insecurity. My intention is not to suggest Jacobs is participating in marronage in its most traditional sense, but rather, I am interested in what is made possible when thinking through fugitivity and flight, refuge and precarity, as concurrent ongoing practice in place and time. The encounter with the mulatto family, and reluctant presence of the master, accounts for further examples of precarity when one wonders into the gaps of Byrd's log. Nevius's (2020) historical account of the swamp reiterates that even with acts of petit-marronage, it was in part made possible through precarious and perilous engagement with plantations positioned on the outskirts of the swamp. Those who sought marronage were also among those who explicitly interacted with the Dismal Swamp Company—which recruited slaves and maroons to maintain its workload (Nevius 2020: 14).

While Jacobs's account occurs over a century after Byrd's sighting of the mulatto family and the *Wilmington City Gazette* advertisement, these examples share similarities in the way in which Black life thwarts the conditions of capture while negotiating precarity. These instances—Harriet Jacobs's garretted existence, the mulatto family, and a band of runaways finding refuge in the swamp—require a different orientation to space and temporality in the archive in order to get at their meaning for Black life. For Jacobs we are fortunate to have close to a first-person account, in the form of her neo–slave narrative. The mulatto family and the band seeking refuge in the swamp perhaps require wondering into the gaps of the colonial and slavery archive. While the reader is afforded a glimmer into the mulatto family through Byrd's travel logs, the author's blind sightedness leaves considerable omission. Imagining into the temporality of Byrd's encounter with the mulatto family, I wonder, what are the conditions that make it possible for a *mulatto family* to be a family in this context, in this environment, and in this timespace, for this grouping to "call themselves free" and be legible, or strategically illegible? Reading into this example of marronage in the Dismal Swamp registers assemblage temporalities that move among unknowability, flight, and precarity.

I turn to the contemporary moment with assemblage in mind. I propose characteristics of temporalities that can account for movements away from captivity and annihilation and toward worldmaking. I argue that such a process of looking for marronage as assemblage allows for Black life and its relationship to the past to be a discontinued one, shaped by absences, presences, shadows, and hauntings. This proposition is premised on the fact that we resist romantic narratives of overcoming in the past, present, and future. Temporality with a difference requires that—instead of simply suggesting future is not enough or the time of futurity has not yet happened—temporality, much like the Deleuzian fold, might be imagined with spatial differentiation that can hold the breadth of social configurations of time (Black temporality) in assemblage. This reorientation to temporality is not meant to occur outside history; quite the opposite, and to use Roderick Ferguson's provocation, such a temporality imagines history as one where "recruiting previously excluded subjects into a nationalist regimen can be a way of using time to unmake forms of non-nationalist relationality" (Dinshaw et al. 2007: 185). Can we think of Harriet Jacobs's escape to her grandmother's garret and the subsequent methods of evading capture as movements of marronage temporality? Can Jacobs's movements of maroon temporality be thought alongside those of the petit maroons of Virginia and North Carolina? Cummings informatively notes, "Marronage is marked by strategies of contingency and survival. It is an experience of time which 'invite[s] futurity even as it refuses to script it'" (Cummings 2018: 15; Puar 2007: xix). Rather than evoking a unilateral directionality for reading temporality in these instances of contemporary Black life in crisis, through Black life temporality as assemblage I consider the way in which contemporary examples of Black life in the dual pandemics of racial unrest and COVID-19 continue to orient time as assemblage of scarcity, precarity, refuge, and flight. I turn to several personal examples of time through the everyday experience, somatic movements, and conversations among a small group of interlocuters to think time, to think its passing, its retreat, its rebellion, its acknowledgment, its mathematics, its formula, its insurgency, the vessel of it, and the formation of it.

Movement Study No. 1

Over the course of the last year and a half I have been in conversation with three other people, and in particular we discussed the state of their experience of the global pandemic and racial uprisings. One of these individuals is based in the United States as I am (they in New Orleans and I in Washington, DC) and the other two are located in the United Kingdom (Nottingham and London). We four have known each other for over ten years. Over the course of that time, we have had semi-regular intervals of communication as friends, colleagues, and collaborators. Most recently through voice memos, video and photograph shares, and Zoom calls, we have continued a mode of communality. At one point during the pandemic, I revealed I was thinking about Black people, time, and crisis and, in a very open-ended manner, invited them to talk with me about their experiences of the present moment. The

Figure 2. Photograph and image capture from video. Courtesy of Celestin Edward, 2021.

experiences shared all took place over the course of the last eighteen months at the height of the pandemic and contemporary racial unrest.

≡

A subject sits in the expanse of a green space. The subject is stretched up, or they are reclining, or we get a glimpse of a glistening knee embraced by an arm, or an upper torse as hands are held up toward the sky. When we are invited into a more fine-tuned perspective of location, the image capture opens up into a manicured lawn. A forest of trees frames along three points of the rectangular space. This location could be many and multiple, carrying with it common elements of geographies of some places—greenery, trees, grass, field, fence, a horizon—alongside its uncanny specificity of Hertsford-shire. In a video clip that corresponds with the same event, the same loca-tion, and the same subjects, the person is on a bicycle, and I (and the others to whom these documents have been sent) get to observe a glee-filled experi-ence as the person rides away from the camera lens. The cyclist follows the implied trail of the outside garden, first on the right-hand-most part of the video, then toward the outer upper position, and on toward the left, until the clip ends in time. There is audio, and I am grateful for it, as it brings another layer of glee, joy, and silliness to the video clip, sent to me from thousands of miles away, across an ocean, to view and be with. Off camera, you hear the voice of Cousin, who has always been present. There, of course, is ambient sound—rustling of leaves, buggy noises, et cetera.

> There she goes. She riding. Let's see if she can take this corner. You know Fred, last time she couldn't take the corner (voice change), yeah, I know, she stumbled a lil bit (voice change) . . . Oh look Fred (shouts of glee and affirmation), look Fred, she took the corner (voice change) . . . well done, that's a really good corna (voice change) . . . Fred, I agree. She took the corna nicely. She learned from her previous lack, knew what . . . (Sound cuts off, video ends).[11]

Given the conditions of the pandemic, where protocols of safe social distancing are in place, at the time of this video capture, what is extraordinary about Edward's seemingly unextraordinary vernacular snapshots and video of a weekend in the country is the urgency of continued connection and living a life in the lines of meaningfulness. Without the context of time (this was shared in July 2020), we know little of the series of media. In fact, the series of media might simply be one of many outlets of public communality, viewed on Snapchat, Instagram, or Twitter. For this instance of communality, Edward fleshes out the conditions that bring them to this location with family—on the occasion to celebrate their niece's fourteenth birthday—in the midst of the United Kingdom's first several months of lockdown. "I think we were thinking way, way ahead of those time scales."[12] Given the current constraints by the government, Edward's remarks hold up for scrutiny the tensions between isolation and the protocols of sociality now. Edward continues, "So yeah, that became an important thing to do, and again being a Black family, and being used to just seeing each other on a weekly basis, to then go to nothing, would just be very detrimental to all of our mental health."[13]

I am struck by a doubled gesture that travels across this collection of images and video. For what is the way forward of *those* time scales that Edward speaks of? What is the forethought that Edward maps into a temporality of the now? Might this be a way forward that may seem reckless to some, but also health centered toward the collective? This question seems even more prevalent now, when the conditions of health, crisis, wellness, and well-being are set through a litany of constraints by governmental offices, ableist belief and value, and overall precarity. This is acerbated by a lack of cohesion and consistency. As I write revisions into this article—in the late stages of the pandemic, in June 2021—my own family grapples with social interaction among those who choose to vaccinate and those who choose not. I bring this personal example up not to redirect focus from

Edward's constellation of images and concerns, but rather to fold into such a discussion of temporality and crisis the many ways periods of contact with crisis (in this instance, the proliferation of COVID, but certainly not only; we are in multiple crises) produce moralistic belief and value about risk averse behavior and less risky behavior.

This brief description of Edward in the country, for me, invites an opportunity to think deeply about multiple movements conceived in marronage as assemblage. I see this act of sociality and rest as an example of movement away from capture (slavery) and Black annellation and toward other practices of collaborative worldmaking. Acts against annellation and toward other modes of existence happen inside and outside the plantation (or spaces of captivity). Marronage as assemblage negotiates temporalities of crisis through *process*—repeated acts of flight, escape, and fugitivity even in continued precarity and surveillance.

Further, Edward's remarks highlight the problem of modern/capitalist time. Time as it pertains to modernity is marred with absolutes. Late capital has oriented a particular understanding of time and temporality as productivity, product driven, and alienated from the body's own labor. In instances of Black life with histories linked to transatlantic slavery, coloniality, and empire, capitalist time has a long history of characterizing Black movement. For an example of such characterization you need only return to my early example of the *Wilmington City Gazette* in which runaways hiding in the swamps of the Dismal are characterized through their threat of insurrection. Certainly, in the context of these last eighteen months, those that have not visibly felt the constraints of temporality on their being are having to negotiate that.[14] Edward's insistence on familial sociality, as a means of mental health, challenges the totalizing time of the modern state, but also the ways Black life is produced and incorporated into it. In the above example, in addition to an encounter with life and joy, we might be made privy to a glimpse of what Amanda Lagji (2018) understands as disruptive waiting and idleness. This idleness goes against the grain of tropes of lazy, sleepy, or ambivalent Black movement for one that rejects (or at least disrupts) the labor demands of European late capital through its "refusal to be read as active or passive, and its potential to disrupt systems of meaning" (202). In another voice memo, giving further context to this *time off*, Edward recounts a point of tension in their work environment. Edward and their colleagues have been asked to participate in a series of discussions about racism in the workplace. After a presentation, the facilitator asks for comments, and the workspace, largely comprised of white employees, responds with complete silence. Edward's anger is made plain, as they consider the silence of their peers. We might make sense of this instance as marronage as assemblage within the context of contemporary diversity, equity, and inclusion (DEI) initiatives that at once suggest an interest in unifying practices and liberation but doubly place Black and POC in continual spaces of precarity. The workspace is where Black folks are called on to connect dots, suggest moments of intersectional racisms, while surveilling their movements around what type of Black person they might be in the workforce environment. Several days later, around the time of Edward's sociality with family, Edward turns their reflection to sociality, isolation, and racial unrest: "how I am protesting, or how I am dealing with crisis, seems to stem from a space of joy, in particular, as a form of resistance."[15] Edward's experiences negotiate isolation, intentional sociality, and everyday encounters through a range of emotion. I understand this vacillation between anger and isolation, care and reflection, as maroon assemblages, in that new instances of insecurity warrant new strategies of coping and worldmaking. This example puts into view the ways in which marronage as assemblage invites us to think about Black life and crisis as a set of processes that enact continual flight *and* precarity. I argue that Edward's vacillation between joy and pleasure, anger and grief, is a constellation of processes on time and place that cannot be captured through a dialectic of freedom and precarity.

Edward negotiates a move away from captivity/annihilation and toward worldmaking. How then does the body factor into a discussion of temporality and crisis? What ways do gestures within the body's repertoire invite marronage as assemblage as a point of thinking? I turn to the next section, to highlight a third movement of spatial and temporal difference that I see present in these conversations with the four. This third gesture looks closely at embodiment and bodily autonomies.

Movement Study No. 2

This section turns to embodied temporalities of marronage as assemblage. I turn to Dennis's practice of somatic movement. In somatic movement, the internal movement of the body is the focus, rather than the external experience or result of the movement in the outward sphere (Eddy 2002; Selfish Activist 2020). In addition, one might think of the body in relation. Cultural somatics are those thinking, feeling, and sensing bodily gestures that emerge out of networked complex relationships. This is a way of being in the world that functions as a form of lived experience and embodiment (Selfish Activist

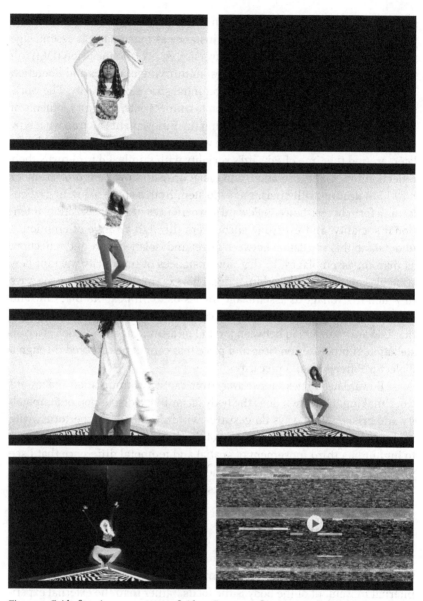

Figure 3. Grid of ten image captures of video. Courtesy of artist, Angela Dennis.

Figure 3. (continued)

2020). While I only focus on two somatic movement exercises by Dennis, she has published numerous video clips; many that remain on Instagram and TikTok and others that are temporary, deleted after a few days or months. When I first introduced the topic for discussion with the four, Dennis had recently relocated to Nottingham, a suburb about two hours outside of London, where her family lived. Of the transition, Dennis remarks, "I have been thinking about it [race, time, the pandemic] for a couple of days, in the back of my mind, and feeling into it."[16] Dennis continues, "Then being in Nottingham, feeling into a slower pace of life; as opposed to London and living with elderly people. Feeling into a slower pace of life, trying to accept that, then also feeling impatient and waiting . . . this thing [COVID] has not yet arrived but feels so close."[17] Dennis's remarks highlight the prevalence of *feeling into* a pace of existence that had significantly been altered. While Dennis recounts that the urgency of non-contact in Nottingham was less prevalent than in other parts of Great Britain, the anticipation of its arrival was a presence. This time frame corresponds with Dennis's increased participation and study of somatic movement.

The not-quite-here but presence of the pandemic corresponds with a state of precarity that Dennis experiences as she quarantines and also reaches toward her somatic practice. Given the theory behind somatic movement, as a researcher, I attempt to resist the need to define a fixed set of practices in order to engage with Dennis's movement studies; and yet the challenge of media—the video clip—which captures a set of images—in some ways acts against this urgency.[18] In this way, I think of an application of marronage as assemblage through the unknowable. Somatic movement, if the movements are generated through an internal dialogue, one that in some ways is pre-sensory to its language meaning, means that there is a distinction between things Dennis might do as rituals to "get into the head space of movement" and the things the body leads her to do when in the moment of a somatic gesture.[19] In the first instance, we are invited into one of Dennis's dance rituals. The three-minute video clip invites us into a white space with a checkered rug. The dancer/body/subject is in a white space at the intersection of two white walls connecting in the corner. The checkered rug frames out the remaining element of the environment. Body in burnt orange pants, long-sleeve sweatshirt with picture of a green space with sky in the upper one-third of the shirt. The clip starts and restarts; because of this, there are several (two to three) affective spaces that emerge over the course of the three-minute video. The first encounter is a coming into the space; there is no music, and the sound we hear is that of ambient static. The opening frames show the performer, hands over heart. Then the subject brings hands and arms above the head, and then down, to bring in, build up the breath. Temporally, as a viewer, one might connect with the subject's movement of energizing the space by bringing the ephemeral into contact with the heart center. The subject is visibly breathing, and then the eyes open. The first shift is marked by a black frame and the introduction of rhythmic music. Arms outstretched, legs move, and there appears to be a kind of affirmation to the viewer, then, with arms on hips, and the performer gyrates forward to the point of contact with the camera. The performer opens up their stance and begins to move within the confines of the frame.

The second shift is marked by a kind of reset environment—the viewer sees the white walls and carpet, without a figure. It is clear the video has been edited together. The performer is not visible in the first frames of this shift, and then materializes again, in the upper-right foreground, walking into the frame. The music has shifted again, and this is compounded by the performer's selecting another tune. Audible above the sound shift is the performer's affective vocalization of "okay, humpf." This temporality is brief, lasting only a few seconds, visualizing a kind of pause, a waiting or perhaps a shifting, both in the visual movements of the performer and the audible ambient sound of *okay, humpf.* In those few seconds the performer walks into the frame and back to the conjoining wall corners, slides down the corner section, arms splayed. The third and final shift is marked by the change in video quality/color from a negative-positive affect, and the color spectrum bars. This shift is fractal, a fraction of time (three frames long). In this instance the sound frequency shifts, a raised vibration. "Why in the state that I am in, everybody is dancing," followed by the repeating refrain "Like Sugar, Like Sugar." Resisting uniformity and in some sense the time-based medium of the video snapshot, I find the break spaces (e.g., reset wall space, negative-positive affect) between gestural movements of interest. These spaces, these lag times, present a temporal shift within the confines of the

Figure 4. Ten image captures from "Seven Sisters Cliffs." Courtesy of artist, Angela Dennis.

Figure 4. (continued)

medium—video capture. Dennis resets the encounter, returns, and, in Fred Moten's (2003) parlance, enacts a sonic registry that is in the break. We do not encounter that kind of sonic resonance until the third and final shift. In this instance the sonic break occurs alongside a visualized element—the negative-positive screen, the color bar screen, and the subject walking off and out of the frame.

The second instances of somatic movement might bring into closer focus consideration of this relationship between the break, excavation, and discovery as it relates to marronage as assemblage. At one and half minutes long, this clip takes place on location, at the Cliffs of Seven Sisters in the southeastern most portion of the United Kingdom. Located in east Sussex, the area is comprised of a series of chalk cliffs within the South Downs National Park. The series of cliffs are in part bound by the southernmost coast, letting out into the English Channel and onward to the North Atlantic Ocean. The subject is against the background of a cliff; this background, white, sandy, and rocky environment. In the upper-right corner of the screen, we see a slice of the sky. The sky is gray/overcast with little detail in the form of clouds; opaque. The performer opens the sequence in the center of the shoot, arms overhead, dip movement, arms overhead and then cartwheeled across the body. Then grounding the right foot into the earth before kicking out, grounding the right foot into the earth again, into a split and sliding back. The next sequence of movements involves the performer picking up grit and sand and hurling it into the four corners of the environment, away from the body. This sequence of movements begins, first right, then adjacent corner, then left background corner, and then center corner. On the fifth throw, we hear an audible grunt before the performer walks off and out of view of the frame. Dennis's "Seven Sister Cliffs" resonates marronage as assemblage through the self, bodily autonomy and movement, as a process of digging into, quite literally to a discovery. In the second pairing of image stills, Dennis digs into the earth and kicks up and out. This first act of digging in with the foot is followed by a sequence in which the hand becomes the site of excavation, throwing gravel and ground and earth at the four corners of the visual frame—a figurative north, west, east, and south. Byrd excavates and examines lands for conquest. This is a different kind of excavation, exemplified in Dennis's gestures. Movement of the body as assemblage. In this way the body is a house, a home for a number of practices that are projected onto the body and that the body creates from within.

Late capital temporality produces the assumption that there is no captivity—free markets, free movements between goods and ideas. How do you make sense of such an obvious captivity (pandemic), where the entire United States and other configurations across the Global North and Global South (global pathways) must negotiate the pandemic's captivity? The entire United States as a dismal swamp; the swamp being exploded. Ahmaud Arbery, shot while running. How does the present moment's late-capital temporality comply with a kind of captivity, one made more visible to some (white people) against their freedom to not wear a mask, not respect six-feet policies as a breach of their freedoms? How do the bodily autonomies, bodies in motion, in interaction, in non/relation, tell us something about freedom and precarity?

By Way of a Conclusion: A Passing, a Rebellion, a Retreat

It has now been over eighteen months since the first *public* reports of COVID. August 2021 marked the anniversary of my trip to the Great Dismal Swamp and Lake Drummond. The almost uncanny quiet of that space, where I sat for almost forty-five minutes, alone, no other in sight, is a phenomenon I suspect is long gone, specific and perfect to that one moment in time. Washington, DC and western Massachusetts, where I have written most of this text, are now undergoing reopenings, whereby most restaurants, gyms, and public spaces are widely open. Masks do not have to be worn while outside. Most notable is the increased amount of traffic I can view from outside my window. For DC a phenomenon which is significantly lighter than its most arduous traffic but, nevertheless, a sign of the increasing assumed returns to "business as usual." Many have died. I write this, with considerable trepidation, again. I have learned, most acutely in the last eighteen months, but certainly a learning I return to, that so much is unresolvable, unprocessed, and out of reach of a clarity of mind and meaning. I try not to strive quite so much for resolving.

For the dead and for the living. For our dead, for our living. I learned of the passing of a friend's mother over the month of February. I learned of the ending of a marriage over the fall of 2020. I learned of the passing of my aunt (not by blood) over the summer. She took me in, let me do laundry at her house when I was in college. I learned of the passing of a mentor's cousin; they were like siblings, and she shared their passing with me. My mentor tells me it has been difficult to write. I understand that grief. I learned of the death of Ahmaud Arbery in February 2020. I know of the death of Breonna Taylor in March 2020. I heard of the death of George Floyd in May 2020. These were the first months of the pandemic. I know of the passing of my partner's aunt. Aunt was recovering from diabetic complications in a health facility in Harrisonburg, Virginia. She did not survive the stay. They think it might have been complicated by COVID. I learned of an auntie's return from a nursing home after an outbreak. Auntie is the parent of my namesake—we share the same last name, not blood, but chosen. His parent has been back and forth between assisted living and the hospital. My namesake still visits bi-weekly, preparing weekly with a test. I learned of the passing of a grandmother. I know of the passing of Duante Wright in April 2021. I read and listened and saw of the passing of Ma'Khia Bryant in April 2021. I learned of a grandmother's COVID-related death. A death, a passing, a crossing, too soon. For the dead and for the living.

Notes

Many thanks to Habiba Ibrahim and Badia Ahad for their editorial comments, graciousness, and the much-appreciated invitation to participate in this project. I also thank Dennis, Edward, and Lake for their collaboration and communion over the course of these ten years, and for their willingness to help me think through the important constellation of Black life in crisis. Thank you to Natasha Oladokun for being an early reader of this text, and to Manuel Cuellar and Laura Kwak for your comments. Finally, warm thanks are due to my research assistants Peri Conroy-Baarch and Mirushe Zylali for your hard work gathering materials and transcription for this publication.

1   The Great Dismal Swamp is located in southeastern Virginia and northeastern North Carolina, with an estimated original size of one million acres. Lake Drummond, which sits on the swamp, is one of two natural lakes in Virginia.

2   Byrd, a wealthy Virginian planter, set out to survey the land in 1728, specifically to delineate the boundary of North Carolina. He recorded this experience in a travel journal, *The History of the Dividing Line betwixt Virginia and N. Carolina.* In this record, Byrd's team recounts encountering a Mulatto family who communicated themselves as free. In this record, Byrd is skeptical, questioning the family's freedom.

3   *Maroon* broadly refers to people who escaped slavery to create independent groups and communities on the outskirts of slave societies. Scholars generally distinguish two kinds of marronage, though there is overlap between them. *Petit-marronage* refers to a strategy of resistance in which individuals or small groups, for a variety of reasons, escaped their plantations for a short period of days or weeks before returning. It also is used to account for the scale of the refuge sought in neighboring swamp lands, forests,

and environments, albeit without long-term sustainability. *Grand marronage*, much less prevalent, refers to people who removed themselves from their plantations permanently. Grand marronage could be carried out by individuals or small groups, or it could be the result of plantation-wide breakouts, or even colony-wide rebellions.

4   Settler-colonial subjects were hesitant to settle in those regions due to the harsh climate, and instead sought to manage the land. The first base of swamp operation took place in the 1760s and used slave labor in attempts to drain the swamp land. See, e.g., Nevius 2020: 12.

5   This section takes its title from a series of decrees in 1705 and 1741, in Virginia and North Carolina, respectively, enacted to curtail the movements of slaves. In 1741, for example, North Carolina, Chapter XXIV, sections XV–XLVII, prohibited the arming of slaves in forests and swamps. Lawmakers noted, "Many times slaves run away and lie out hid and lurking in swamps, woods, or other obscure places" (Nevius 2020: 17; Iredell 1791: 85–95).

6   *Wilmington City Gazette*, July 18, 1795; also quoted in Nevius 2020: 38.

7   Cummings's use of "marronage as assemblage" is to disrupt the space of resistance and freedom/ fugitivity, in order to also think about reoccurring arcs of vulnerability and insecurity. Cummings is also interested in placing maroon studies in direct conversation with security studies.

8   Cummings uses Jasbir Puar's terminology of "terrorist assemblages" to conjoin a discussion of surveillance studies with maroon studies, specifically through the ocular and the unknowability of how the maroon moves, is surveilled, and is viewed in relation to the colonial/plantation state.

9   I am thinking alongside the work of Hortense Spillers, Katherine McKittrick, Fred Moten, Ashon Crawley, and Tina Campt/Loophole of Retreat among others who turn to Harriet Jacobs's among other Black feminist narratives in early neo–slave accounts to think about the spatial and temporal resonance of Black life inside and outside captivity.

10 The series of events leading to Jacobs's decision to run away include death and sending family away, being sent to work on a relative's plantation with harsh treatment, and the grotesque beating of a sibling, among other things.

11 Edward, voice memo conversation with author, July 23, 2020.

12 Edward, voice memo conversation with author, July 2020.

13 Edward, voice memo conversation with author, July 2020.

14 Here I am thinking of the wonderful writing that has come out in the last two years, in response to and in the context of COVID, but also continual forms of alienation, temporality in crisis. The special issue of *SAQ* on crip temporalities (121, no. 2), for example, invites readers to contend with ableism and its intersections with race, gender, and sexuality. See also "Radical Care: Survival Strategies for Uncertain Times" (*Social Text* 38, no. 1).

15 Edward, voice memo conversation with author, July 23, 2020.

16 Dennis, voice memo conversation with author, July 17, 2020.

17 Dennis, voice memo conversation with author, July 17, 2020.

18 Dennis has chosen a time-based medium to explore and exemplify movement and gesture and location and space and temporality. In the material of video, already temporality is implied in its making. Each second twenty-five to twenty-eight frames of image make visible a fractal-like sequence of sound, body, environment to view, sense, and feel with.

19 Dennis, voice memo conversation with author, July 2020.

References

Byrd, William, and Edmund Ruffin. 1841. "The Westover Manuscripts: Containing the History of the Dividing Line Betwixt Virginia and North Carolina; A Journey to the Land of Eden, A. D. 1733; and A Progress to the Mines. Written from 1728 to 1736, and Now First Published." docsouth.unc.edu/nc/byrd/byrd.html (accessed June 28, 2020).

Cummings, Ronald. 2018. "Maroon In/Securities." *Small Axe* 22, no. 3: 47–55.

Dismal Swamp Canal Welcome Center. n.d. "History of the Dismal Swamp." dismalswamp welcomecenter.com/history/ (accessed June 4, 2021).

Eddy, Martha. 2002. "Somatic Practices and Dance: Global Influences." *Dance Research Journal* 34, no. 2: 46–62.

Dinshaw, Carolyn, Lee Edelman, Roderick A. Ferguson, Carla Freccero, Elizabeth Freeman, Judith Halberstam, Annamarie Jagose, Christopher Nealon, and Nguyen Tan Hoang. 2007. "Theorizing Queer Temporalities: A Roundtable Discussion." *GLQ: A Journal of Lesbian and Gay Studies* 13, nos. 2–3: 177–95.

Iredell, J. 1791. *Laws of the State of North-Carolina. Electronic Resource: Published, According to Act of Assembly, by James Iredell, Now One of the Associate Justices of the Supreme Court of the United States.* https://go-gale-com.proxy.mtholyoke.edu:2443/ps/retrieve.do?tabID =Monographs&resultListType=RESULT_LIST&searchResultsType=SingleTab&hit Count=1&searchType=AdvancedSearchForm&currentPosition=1&docId=GALE%7 CCB0127068198&docType=Monograph&sort=Pub+Date+Forward+Chron&content-Segment=ZCFE&prodId=ECCO&pageNum=1&contentSet=GALE%7CCB0127068198 &searchId=R1&userGroupName=mlin_w_mounthc&inPS=true (accessed June 16, 2021).

Kars, Marjoleine. 2013. "Maroons and Marronage." In *Oxford Bibliographies Online.* https://www.oxfordbibliographies.com/view/document/obo-9780199730414/obo-9780199730414-0229.xml (accessed September 9, 2021).

Lagji, Amanda. 2018. "Marooned Time: Disruptive Waiting and Idleness in Carpentier and Coetzee." *Safundi* 19, no. 2: 190–211.

McKittrick, Katherine. 2006. *Demonic Grounds: Black Women and the Cartographies of Struggle.* Minneapolis: University of Minnesota Press.

Moten, Fred. 2003. *In the Break: The Aesthetics of the Black Radical Tradition.* Minneapolis: University of Minnesota Press.

Nevius, Marcus. 2020. *City of Refuge: Slavery and Petit Marronage in the Great Dismal Swamp, 1763–1856.* Athens: University of Georgia Press.

Puar, Jasbir. 2007. *Terrorist Assemblages: Homonationalism in Queer Times.* Durham, NC: Duke University Press.

Roberts, Neil. 2015. *Freedom as Marronage.* Chicago: University of Chicago Press.

Selfish Activist. 2020. "Cultural Somantics," selfishactivist.com/cultural-somantics/ (accessed May 15, 2020).

Smith, Sarah Stefana. 2019. "Performing Bafflement: Time and Space in Photographer Ayana Jackson's *To Kill or Allow to Live.*" *Black Scholar* 49, no. : 17–27.

Spillers, Hortense J. 1987. "Mama's Baby, Papa's Maybe: An American Grammar Book." *Diacritics: A Review of Contemporary Criticism* 17, no. 2: 65–81.

Frederick C. Staidum Jr.

The *Durée* of Emancipation and the Crisis of Freedom in Antebellum Black Writing

In the closing chapter of *Incidents in the Life of a Slave Girl* (1861) by Harriet Jacobs, the author tells of her second northern employer Mrs. Bruce and her willingness to buy Jacobs's "freedom" in order to put an end to her anxious existence as a fugitive and thwart the continued torment from slave-catchers and Mr. Dodge, Miss Emily Flint's new husband, "who claimed [her] as his property" (Jacobs 2019: 165). However, Jacobs is unsettled by this proposition and asks Mrs. Bruce to refrain from such a plan, since to go through with it would ironically concede to the terms of slavery that she or any person could be "an article of property" (165). Jacobs expounds on how she "wrote to Mrs. Bruce, thanking her, but saying that being sold from one owner to another seemed too much like slavery" (165). Her phrasing "from one owner to another" marks the positionality and thus privilege of the white Mrs. Bruce, placing Jacobs's would-be benefactor into the role of a slaveholder with agency to transact in Black flesh. Despite its intended benevolence, its transactional properties concede the idea that one person can own and hold the person of another—that personhood, labor, and thus freedom can actually be held outside of the

The South Atlantic Quarterly 121:1, January 2022
DOI 10.1215/00382876-9561517 © 2022 Duke University Press

self, which is the aporia Jacobs announces with the simile of "being sold . . . seem[ing] too much like slavery."

Jacobs evinces the suppressed terms by which Mrs. Bruce's scheme works and thus betrays the deconstruction of the freedom concept and practice as contrived by nineteenth-century US democratic republicanism under racial capitalism. Jacobs reveals the discrepancy between how Mrs. Bruce sees such a transaction as "buying . . . freedom" versus Jacobs's own perception of it as buying an enslaved person. Legally, Mrs. Bruce and the State of New York would have to first recognize Jacobs as a piece of movable property in order to enter into the contract with Mr. Dodge, and in this way, Mrs. Bruce, no matter how well meaning, would certainly not be buying freedom. Nevertheless, ignoring Jacobs's protestations, Mrs. Bruce proceeds with her plan, and when Jacobs learns of the news, her response is not at all what the sympathetic nineteenth-century reader might expect. There is a deep gulf between her arduous longing for freedom as enumerated throughout the narrative and the author's horror-struck and visceral response to the message announcing her freedom:

> My brain reeled as I read these lines. A gentleman near me said, "It's true; I have seen the bill of sale." "The bill of sale!" Those words struck me like a blow. So I was *sold* at last! A human being *sold* in the free city of New York! The bill of sale is on record, and future generations will learn from it that women were articles of traffic in New York, late in the nineteenth century of the Christian religion. It may hereafter prove a useful document to antiquaries, who are seeking to measure the progress of civilization in the United States. I well know the value of that bit of paper; but much as I love freedom, I do not like to look upon it. I am deeply grateful to the generous friend who procured it, but I despise the miscreant who demanded payment for what never rightfully belonged to him or his. (165–66; original emphasis)

The note and particularly the words "the bill of sale" send the author into a disoriented state; she is dazed and taken aback. Undermining the conventional gratitude or humility of abolitionist discourse, Jacobs registers a sort of melancholia (McBride 2001: 44–51, 128). Her subsequent avoidance of "that bit of paper" suggests that the bill of sale is not a documentary artifact of freedom but rather a mnemonic, a physical reminder, of the status of chattel, which, according to the author, was the prerequisite of this iteration of freedom. Further, the phrase *"sold* at last!" standing out with its italicization mimics the title of the chapter in which this scene is contained—"Free at last." The title "Free at Last" announces a temporality of waiting, delay, and expectation—a long held expectation—only to be "*sold* at last" instead. This assumptive inclusion of the adverbial phrase "at last" conjoined to "free" seems to reinforce the linear progressiveness often attributed to the slave narrative, where freedom sequentially follows enslavement "at last." And yet, the ease by which the transactional economics of the slavocracy supplants freedom in both this grammatical unit and the larger plot of *Incidents* vis-à-vis the means by which Mrs. Bruce purchases Jacobs's freedom qua chattelhood exhibits the twisting, recursive, concurrent, and interspersed temporalities of emancipation.

Jacobs's affective and semantic dysphoria as illustrated by the above episode, when her anticipation of freedom gives way to a recapitulation of slavery's racial capital at the very moment of emancipation, heralds a pluralism of tenses (i.e., pasts, present, and futures) and temporalities (e.g., expectation, recurrence, cyclicality, and beginning) appertaining to Black liberty. Jacobs registers a temporality of emancipation that is a time of nonfreedom, when the change in legal status does not initiate freedom in the broad liberal sense. Across select nineteenth-century slave narratives, like *Incidents* but also Solomon Northup's *Twelve Years a Slave* ([1853] 2007), and their fictional interlocutors, such as Harriet E. Wilson's *Our Nig* ([1859] 2003), emancipation, which is traditionally understood as a time of progressive transition from bondage to freedom and liberal personhood, is very often fraught with nonlinear recursiveness, pause, anticipation, anticlimax, and entropy. These temporal pluralisms and nonlinearities of Black (non)freedom may be best understood as the *durée* of emancipation. Despite its connotations of lengthiness as in the historiographic *longue durée*, my adoption of this term is not so much tethered to a sense of the inordinate length of a "postslavery, prefreedom temporality" as astutely termed by Derrick Spires (2018: 49), although it could be. The interstitial or in-between time of such a formulation like "post-slavery, pre-freedom," which itself is a challenge to the assumed immediacy of the conventional bondage-to-freedom plot, maintains the sequentiality (e.g., after 1, before 2) of the more recently maligned belief in linear progress (Wright 2015: 25–27). Instead, the "*durée*" in the "*durée* of emancipation" describes a matrix of "untimely" freedoms, when and where the political, cultural, and material strictures rehearsed under slavery and practiced by whiteness foreclose any unfettered sequential passage into liberal freedom (Laski 2017: 4). As experienced by Jacobs, Northup, and Frado, the protagonist of *Our Nig*, these (non)freedoms are variably premature, delayed, provisional, or revised and are thus illiberal.

In what follows, I offer a meditation on the utility of thinking through this crisis of freedom—that is, the circumscription of Black freedom under a regime of antiblackness—alongside the concept of *durée* by nineteenth-century French thinker Henri Bergson. As I outline below, *durée*, or duration, when refracted through postcolonial and Black studies interlocutors, offers a richly multivalent way to conceptualize the contemporaneousness of slavery's past alongside and within the present and its myriad futures, while conceiving the multidirectionality of these tenses (e.g., the present can also create a past) and acknowledging the agentive creativity of Black fugitive pursuits. After fleshing out this framework using *Incidents in the Life of a Slave Girl* and Wilson's *Our Nig*, the second half of the essay offers a case study extracted from Northup's *Twelve Years a Slave*. Solomon Northup's freeborn yet ex-slave status in the narrative's present (re)constitutes ex post facto the past freedom of his father and mother to whom he was born free. In *Our Nig*, the formerly indentured protagonist Frado experiences a fleeting freedom in the form of a repetitive cycle of public dependence and adverse self-reliance. In so doing, Jacobs, Northup, and Wilson contribute important and unique philosophizing about the limits *and* possibilities of slavery's abolition.

Together, the three aforementioned works depict the duration of emancipation as a time compounded with slavery in contradistinction to the archetypical structure of the antebellum slave narrative with its episodic linear trajectory from slavery to freedom, such as relayed in *Narrative of William W. Brown, a Fugitive Slave, Written by Himself* (1847), *Narrative of the Life and Adventures of Henry Bibb, an American Slave, Written by Himself* (1849), and *The Fugitive Blacksmith; or, Events in the History of James W. C. Pennington* (1849). The outline of the conventional slave narrative proceeds from the narrator's fragmentary description of their birth and parentage to an extensive chronicling of various conditions of the enslaved, including the brutality of "a cruel master, mistress, or overseer" and the callousness "of a slave auction [and] families being separated" (Olney 1991: 153). The narrator then recounts a revelation about their condition and a decision to get free; a "failed attempt(s) to escape"; and *finally* the "description of successful . . . escape," "reception in a free state," and the "taking of a new last name . . . to accord with new social identity as a free" person (153). This conventional structure follows the form of a linear progress narrative, where the comprehension of the narrator's own enslavement and a subsequent flight from that enslavement to freedom is the core organizing schema around which the narrative turns (Sinanan 2007: 71; Olney 1991: 153; Foster 1979: 85). As is frequently the case, the *Narrative of the Life of Frederick Douglass, an American Slave* (1845) is both the paradigm and the exception (Olney 1991: 153–54). At once, Douglass upholds this trajectory via a "fundamental American plot, the myth of the self-made man . . . telling the story of one man's rise from slavery to the station of esteemed orator, writer, and statesman" (Smith 1987: 27), while also narratively juxtaposing the present against the past in decidedly nonlinear ways by moving "back and forth . . . from the person written about to the person writing" (Olney 1991: 158), such as in the line "My feet have been so cracked with the frost, that the pen with which I am writing might be laid in the gashes" (Douglass 2017: 27). And yet, despite the nonlinearity of the narration, Douglass's vacillations still embody a type of progressivism, since the presently free Douglass inserted within the narration of his past codifies a thoroughly modern and literate future iteration of that former self.

The works by Jacobs, Northup, and Wilson differ. Jacobs's escape to the confined attic crawlspace at her grandmother's house ushers in a relatively elongated pause in the conventional trajectory, and as we witnessed above, Jacob's account does not end with perpetual fugitivity, at least in the traditional sense of the term, but with her twinned purchase and manumission. Northup, Wilson, and Wilson's autobiographical protagonist, Frado, are all born into a free status to free women. Northup is kidnapped into slavery only to be rescued by the white son of his father's former owner, and Frado, who is virtually orphaned and literally abandoned by her white mother, Mag Smith, is kept as an indentured servant by a Northern white family, where conditions are analogous to slavery "Showing That Slavery's Shadows Fall Even There" (Wilson [1859] 2003: 1). The last two, in particular, while often classified as a slave narrative (*Twelve Years a Slave*) and the adjacent novelization of one (*Our Nig*), stand apart. With a freeborn narrator and protagonist, respectively, these works have a temporal structure more akin to the African-born Afro-British writings of the eighteenth-century Atlantic World, such as *Narrative of the Remarkable Particulars in the Life of James Albert Ukawsaw Gronniosaw, An African Prince* (1772) or *The Interesting Narrative of the Life of Olaudah Equiano; or, Gustavus Vassa, the African* (1789), than the US antebellum slave narrative (Carretta 2004: 1); however, unlike Gronniosaw and Equiano, the freedom into which Northup and Wilson/Frado are born is the postenlightenment, postrevolutionary individual liberty of classical Western liberalism, which shifts the meaning of their bondage and emancipation. Overall, the generic unorthodoxies of *Incidents*, *Twelve Years a Slave*, and *Our Nig*, especially their differences in transitions from enslaved to ex-slave as encapsulated by Jacobs's purchase, Northup's rescue, and Frado's discharge, provide uniquely useful material to mine the temporal and ontological crises (and possibilities) of nineteenth-century Black freedom.

The Context of the *Durée*

As mentioned, my use of the word *durée* intentionally alludes to Henri Bergson's philosophy of time. Bergson's concept of *durée*, or duration, is scaffolded by several key suppositions conceding the distinction between clock time (quantitative) and duration (qualitative); the inability of the former to measure the latter; the multiplicity of time as heterogenous yet continuous; and that duration is a "mental synthesis," which is "carried out by our consciousness" (2014b: 78, 86). Duration is the subjective experience of time as a type of flow. As one scholar has defined it, "Duration is time as experienced by consciousness;" that is, "time at its most timelike" (Lacey 2005). Bergson contrasts this sense of lived time against clock time or scientific time, since any measurement of time designated by numerical representations (e.g., seconds, minutes) only marks the termini—the beginning and the end—and not the actual duration itself (Bergson 2014b: 83). Whereas this mathematized time is a homologous form divisible into equal and quantifiable intervals, duration, Bergson proposes, is composite, dynamic, and indivisible. Bergson observes that humans (and later Bergson extends duration to all lifeforms and even inanimate matter) do not encounter, endure, and register the myriad happenings of life, their environment, or society from one single isolated juncture to another. That is, humans do not inhabit their milieu second by second or minute by minute at the extreme edges of duration as marked by clock units but rather in a manner that is necessarily fluid, because time is encountered and felt through consciousness (Bergson 2014b: 76–77).

Therefore, time is qualitative in addition to quantitative, and *durée* describes that qualification. Put differently, one minute is technically equal to any other interval of 60 seconds; however, those 60 seconds elapsed cannot be exchanged nor substituted for any other 60-second interval despite being numerically equal as with scientific formulae, since the experience of that stretch of time is qualified by external and internal conditions and context and human perception, which are always dynamic and in flux. A measurement of 60 seconds of clock time gives the impression that any equal interval is interchangeable, although the quality of that time is discrete and irreducible to quantity. We might consider one of Bergson's examples as paraphrased by philosopher Mark Sinclair, who draws on Bergson's frustration with melting sugar in water: "My impatience, the experienced quality of the passage of time being a burden, is constitutive of that interval of time itself. This is what the passage of time, as we might say, 'feels like' for me— and what, at bottom, it 'feels like' for me according to Bergson, is what it is"

(Sinclair 2019: 38; see also Bergson 2014a: 215). Bergson's impatience defines the time of the sugar's melting, and there is no conception of that period, at least for Bergson, outside of this impatience.

Furthermore, time as duration is not contiguous, where units (e.g., seconds, minutes, hours) or even broad tenses (e.g., past, present, future) exist discretely and exclusively next to others, but rather intervals of time expand multidirectionally, melding into and co-constituting other intervals—a process Bergson describes as "interpenetration" or "mutual penetration" (2014b: 77, 73). The comprehension of a musical melody, another one of Bergson's famed examples, illustrates how the interpenetration of duration works (75–76). A melody's sequence of notes cannot be legible as a whole without simultaneously experiencing, through consciousness, its past notes in the present. Otherwise, if past, present, and future were intrinsically divisible and distinct, then the notes would be heard as isolated, detached sounds and thus rendered incomprehensible as a whole. This phenomenon of heterogeneity yet continuous interpenetration is what Bergson names *qualitative multiplicity*, which is fundamental to *durée*. The framework of *durée*, thus, makes decipherable the continuity or mutual penetration among the past, present, and future tenses of experience, while also acknowledging the qualitative dynamism and uniqueness of any given moment without the reductive-ness of mathematical or quantitative equality, which renders futures predictively determinable and humans nonagentive. The concomitant interpenetration and creativity of *durée* can be an exceedingly useful point of departure for interpreting the temporalities of slavery and freedom in Black studies by providing for the ways in which the political economies and anti-Black ontologies of colonization and slavery's past inform our present and myriad futures while also appreciating the creative possibilities of Black life, escape, and fugitivity that are not yet foreordained.

Although a potentially outmoded choice for a theoretical interlocuter, in recent years, scholars from postcolonial philosophy to Black queer performance studies have productively reengaged Bergson and have found duration generative, specifically the seemingly contradictory interpenetration among tenses (e.g., the continuation of the past into the present) and the dynamism of qualitative multiplicity. Despite Bergson's negligent sidestepping of French colonialism in his own criticism of German "imperialist expansion" (Sinclair 2019: 20), Souleymane Bachir Diagne (2008) and Alia Al-Saji (2004) have insisted on Bergson's utility. In an effort to make sense of why Léopold Sédar Senghor would take up Bergsonian ideas within his decolonial project, Diagne focuses on Bergson's break with the mechanism and fatalism of mathematized time in order to "philosophiz[e] otherwise" and conceive "time that really *does* something (instead of just measuring movement, as with Aristotle's definition) and that also endures" (2008: 128). In a similar vein, Al-Saji critiques the latent hierarchical and teleological view of culture in Bergson's later writing by returning to duration with its "nonhierarchical coexistence of rhythms of becoming and ways of life" and "nonlinear theory of time" (15, 29). Duration as a potentially decolonial approach to temporality resonates with Tavia Nyong'o's engagement with Bergson in *Afro-Fabulations: The Queer Drama of Black Life*. I am particularly taken by Nyong'o's crossing of Bergson's *durée* with Amiri Baraka's "'changing same' of black aesthetics" (Nyong'o 2019: 4) and its "intertwining of 'tensed' and 'tenseless' time" (9). In his essay "The Changing Same (R&B and New Black Music)," Baraka builds out a framework of the "changing same" to wrestle with the concurrent evolution and consistency in US Black music. In Baraka's explanation, our ever changing context (i.e., the passage of time) and its attendant alterations to social conditions and materiality necessarily produce transmutations in Black culture ("mixtures . . . transfers and imitations"), and yet, the motivation or "impulse" of Black cultural production and creativity remains the same—that is, a commitment to and thrust toward self-determination—either freedom from the constraints of Western whiteness or Blackness and a freedom toward self-definition (i.e., to be "The Black Man in the West") (Jones [1968] 1998: 180). The sameness of the changing same is more akin to an approach or modus operandi rather than an essential racial essence (although Baraka certainly leaves room for that). Nyong'o picks up on this significance of context and modality while interpreting the temporality and "deeper history" of queer and trans* of color art and performance. In order to unfold the contours of Black queer duration, Nyong'o turns to the doubled and "out of nowhere" interpolation of Black trans and drag icon Crystal LeBeija within the performance film *for how we perceived a life (Take 3)* (2012) by Wu Tsang, who interposes LeBeija's boisterous denunciation of white normative beauty standards as captured in the earlier film *The Queen* (1967) within the already quoted dialogue of *Paris Is Burning* (1990) (Nyong'o 2019: 9). Nyong'o insists that this interpolative composition is not "a corrective or rebuke to these earlier queer films," but rather it demonstrates the duration of Black and queer time, since LaBeija's inhabitation of these other moments—1990 and 2012 in addition to 1967— remains apropos (Nyong'o 2019: 9). While certainly changed, the persistence of exclusionary cis-normative and misogynoir conditions structure access to funding sources for film production in the 1980s, for example, or the dissonance between major judicial victories toward marriage equality in 2012 and the disproportionate death of Black trans women in that same year. This shared "coeval presentness" of a historical figure (or event, idea, etc.) within a tense to which she allegedly does not belong marks the contrapuntal existence of "both tensed and tenseless" times, which Nyong'o likens to Bergson's duration (Nyong'o 2019: 9, 10). LaBeija, her prescient critique, and the Black trans* self-affirming point-of-view from which it emerges are not anachronistic or "out of context," or as Nyong'o writes, "rather than taking this historical audio-image from the 1960s out of context, Tsang's performance film is perhaps better described as *creating* a new context for it" (8).

Although these scholars, who are thinking through the conditions of coloniality and anti-Blackness in conversation with Bergson, are probing different eras, their adaptations of duration are exceedingly fruitful to the present study, specifically the reframing of anachronisms within Black cultural productions as not always out of context, which, of course, has all of the connotations of Hegelian African ahistoricity and the like, but as the creation of new context—that is, making legible the conditions constituting the changing same. So, in the above episode from *Incidents in the Life of a Slave Girl*, Jacobs's sensation of disillusionment and repetition are not anachronistic or out of context. Instead, Jacobs's description of her affect makes legible the potentiality of slavery's return even after her fugitivity, during her emancipation, and in the North, because the circumstances after escape, during manumission, and in the North (e.g., Fugitive Slave Clause of the US Constitution, Fugitive Slave Act of 1793, and the human chattel principle more generally) make possible slavery's reprisal at the moment of emancipation. Jacobs's, and by extension Northup's and Wilson's, creation of new contexts for slavery within their cultural productions forces the question, What is this new context that allows slavery to exist in a tense to which it allegedly does not belong? What are these conditions—economic, epistemological, or the like? These get at a different constellation of questions, answers, and times for abolition—one not built on negation (i.e., freedom is the absence of slavery) but rather on presence (i.e., freedom is the existence of life-affirming conditions).

Jacobs's preface to *Incidents* offers a useful specimen of how ex-slave temporalities operate as *durée* and how the interpenetration of past, present, and future accentuates a changing same context. The new conditions within which Jacobs finds herself embroiled in the US North encourage her to draw parallels, albeit metamorphosed between the illiteracy of her past bondage and the irregular writing of the present narrative. The manner by which Jacobs contextualizes the alleged deficiencies of her writing and the justification for producing and publishing her narrative abounds with the interpenetration of past, present, and future. Under the pseudonym Linda Brent, she writes,

> I wish I were more competent to the task I have undertaken. But I trust my
> readers will excuse deficiencies in consideration of circumstances. I was born
> and reared in Slavery; and I remained in a Slave State twenty-seven years.
> Since I have been at the North, it has been necessary for me to work diligently
> for my own support, and the education of my children. This has not left me
> much leisure to make up for the loss of early opportunities to improve myself;
> and it has compelled me to write these pages at irregular intervals, whenever
> I could snatch an hour from household duties. (Jacobs 2019: 5)

There are several experiments with temporality in the entire preface—first,
the past melts into the present via Jacobs's incapacities; second, Jacobs diffu-
sively parallels her present lack of time to her past dispossession of time
under slavery; and, third, she charges the reader with changing the future.
Through the first two, Jacobs creates a *new* context for enslavement, since her
self-described writerly deficiencies and dearth of time to write her narrative
turn on a similar axis—the changed yet same exploitation of Black labor.
Through a mélange of temporalities, Jacobs chronicles the conflation and
accumulation of the contrived material and intellectual depravations of slavery and how they persist across time. She deploys diverse verbal tenses and
forms and also a diction of dispossession and contradiction in a way that communicates the nonlinearity, or at least "irregular intervals," of ex-slave time.
Superficially, Jacobs outlines a linear trajectory from enslavement to freedom;
she was first "born and reared" under the institution of slavery and then
"remained" subjected to this existence for a span of twenty-seven years. The
present perfect form that follows ("Since I have been at the North") alludes to
her ongoing ex-slave status. However, the remainder of the passage and its
prefacing of her slave narrative reveals as much about the circumscription of
Jacobs's present status as it does about her past captivity. For example, through
both placement and capitalization, "in Slavery" and "at the North" are syntac-
tically joined and contrasted as antithetical states of being, and yet the paral-
lelism is skewed since the US North is a geography and not an explicit social
position. Jacobs curiously avoids the diction associated with unencumbered
liberation and, instead, communicates a continued dispossession, specifically
of time and capacity, as engendered by what Saidiya Hartman might desig-
nate as "the burdened individuality of freedom" (Hartman 1997: 115–24).
This dispossession of time—by way of both labor exploitation in an industri-
alizing North and the accumulated disabilities originating under slavery—is
the axis on which the potential of the ex-slave is curtailed. It demonstrates the
accumulation of white slaveholders' restrictions on enslaved people's literacy

and appropriation of their time, where the educational deprivation and economic theft of the past materially affects the present, including the production of the very text the readers are reading.

The notion of dispossession is heightened by the author's word choices of "snatch" to describe her appropriation of the requisite time to write her narrative and "leisure" to characterize the type of time essential to improving the literacy skills denied her under bondage. *Snatch* disrupts her otherwise normal use of time to attend to "household duties." The phrase "household duties," although potentially referencing Jacobs's personal domestic chores, dissembles and refers to her diligent work outside the home by way of the determiner "This," which opens the sentence. This connection to alienated labor attributes the possession of this time to someone else other than Jacobs, so then "snatch" also ushers in a connotation of theft. Jacobs's theft of her own(ed) time as she describes it in the preface foreshadows the many instances and allusions to stealing and fraud throughout *Incidents*, especially the paradox of slaveholders' definitions of theft, including in the cases of an enslaved person brutally punished by "Mr. Conant" for taking "a pig from his master, to appease his hunger," and of the trickster-like Luke, who hides some of his dead master's money in a pair of trousers, which he is sure will be benevolently given to him (Jacobs 2019: 43, 159–60). In addition, Jacobs's use of *leisure*, a now-rare historical usage meaning an "opportunity afforded by [a] freedom from occupation," a "duration of opportunity," and "a period or spell of unoccupied time," qualifies the type of time Jacobs anticipated and the relationship that she would have with that time after slavery.[1] The point, here, is that the past of slavery materializes into the present by way of Jacobs's self-described incompetence, which is the interpenetration to which Bergson alludes. That is, like the melody, Jacobs's struggle to write and write well would not make sense without the consciousness of the past. In addition to the content of *Incidents*, the very materiality of the narrative's production would be illegible or at least mistaken without the imbrication of the past. But what's more, those earlier conditions continue in an altered form. The US North certainly lacks the antiliteracy laws of the US South; however, the form of Jacobs's employment in the North has maintained a similar effect.

Jacobs echoes the disabling dispossession of Frado as depicted in the autobiographical novel *Our Nig*, by Harriet Wilson. The slave-like conditions of her time indentured to the white middle-class Bellmonts, which includes physical torture and nutritional neglect, accumulates within her body and manifests as bouts of debilitating illness that reduce her capacity to subsist and support her young son. Her slave-like indentured past is thus imbricated within Frado's present via the cyclical disability of her body, and yet Wilson's very writing of the autobiographical novel by the real-life Frado in an effort to eke out an existence and retrieve her son from the county house demonstrates a commitment to creating a different future from the one foretold from within that cycle. As a work set in New England and among its gradual abolition of the institution of slavery, Wilson's autobiographical novel furthers considerations of the interpenetration of past and present and its circumscription of freedom, particularly freedom in the form of independence.

The last two chapters of the work, in particular, demonstrate the cyclicality of emancipation and dependence amid the interstice of "post-slavery, pre-freedom." Although formally free, the novel's orphaned protagonist Frado is trapped in a cycle of dependency, first as a deserted indentured servant in the white Bellmont household, and second as a disabled ward of the state after her formal emancipation at the end of her indentured term. Her temporal experience of freedom is characterized by fits and starts, gradualism, anticipation, disenchantment, cyclicality, and return. On that last point, whereas for Jacobs slavery returns to her, Frado, although emancipated, is made to return to "indentured" servitude or similar conditions of dependence. Her seeming autonomous decisions to depend on the state and charity are continuously coerced by social inequality, material lack, and, especially, the ways in which years of exploitation and abuse at the hands of Mrs. Bellmont and her daughter have accumulated in her body, rendering Frado frequently sick and disabled. In this way, *Our Nig* betrays another temporality of emancipation's *durée*—latency. The enslavement-like conditions of Frado's orphaned freedom latently linger in her body, circumscribing her capacity to pursue her goals of independence as defined by the period, a major component of liberal freedom and personhood.

The Multidirectionality of *Durée*

Returning to Jacobs's disheartened and dejected tone accompanying the occasion of her freedom, although unexpected, this affect is not exclusive to *Incidents*. Solomon Northup in *Twelve Years a Slave* similarly expresses a sort of equivocation about the circumstances of his emancipation from slavery. When placed in conversation with Jacobs, their cognizance of *durée* and its interpenetration accentuates the importance of the method by which one is emancipated to the efficacy of one's freedom. Emancipation vis-à-vis the anti-Black terms of slavery and colonization—Black as abject thing, reducible to financialized object, unable to bear witness under the strictures of US legal code and custom—renders freedom conditioned. In addition, since

Northup was born free, his present ex-slave status evinces the precarity of his parents' and particularly his father's historical free status that theretofore bequeathed Northup's own freedom. Liberal, republican freedom of the early American white, landed gentry was always about a linear futurity—about guaranteeing the generational wealth and privilege often financed through the future values (reproductive and otherwise) of enslaved people; the enslavement of Northup's father's progeny is a reflection of the latent circumscription of his father's time as much as it is an attribute of Northup's. The narrative and the recollection of his rescue by the white Henry Northup inadvertently demonstrates the multidirectionality of temporality, since the *present* status of Northup and his more recent experience of bondage retroactively redefine the *past* freedom of Mintus, since the latter was not enough to preclude Solomon from being enslaved, rendering it quasi at best.

After Northup successfully arranged for letters explaining his kidnapping and enslavement to be dispatched to acquaintances in New York, the attorney Henry B. Northup, son of Northup's father's former master, procured evidence authenticating Northup's free status and New York state residency, after which the governor of that state deputized the white Northup to rescue the *other* Northup under New York's 1840 personal liberty law. In early January 1853, Henry Northup arrived at Epp's plantation attesting to Northup's free status, and following an official proceeding "a paper was drawn up and signed by the proper parties, wherein Epps acknowledged he was satisfied of my right to freedom, and formally surrendered me to the authorities of New-York" (Northup [1853] 2017: 175). After conveying these transactions, Solomon Northup opens the subsequent chapter ruminating on his aloof comportment: "As the steamer glided on its way towards New-Orleans, *perhaps* I was not happy—*perhaps* there was no difficulty in restraining myself from dancing round the deck—perhaps I did not feel grateful to the man who had come so many hundred miles for me—perhaps I did not light his pipe, and wait and watch his word, and run at his slightest bidding. If I didn't—well, no matter" (175). Northup's italicization and repetition of "*perhaps*" opens up the possibility that he was not contented nor appreciative of his rescue. The uncertainty produces a tone of ambivalence and near indifference. This tone resonates with Jacobs's own affect of disappointment, and together both reveal something about the *durée* of emancipation and enduring crisis of Black freedom.

Elsewhere, I have interpreted the moment of Solomon Northup's retrieval from slavery and his accompanying emotional morass as his theorization of the relationship between enslavement and quotidian performances of obligation and indebtedness (Staidum 2019: 20–21). I want to extend that analysis and consider it alongside Jacobs's disillusionment, since, together, the authors and their sensations make legible a pattern of occasions when the alleged yet wanton past of slavery inordinately interpolates a dubious inauguration into freedom. For example, the myriad affidavits, especially those of white citizens, presented to the New York governor, are the sources from which Henry Northup's deputized authority to rescue and thus emancipate Solomon Northup exudes. The white male propertied voice can do what the Black(ened) voice is unable to do. The performative and legal power of these attestations evokes the powerlessness of Northup's earlier assertions of his free status directed at his first captor, James Burch, at Williams's slave pen in Washington, DC, nearly twelve years prior. When he awakens in the jail-like conditions, Northup inquires about his situation. He paraphrases Burch's response, insisting that "I was his slave—that he had bought me, and that he was about to send me to New-Orleans" (Northrup [1853] 2017: 28). Northup writes of his retort, "I asserted, aloud and boldly that I was a freeman—a resident of Saratoga, where I had a wife and children, who were also free, and that my name was Northup" (29). After a bit of back and forth, Burch violently replies "with blasphemous oaths" and declares that Northup is "a black liar, a runaway from Georgia" (29). Burch and the jailer Ebenezer Radburn then physically beat him in an attempt to coerce Northup into accepting a false history and timeline of a life as an enslaved person born in the slave state of Georgia. Northup refers to Burch and Radburn as "the authors of my imprisonment," who figuratively re-place him, not on the free soil of New York and the place of his birth but on a landscape of slavery. For Burch, this cartographic fiction offers a justification for Northup's captivity and Burch's alleged ownership over him. The modifier of "black" before "liar," its racial narration of inherent black servitude and subhumanity, and the uneven power of the lash reinscribe this false truth and temporality. In the mouth of Burch, Northup's corporeal complexion and history of freedom is transmogrified into a fungible Black ontology, where and when past, present, and future can be rewritten and made into a truth. As with this originary scene of kidnapping and enslavement, where Burch's word has greater power than Northup's, so too does the white Northup's, and the entire state apparatus that upholds his singular ability to *free* the Black Northup twelve years later.

As with Jacobs's melancholia, Northup's ambivalent *perhaps* signals this nested and precarious aspect of emancipation's *durée*, when the terms of freedom share the terms of slavery. These occasions of unfreedom in spite of emancipation are only made possible through the conditions of slavery's modernity (i.e., the liberal rights discourse materialized through the profits and leisure created by Atlantic colonization and slavery). Hence, slavery does not simply haunt through memory or a traumatized psyche, although certainly it does, but the terms of slavery live into the present ordination of Jacobs's and Northup's manumission and their respective emancipated futures through the very legal and economic institutions and grammars that make manumission conceivable—Mrs. Bruce's purchasing Jacobs's person and not her freedom and Henry Northup's authority to testify on Solomon Northup's behalf, since the Blackness-cum-chattelhood of the latter Northup precluded him from bearing witness against whites' lies about his personal history and enslavement.

For Northup, emancipation is no break, and in fact, Northup's affect betrays how the past merges with the present. Northup's experience of *durée* and the penetration of past into the future reveals how the means and method of emancipation are as important as the state of being free, and that the limitations of attaining emancipation will always threaten and circumscribe freedom—that is, it is a crisis of freedom. Emancipation is not a clean break with the past or an unobstructed induction of freedom. Emancipation is made into a crisis by this conflation of past and present, but since, as delineated by Bergson, the experience of time in general is not successively linear, nor is the transition from past to present terminable, conflation alone does not inherently produce crisis (Morris 1992: 1209). Freedom's crisis emanates from the unequal discrepancy between majoritarian time and Black anticipation, between the social and political conditions that constitute slavery and the professed conditions of liberal personhood. This crisis of freedom is the precarity of Black prerogative and self-determination. Emancipation commences according to Mrs. Bruce's and Henry Northup's time and not by Jacobs's or Solomon Northup's. Instead, emancipation is one more performance of the racial-social power relations of slavery, just one more *"incident* in the life of a slave."

In addition to the penetration of the past into the present as coeval times and terms, Northup's self-reflection reveals how his twelve-year interlude as an enslaved person co-constitutes or interpenetrates those aforementioned tenses. This phenomenon is best embodied by the figure of Mintus Northup, Solomon Northup's father. Mintus and his manumitted free status haunt the entirety of *Twelve Years a Slave* despite being mentioned in only the first chapter, the last two chapters, and the second appendix, which contains the "Memorial of Anne" or the petition of Solomon Northup's wife to the governor of New York consisting of thirteen affidavits and/or signatures from prominent white citizens attesting to Northup's freeborn status. In an effort to establish the legitimacy of his freedom, Northup spends a sizable portion of the opening chapter narrating the biography of his father, highlighting the white Northup family's possession of his "paternal side," his father's removal to New York state with one of the white Northups, and his subsequent manumission "by a direction in his will" (Northrup [1853] 2017: 15–16). Solomon Northup also foregrounds his father's character traits of honesty, morality, regard for education, and industriousness; his property ownership; and his suffrage eligibility. As others have commented, this narrative and biographical grounding in paternal freedom, industriousness, and civic participation "situates[s] his own early life in an unbroken network of family and society that contrasts dramatically with the chaotic family relations found in most other narratives as well as in the later portion of Northup's own story" (Worley 1997: 245). It underlines the temporal perversity of Northup's antebellum narrative, where enslavement follows freedom, contrasting the trajectory of liberal revolution and reform and the plot of the slave narrative. Sam Worley (1997: 247) has demonstrated how *Twelve Years a Slave* eschews the Ben Franklin-esque rags-to-riches temporality that weds subjecthood to rationality and linearity, which removes any "possibility of . . . the return of history, the possibility that prosperity may be as fragile and temporary as poverty has proven to be." Extending this line of criticism, I contend that the *durée* of *Twelve Years a Slave* demonstrates both the "return of history" with the present and the constitution of history by the present.

Mintus's manumission is imbricated within Solomon's rescue decades later, since it is the former's relationship to his former slaveholder that makes Solomon's recovery possible. The previously mentioned affidavits refer to Mintus by name or relation at least fourteen times. Further, Northup acknowledges the salience of Mintus and his paternal relationship with the white Northups to the narrative when, in the midst of the opening chapter and description of his genealogy, he offers this gracious aside:

> Henry B. Northup, Esq., of Sandy Hill, a distinguished counselor at law, and the man to whom, under Providence, I am indebted for my present liberty, and my return to the society of my wife and children, is a relative of the family in which my forefathers were thus held to service, and from which they took the name I bear. To this fact may be attributed the persevering interest he has taken in my behalf. (Northrup [1853] 2017: 16)

The textual and formal imbrication of Henry Northup's role in Northup's renewed freedom in the middle of the narration of Mintus's manumission links these two moments even though they are separated by "some fifty years," suggesting that Mintus's free status saves his son (Northrup [1853]

2017: 16). Solomon Northup's deferred liberation, or put differently, the interlude of enslavement carving open his free status, informs retrospectively Mintus's freedom despite the nearly fifty-year gulf between the two events. Mintus's freedom, his status's capacity to protect his progeny, is circumscribed or is revealed to be deficient ex post facto by his son's kidnapping and subsequent "twelve years a slave." It is not patrimonial freedom alone that restores Northup but Mintus's connection to the white Northups, a relationship defined by a legacy of slavery, extractive economics, and unequal power. In this way, we might understand the duration of Solomon Northup's emancipation as a composite of myriad moments sharing multiple inceptions. The *durée* of Northup's emancipation certainly encompasses his rescue from the Epp's plantation, but it also involves his first protestations at "Williams' slave pen in Washington," *and* his decision to pursue employment with the conniving Brown and Hamilton, *and* his "having been born a freeman," *and* the manumission of Mintus Northup, his father.

I use *durée* of emancipation rather than *durée* of slavery or *durée* of freedom to describe the qualitative multiplicity and temporal interpenetration of the two. Emancipation is an ongoing process; it does not simply signify a finality or new state of being. Emancipation, the time of getting free, has always been embedded in slavery, since the first Africans struggled on the early ships crossing the Atlantic or while waiting in the dungeons of a coastal slave castle. This process of getting free has been coeval with slavery and vice versa. What I am suggesting is an adjustment in scale and directionality—that the time of slavery was always already interpenetrated by the time of emancipation. The *durée* of emancipation stretches into slavery as much as slavery and its afterlife (as in "the afterlife of slavery") do into "the future of the ex-slave" vis-à-vis abolition's "skewed life chances, limited access to health and education, premature death, incarnation, and impoverishment" (Hartman 2008: 6, 107). As such, emancipation is not only "the nonevent" but is also *the* event (Hartman 1997: 116). The negative space left by the *longue durée* of emancipations that were, would have been, are, and are yet to be makes legible the contours, context, and conditions inducing the concomitance of slavery and freedom, and the limitations of the latter.

Note

This publication was supported by a Career Enhancement Fellowship from the Institute for Citizens and Scholars (formerly the Woodrow Wilson National Fellowship Foundation) and the Andrew W. Mellon Foundation.

1   *OED Online*, s.v. "leisure, n." www.oed.com/view/Entry/107171?rskey=94VmGZ& result=1&isAdvanced=false (accessed June 13, 2021).

References

Al-Saji, Alia. 2004. "The Memory of Another Past: Bergson, Deleuze and a New Theory of Time." *Continental Philosophy Review* 37, no. 2: 203–39. doi.org/10.1007/s11007-005-5560-5.

Bergson, Henri. (1889) 2014. "Time and Free Will." In *Key Writings*, edited by Keith Ansell Pearson and John Ó. Maoilearca, 57–94. New York: Bloomsbury Academic.

Bergson, Henri. (1907) 2014. "Creative Evolution." In *Key Writings*, edited by Keith Ansell Pearson and John Ó. Maoilearca, 207–48. New York: Bloomsbury Academic.

Carretta, Vincent. 2004. Introduction to *Unchained Voices: An Anthology of Black Authors in the English-Speaking World of the Eighteenth Century*. Lexington: University Press of Kentucky.

Diagne, Souleymane Bachir. 2008. "Bergson in the Colony: Intuition and Duration in the Thought of Senghor and Iqbal." *Qui parle* 17, no. 1: 125–45.

Douglass, Frederick. 2017. *Narrative of the Life of Frederick Douglass, an American Slave, Written by Himself: Authoritative Text, Contexts, Criticism*. Edited by William L. Andrews and William S. McFeely. New York: W. W. Norton.

Foster, Frances Smith. 1979. *Witnessing Slavery: The Development of Ante-bellum Slave Narratives*. Westport, CT: Greenwood Press.

Hartman, Saidiya V. 1997. *Scenes of Subjection: Terror, Slavery, and Self-Making in Nineteenth-Century America*. Oxford: Oxford University Press.

Hartman, Saidiya. 2008. *Lose Your Mother: A Journey Along the Atlantic Slave Route*. New York: Macmillan.

Jacobs, Harriet A. 2019. *Incidents in the Life of a Slave Girl: Authoritative Text, Contexts, Criticism*. Edited by Frances Smith Foster and Richard Yarborough. New York: W. W. Norton.

Jones, LeRoi (Amiri Baraka). 1998. *Black Music*. New York: Da Capo Press.

Lacey, Alan. 2005. "Bergson, Henri-Louis." In *The Oxford Companion to Philosophy*, edited by Ted Honderich. New York: Oxford University Press.

Laski, Gregory. 2017. *Untimely Democracy: The Politics of Progress after Slavery*. New York: Oxford University Press.

McBride, Dwight. 2001. *Impossible Witnesses: Truth, Abolitionism, and Slave Testimony*. New York: New York University Press.

Morris, Thomas D. 1992. "Slaves and the Rules of Evidence in Criminal Trials." *Chicago-Kent Law Review* 68, no. 3: 1209–40.

Northup, Solomon. (1853) 2017. *Twelve Years a Slave*. Edited by Henry Louis Gates and Kevin M. Burke. New York: W. W. Norton.

Nyong'o, Tavia. 2019. *Afro-Fabulations: The Queer Drama of Black Life*. New York: New York University Press.

Olney, James. 1991. " 'I Was Born': Slave Narratives, Their Status as Autobiography and as Literature." In *The Slave's Narrative*, edited by Charles T. Davis and Henry Louis Gates. New York: Oxford University Press.

Sinanan, Kerry. 2007. "The Slave Narrative and the Literature of Abolition." In *The Cambridge Companion to the African American Slave Narrative*, edited by Audrey Fisch, 61–80. Cambridge: Cambridge University Press.

Sinclair, Mark. 2019. *Bergson*. London: Routledge.

Spires, Derrick R. 2018. " 'I Read My Mission as 'Twere a Book': Temporality and Form in the Early African American Serial Sketch Tradition." In *A Question of Time: American Literature from Colonial Encounter to Contemporary Fiction*, edited by Cindy Weinstein. New York: Cambridge University Press.

Smith, Valerie. 1987. *Self-Discovery and Authority in Afro-American Narrative.* Cambridge, MA: Harvard University Press.

Staidum, Frederick C. 2019. "'Are We MEN!!': Blackness, (Non)masculinities, and the Grammar of the Interrogative in Early Anti-slavery Discourse." *Black Scholar* 49, no. 2: 11–26.

Wilson, Harriet E. (1859) 2003. *Our Nig; Or, Sketches from the Life of a Free Black; in a Two-Story White House, North., Showing That Slaverys Shadows Fall Even There, by Our Nig.* New York: Vintage.

Worley, Sam. 1997. "Solomon Northup and the Sly Philosophy of the Slave Pen." *Callaloo* 20, no. 1: 243–59.

Wright, Michelle M. 2015. *Physics of Blackness: Beyond the Middle Passage Epistemology.* Minneapolis: University of Minnesota Press.

Eve Dunbar

Genres of Enslavement: Ruptured Temporalities of Black Unfreedom and the Resurfacing Plantation

> If you're ever down in Houston,
> Boy you better walk right
> And you better not squabble,
> And you better not fight
> Bason and Brock will arrest you,
> Payton and Boone will take you down
> You can bet your bottom dollar,
> That you're Sugar Land bound
> —Huddie "Lead Belly" Ledbetter,
> "Midnight Special" (1934)

> You can hide a lot in an acre, in the dirt.
> —Colson Whitehead, *The Nickel Boys* (2019)

In July 2018, the *New York Times* began reporting on the remains of some ninety-five people discovered on a construction site in the Houston, Texas, suburb of Sugar Land (Mervosh 2018). The archaeologists called in to exhume and identify the remains determined that they likely belonged to African American laborers who worked between 1878 to 1911 on the Imperial Sugar Company's plantation as part of Texas's convict-lease system. Minimal state regulation regarding the quality of care for the incarcerated meant that they were treated to dreadful and deadly work conditions. Public outrage regarding these conditions resulted in the

The South Atlantic Quarterly 121:1, January 2022
DOI 10.1215/00382876-9561531 © 2022 Duke University Press

Texas legislature outlawing convict-leasing to private companies in 1910. Without easy access to cheap labor, Imperial Sugar sold the fertile plot of land to the state of Texas in 1908.[1] Although Texas Corrections renamed the plot Imperial State Prison Farm, little changed in the conditions of the laborer's lives during or after the land's transition from private to public ownership—those imprisoned, while no longer leased, remained property (of the state), working the land for no wages under an ungodly Texas sun. Change came in name only such that by the 1930s the prison was again renamed the Central State Farm. Around this time, "Lead Belly" Ledbetter was known to sing a version of his blues song "Midnight Special" in which the Sugar Land prison remained a threat for those passing through Houston. This version of the song stands as a testament of the prison's place in the Black imaginary. Central State Farm remained a working prison farm until it was permanently closed in 2011.

Despite this transfer of land from private to public ownership and promises of penal reform, Texas's prison system, like most US prisons, was and continues to be bound to the racial logics of enslavement and Jim Crow. For example, it is not mere coincidence that just as legalized slavery was constitutionally shuttered in the United States, Texas prisons found themselves with an exploding population. Unable to house and pay for the care for an expanding population, Texas made use of the exception of the Thirteenth Amendment (1865) which states that while "neither slavery nor involuntary servitude, shall exist within the United States, or any place subject to their jurisdiction," an exception can be made when servitude is a "punishment for crime whereof the party shall have been duly convicted." Whether one calls it a marriage of convenience or something less benign, deep South prisons outsourced prisoners, the majority of whom were Black, to work and live on privately owned plantations that had been able to weather the storm of slavery's abolition. By 1867 Black men and some women made Texas state property even after abolition lived and died in the exception of the Thirteenth Amendment, their bodies resurfacing to remind us of the illusory nature of freedom in the United States. As historian Sarah Haley notes more generally about the convict leasing system, it "perpetuated both the white South's acceleration of industrial capitalism and its attendant development of Jim Crow modernity" (Haley 2016: 28).

The present-day portion of the Central story is tethered to labor, as well. The Fort Bend Independent School District sought to build the James Reese Career and Technical Center (JRCTC) on the site of the former prison's agricultural fields. During the JRCTC'a building process, the remains of those

who died while incarcerated and conscripted into labor resurfaced just outside of the Old Imperial Farm Cemetery, the prison's official site of intern-
ment. This official site holds thirty graves of incarcerated men and their
guards who died at the prison farm. The unofficial site holds three times as
many who might have been lost to history had they not been disinterred for
the JRCTC's construction.[2] While the discovery of their remains is framed as
a surprise within national news coverage, I believe the dead people's return
to this temporal world illuminates what Toni Morrison refers to as the "grief"
of African American history. Moreover, the power of such unburied Black
grief is that it threatens to unexpectedly disrupt narratives of US progressive
racial history, justice, freedom, modernity, and geography's capacity to contain and overwrite the past. The emergence of the remains of the incarcerated brings to a national light the long shadow of slavery's afterlife. Thus, I
open in Sugar Land and with these resurfaced remains to highlight how
close we live to the plantation. And as Sharon Holland (2000: 4) reminds us,
"raising the dead, allowing them to speak, and providing them with the
agency of physical bodies in order to tell the story of a death-in-life" is a productive counter to the American desire to render slavery, conquest, and
removal unspoken. The plantation's proximity requires we think the plantation not as legacy but as a living site that invites a continued deliberation on
the meaning and modes of Black emancipation.

Within literary studies, we often refer to those texts that explore the
long-lingering impact of enslavement and the way it resurfaces in the contemporary moment as "neo–slave narratives." In this essay, I will explore
how James Hannaham's *Delicious Foods* (2015) and Colson Whitehead's
Nickel Boys (2019) fictionally invite considerations of genre and slavery's
toxic hold on the United States. Taken together these novels push readers to
think beyond generic convention and historical periodization toward states
of freedom in the new millennium. Both texts invite reflection on how the
neo–slave narrative intersects with the past and present, allowing for a
more iterative reflection on how African American literary production
might not only illuminate the living history of enslavement. Literature may
also renew consideration of unfreedom within a more contemporary
moment at the level of genre. My analysis of these novels focuses on how
they extend the neo–slave narrative beyond encounters with the antebellum
period. I offer some preliminary considerations for thinking with and
beyond the neo–slave narrative as a literary genre in the 21st century.
Toward that, one consideration takes the form of exploring the generic
breaks each novel takes from sentimental forms of abolitionism to expose

national frameworks that are discursively and materially integral to continued anti-Blackness and Black death. Additionally, I contend that through their critical investments in elements of the slave narrative—such as the escape plot, the power of education, and negotiating threats of violence—writers like Hannaham and Whitehead consider various ways in which African American characters navigate unfreedom that is often narrated as analogous to enslavement. Through these novels, then, I trace how contemporary African American novels might evolve elements of the neo–slave narrative so that it is freed from the temporal constraints of the antebellum period. In so extending the metaphors of enslavement beyond the period of enslavement in the United States, these authors provide a critique of the national relationship to Black suffering, but also imagine an ongoing legacy of Black life in the face of state-sanctioned violence.

To talk of plantation logics is always to speak in a way that resists the fiction the United States weaves regarding both its exceptionalism and slavery's end as the end of Black exploitation. This fiction is countered by the reality that the plantation is as much a way of structuring relationships to power as it is a site relegated to a period in time. As such, the plantation moves through time and space (McKittrick 2013: 9). In narrative moments when the plantation is revealed, we are reminded not only where we have been in the United States but also of the possibility that we might live and relate to each other in other ways. For instance, we see such revision modeled by Ashanté M. Reese, who seeks to undo "the violence of abstraction" experienced by the men who died while in the hands of the state, and whose lives and deaths remained shrouded in anonymity conditioned by the Central State Prison Farm (Reese 2021). Considering the tension between her training as an anthropologist and how she might acknowledge and restore the humanity of those ninety-five people, Reese bridges the divide through ritual. She names as many of the dead as she can, narrating their personal stories gathered from prison archives, and offers the dead a bit of sweetness at her home alter. Her offering is a family favorite, tea cakes, which she makes in honor of those who died. She asks "for permission to explore their lives," asks them to "bless [her] ongoing work," and invites them to "tarry" with her as long as they see fit. In exchange she holds a place for their lives and bodies "that will not be scarified on the altar of capitalism" (Reese 2021). This is the sort of care I trace through Hannaham's and Whitehead's narratives in order to think the plantation beyond the prison-house of Black death.

While acknowledging the plantation as a site of anti-Black violence and death, the prospect of heralding a future is what Katherine McKittrick evokes to remind us that we must also think other possibilities when we think plantations—the structure is dynamic in its return, and its inhabitants might reveal new ways of being in the world. Suppose the plantation moves and refuses its marginalization to memory, its "relegation to the dustbin of history," as Clyde Woods notes (Woods 1998: 4). How might and must it be made usable by its former inhabitants' many decedents? Not merely a reminder of a past, conjuring the plantation functions as a refusal to close a wound of the plantocracy. If redress is impossible, what does the constant unburying of the past produce for Black people in the United States (or the Americas, for that matter)? The question of redress becomes especially significant in the exception of the Thirteenth Amendment, because there are always those still mired in and available to enslavement. In other words, if Blackness is always akin to crime within the American imagination, how might the exception of the Thirteenth always be at play? How are Black people marked as available for conscription, even if they aren't "duly convicted," turned "state's property"? For my work, the plantation and the African American literary imagination meld to have us rethink genre, geography, and Blackness in this moment so we might imagine other possibilities for Black life that exist amid but also in excess of enslavement's long shadow.

For my own thinking on plantation logics, I offer a mode of encounter that I call the "plantation futures blues," which entails thinking through the materiality of the plantation that continues to raise itself in the present and considering the role of the contemporary novel, and specifically the neo-slave narrative, in accounting for the experience and sites of enslavement not as a past event, but as an always present-future. Undergirding this work of revisitation is an abiding faith in what Ralph Ellison so eloquently describes as the blues: "the impulse to keep the painful details and episodes of a brutal experience alive in one's aching consciousness, to finger its jagged grain, and to transcend it, not by the consolation of philosophy but by squeezing from it a near-tragic, near-comic lyricism" (Ellison 1945: 199). Ellison opens the blues beyond literary or musical form to a form of affective belonging and being capable of recognizing trauma and creating beauty in its wake. Thus, this essay's blues-oriented approach allows for encountering the plantation and its violence and terror while also tending to the plantation's dynamic possibility for those racialized by Blackness. The blues offers the opportunity of holding terror and possibility simultaneously.

What Tiffany Lethabo King (2016: 1023) refers to as "Black Fungibility" is another useful analytic frame to describe the simultaneous manipulation of colonial conceptions of Blackness by colonial actors while also tending to flexibility as a mode for understanding the fungibility of Blackness as a "conceptual resource." Anchoring in Hortense Spillers's and Saidiya Hartman's scholarship, King works to reconceptualize labor and the material relationship of Black people to the plantation to allow for "open-ended" readings than are typically carried out using an Afropessimist analytic (1024). The open-endedness of Black fungibility under King's work is tuned not to the immanence of the death-bound subjectivity of Blackness, but rather it allows for "a new speculative tableau where Black fungibility can also operate as a site of deferral or escape from the current entrapments of the human" (1024). Particularly impactful in this formulation is how it permits considerations of narratives that explore the forced labor and dispossession and fungibility of Black people facilitated by their removal from spaces commonly used by those marked as worthy of full citizenship and movement to spaces of exception.[3] For this essay, those spaces of exception take the form of a fictionalized farm held by a large agricultural corporation and a boy's state-run juvenile detention farm that justifies exacting labor from its residents as taxpayers' repayment. In both instances, the narrative settings draw attention to biopolitical manipulation in the form of spatial remoteness meant to obscure while also relying upon the notion of Black fungibility within a system that deems Black people a free, landless, and moveable potential labor force. Tending to the residual structure of power from enslavement, I am also interested in how these remote spaces of exception might also function as counter-sites for Black inhabitants to formulate sustaining human and nonhuman socialities amid violence and exploitation.

Thus, I situate plantation future blues as an aesthetic mode that might provide a counter-intuitive engagement with the violence of the plantation imagined as functioning in the Civil Rights and post–Civil Rights eras. In reading with a "plantation futures blues" approach, I seek to finger the jagged grain of narratives of Black enslavement, emancipation, and carcerality as unfolding, unfinished narratives that speak to a longer generic tradition of neo–slave narrative in new and unexpected ways. In so doing, I extend Kathrine McKittrick's (2013: 3) notion of "plantation futures," which centers on tracking "the plantation toward the prison and the improved and destroyed city sectors" and argues for our resistance to the impulse to "analytically ignore" the human life in the plantation context. I emphasize the narrative space for elemental refusal, highlighting the contentious will to labor against ceding the plantation to a simple mirage of Black death. I draw attention to other possibilities. Thus while the Fort Bend Independent School District might have encountered the remains of ninety-five people as a problem, a block in the road to careers for the twenty-first century, I offer a reading of these resurfaced remains that suggests we are always unable to think the future of labor without contending with the Black labor exacted through exploitation. In so creating such a reading, I begin by asking the following questions: What might it mean to think differently about the subjectivities of those who live, escape, or die on the plantation? Moreover, how do scholars of the Black diaspora re/visit the plantation context not merely to mark temporal atrocities but also to consider the forms of self-emancipation and liberation that might emerge within such a space despite deprivation and death? What does the novel of enslavement teach us about resisting poverty and writing ourselves outside of the confines of this "prison nation"? Ultimately, I suggest that just as the plantation and its (former) inhabitants continue to raise themselves in the present, we must consider the role of the contemporary novel of enslavement as a mode for accounting and combating Black national dispossession and exploitation in the current moment.

The Neo–Slave Narrative and Refusing Agri-carcerality

In a *Public Books* interview shortly after *Delicious Foods'* publication, James Hannaham is asked by his interviewer, Stephen Best, to discuss why he decided to write a book about slavery. Hannaham initially concedes that he felt it nearly a rite of passage as a "young, black novelist" to write a book that had something to do with the legacy of slavery in the United States, to tap into and say something about the hold of that legacy on members of the Black Diaspora (Best 2016). Yet, what is revealing in Hannaham's interview is that while he may have imagined his "slavery novel" initially to be about the legacy of enslavement, after encountering the narrative of Black women forced into slavery in Florida as late as the early 1990s, Hannaham found himself compelled to wrestle with slavery not as the past or as legacy but as a present.[4] However, Hannaham's novel presents a generic problem: Does one classify *Delicious Foods* as a neo–slave narrative since it encounters no time travel back to or detailed rumination on the antebellum plantation? What happens when the enslavement and forced labor of Black people in America is not past, is not a metaphor, but is a small group of people's lived experience in the contemporary moment?

Yogita Goyal's exploration of slavery as metaphor and analogy for global literatures in *Runaway Genres: The Global Afterlives of Slavery* provides some framework for understanding the continued relevance of slavery and slave narratives to many contemporary writers of the global South. She notes slavery's utility within an American abolitionist and activist ecosystem that favors sentimentalism as a motivating factor for slavery's metaphorical and slave narrative's elemental employment. While Goyal is interested in the circulation of slavery as an analogy within a global context, she also considers the neo–slave narrative's revival among contemporary African American writers. She explores how Black American writers "trouble" the genre within a "post-black" cultural moment by rejecting the sentimentalism and embracing satire and humor (Goyal 2019: 10540). For my own work on the neo–slave narrative, I am interested not in rejections of sentimentalism of the genre but in how thinking through the genre might decenter and surpass antebellum formulations of enslavement and remain usable to contemporary Black American writers interested in history and futures.

In his consideration of the slavery novel, Hannaham links his work with Octavia Butler's speculative novel *Kindred* or Halli Germa's independent film *Sankofa*. What is kin about those two texts, though very different mediums, is that they rely on a form of time-space travel, a return to a past such that the protagonist (and readers/viewers, alike) might experience and understand the impact of both the transatlantic slave trade and the plantation on the psyche of the modern Black subject. These texts are both generally considered neo–slave narratives. Hannaham's novel contains no such transhistorical movement through time. Instead, readers encounter college-educated Black characters living in the American Gulf South who seek to make the region conform to racial equity standards promised not by emancipation but by the Civil Rights movement. The novel unfolds the region's (and the Nation's) failure to observe promises to protect the African American community from white-supremacist violence and, more importantly, to finally grant full-citizenship protections under the law when their rights have been violated. In the absence of protected rights and disposed by the Nation, *Delicious Foods'* characters live and die without access to machinations of equal justice. Embedded in the Gulf South, a region marked by enslavement, the novel continually asks readers to consider what has and has not changed if Black rights, autonomy, and life are so easily revoked by a social and legal system structured upon anti-Blackness.

Bernard Bell (1987: 289) originated the term neo–slave narrative in *The Afro-American Novel and Its Tradition*, defining it as "residually oral, modern narratives of escape from bondage to freedom." Likewise, in his text *Neo-slave Narratives*, Ashraf Rushdy extends Bell's ideas. Moreover, he defines the genre as composed of "novels that assume the form, adopt the conventions, and take on the first-person voice" of the original texts written during the antebellum period (Rushdy 1999: 3). Rushdy also sources the genre's emergence to the aesthetic and political shifts between the Civil Rights to Black Power moments in the 1970s and 1980s. Similarly, scholars such as Stefanie Sievers in *Liberating Narratives* (1996) and Angelyn Mitchell in *The Freedom to Remember* (2002) add to the scholarly discourse by situating the exploration of slavery's legacy by contemporary writers beyond serving a historiographic function but also suggesting how the texts occasion consideration of Black liberation and the ontological nature of freedom. Unlike Bell's or Rushdy's configuring, Arlene Keizer (2004: 3) opts for the "contemporary novel of slavery" as her descriptive to avoid what she calls the "neologisms" of Bell and Rushdy. She also seeks to expand the geographic scope of analysis to narratives of the Caribbean. Keizer's formulation opens up both the temporal and the literary scope of the genre, which allows me to grapple with the atemporal, and thus, the generic impossibility of periodizing the slave narrative in light of the plantation's constant return to the present.

Hannahan's *Delicious Foods* rests at the point of inflection between the plantation and carceral logics that rely on Black social dispossession (poverty, racism, and addiction) that literally and figuratively feed the Nation. In the novel's construction, poverty, addiction, and Blackness mark one as available for the plantation as it is formulated in the present moment as agribusiness. The twenty-nine chapter novel focuses on modern-day slavery in the Gulf-South region—shuttling between Texas and Louisiana. It is told mainly via flashbacks and mixed narrative points of view—third and first—over alternating chapters. A third-person account of the novel's protagonist, Eddie Hardison, opens the novel. Hannaham shifts in other chapters to the "traditional" neo–slave narrative's first-person narrator and then further collapses that first-person voice with that of the vernacular speaking narrator named Scotty, who is the voice of crack-cocaine. Scotty narrates the addiction and enslavement of Eddie's mother, Darlene Hardison. This narrative-voice twist signals but one of Hannaham's divergences from the neo–slave narrative conventions outlined by both Bell and Rushdy. Crack-cocaine personified through the voice of Scotty allows the novel to shift between narrative realism and surrealism. Beginning in medias res, readers meet Eddie attempting to escape "the farm" by car, pursued by an unknown and unseen aggressor. As the novel unfolds, readers learn that Eddie has escaped Delicious Foods farm, where he has been living and laboring for nearly six years, since he was twelve years old. Readers also come to know that Eddie has been "employed" at Delicious because Delicious employs his mother, a modern-day perversion of the slave codes' *partus sequitur ventrem.* Eddie's escape is only possible through the loss of both of his hands and the sacrifice of his mother and fellow farmworkers who remain behind at Delicious. On one level this escape reinforces the notion of the tenuousness of freedom and sovereignty for Black people in the United States. Additionally, the narrative also bears witness to the embodied stakes of personal sacrifice and collective action amid the terror of the plantation, which King's and McKittrick's scholarship remind us is also necessary to acknowledge.

While it is a sprawling novel in its sense of time and geography, *Delicious Foods* maps onto many recognizable enslavement practices, namely, in its cultivation of Black indebtedness. This fiction of Black indebtedness, Saidiya Hartman (1998: 132) reminds us, is the hallmark of enslavement and creating an unfree subject: "The fiction of debt was premised upon a selective and benign representation of slavery that emphasized paternalism, dependence, and will-lesness." Moreover, "if the slave was dependent, will-less, and bound by the dictates of the master, then the freed individual was liberated from the past and capable of remaking himself/herself through the sheer exercise of will." The lack of free-will and a system of debt most binds the antebellum moment about which Hartman writes and the fictional world of Delicious Foods farm. While the novel's characters never refer to themselves as enslaved, they are locked into a bunkhouse every night, fed drugs to be made more pliable for farm labor, beaten at the will of (similarly abject) managerial workers who oversee their work, unable to communicate with the world outside of Delicious freely, and made to feel indebted to distract from the reality of their exploitation.

The narrative's exploration of indebtedness begins in the form of a promise and contractual obligation initiated under drugs' influence. Darlene and her soon-to-be coworkers are lured away from Houston in the middle of the night and encouraged to enter into a labor contract with Delicious with promises of guaranteed accommodations, a competitive salary, and vacation. Most of the riders who join Darlene in the minivan routed for Delicious Foods farm are similarly situated: unhoused or housing unstable, suffering from addiction, unemployed or employed outside the traditional labor marketplace, and Black. Scotty narrates the moment of contractual obligation as such: "Picture Darlene not thinking. Imagine her ass floating above that bus, having a long-term hopegasm, rivers of happy sliding from her mouth to her crotch and back" and "Picture Darlene starring in a Hollywood voice called *The Lady with the Damn Good Job*" (Hannaham 2015: 71). The signing of the contract and

Darlene's "hopegasm" suggest that she and her coworkers have willfully entered into a legally recognized working contact with Delicious Foods. Yet the narrative suggests that the entering into contractual obligation with Delicious relies upon a captive and intoxicated group of workers, none of whom has read the contract into which they are entering. "Somebody already done folded that sucker over to the last page and put a bright yellow tag in the place where you supposed to sign," Scotty notes. When Darlene's soon-to-be coworker, Sirius B, attempts to read the contract, the recruiter for Delicious, Jackie, leans into "his personal space" and says, "Don't sweat it, bruh, you just sign" (71). The contract stands as a legal document and represents a point at which the narrative calls into question the nature and possibility of consent among a captive and subdued laborers. The contract renders the Black laborers on Delicious Farms free labor, marking them as willfully responsible for their experience of captivity and exploitation.

Just as sharecropping was an extension of plantation logic within a free labor system, Delicious Foods runs on the perpetual indebtedness of those laborers on its property. In the latter case, the influence of addiction and violence denies free will. Enticed, however, the laborers of Delicious Foods never earn enough to outpace the charge of their living expenses on the farm in the form of lodging, food, and drugs. The enslaved's boundness and indebtedness are fabricated to declare them unworthy or unfit for freedom. This logic is illuminated at the moment in the narrative when Eddie, refusing the task of disciplining his mother with corporal punishment, reflects that at Delicious Foods, "obedience came first" and "everyone had to submit to a preposterous system of laws that had nothing to do with justice, logic, or even maximizing company profits" (208). Without logic, relying on submission and the illogical application of punishment as a form of control, Delicious Foods exemplifies slavery's afterlife, its present life.

The second practice of enslavement that Hannaham explores in the novel is the proximity of the Black laborers to nonhuman animals. Within a larger context of the slave narrative, the exploration of enslavement relying on Black people and animals' affiliation is a fairly common trope. For instance, in a pivotal moment in Frederick Douglass's canonical *Narrative of the Life of Frederick Douglass* (1845: 45), he recounts what he describes as an early reminder of his "degraded condition" during a property evaluation for his recently deceased enslaver: "We were all ranked together at the valuation. Men and women, old and young, married and single, were ranked with horses, sheep, and swine. There were horses and men, cattle and women, pigs and children, all holding the same rank in the scale of being, and were all subjected to the same narrow examination." The repetition of the human and nonhuman animal pairings punctuates Douglass's argument regarding not only the property status of Black people under enslavement but how Black humanity is rendered null and void by the system.

Hannaham takes up this trope of Black and animal pairings within *Delicious Foods*, establishing a clear connection to the slave narrative tradition, thereby suggesting the laborers' conditions mark them as far from free persons. As Darlene and the other newly "employed" workers approach Delicious Farms to begin their employment, they see a chicken cross in front of the minivan that has transported the human cargo across state lines from Houston to rural Louisiana. Scotty narrates that Jackie "frowned and squinted, tryna see where the chicken had went, like maybe she gonna have to chase it down. How did she get out? Jackie muttered under her breath" (Hannaham 2015: 98). The narrative further links the chickens and the human cargo that Jackie transports when, smelling the fecal matter, hearing clucking, and wading through the errant feathers and feed pellets as they enter their permanent housing at Delicious, Darlene exclaims: "This is a chicken coop" (99). In response and with a sweep of the hand, Jackie dismisses Darlene's assertion with, "It's people on this side, not no chickens. This the no-chicken area. She moved her hand in a half circle and went, Chicken, no-chicken" (201, 100). The line of demarcation that Jackie suggests is arbitrary and nonexistent. Like Douglass's pairings in the plantation's property valuation day, the laborers at Delicious Foods are sleeping and eating with the chickens.

Delicious Foods, in these ways, asks us to encounter the plantation anew, not as history but as the present. But it also asks that we consider the care that the dispossessed can muster for one another. For instance, while Darlene has been conscripted into labor at Delicious Foods, working with no hope of relief or escape beyond those provided by her drug highs, she finds some solace in imagining who will eat the food she picks. Scotty narrates, noting that she takes off her gloves to leave fingerprints on the sticky watermelon skins,

> hoping somebody gonna dust that damn melon for evidence and let her son know where she at. Way far away, folks from America and Canada and even father be dropping them Sugar Babies and Golden Crowns on they Italian marble counters; blond children be biting down on that juicy red flesh, letting the sweetness ooze and dribble over they tongue and out the corner of they mouth. They wasn't looking for no fingerprints on no dam melon. (166)

This call to awareness and the materiality of this message makes Hannaham's unconventional neo–slave narrative significant. Darlene's attempt to speak beyond the gates of Delicious Foods through the commodity chain may be illogical, as Scotty notes; however, the gesture reminds the novel's readers that change begins with taking notice, with care. As Christina Sharpe (2016: 120) notes, care among the Black diaspora is "different" and requires a "different optic," which needs one to be attentive to the "life, however precarious, that [is] always there." The pathos of Darlene's gesture suggests the plantation is a structural force, even when made invisible, that continues to feed the world. Contrary to Scotty's critique, I want to suggest that Darlene understands that care and consumption might be a site to counter the invisibility and remoteness that ensures enslavement in the contemporary moment.

I also want to distinguish care from the myth of conscientious consumption, because the latter is ineffectual within a capitalist labor market. For instance, when all the laborers at Delicious are set free and the farm is dismantled, Darlene returns to the world outside of the farm. Not only does she get clean of her addiction to crack-cocaine, she also sets out to give up what she calls "unhealthy living" (Hannaham 2015: 353). We can see evidence of her recovery in the fact that Darlene narrates her own life in the first person. Scotty no longer mediates the narrative on her behalf. But more than merely living clean, she attempts to acknowledge and source the food that contributes to her health. She says, "I would always think about the people whose hands had touched those apples and that cantaloup before I ate. Sometimes, at the supermarket, I asked questions about the growers that nobody could answer, and eventually the stock boys started to hide when they saw me coming" (Hannaham 2015: 354). While this might be misunderstood as a sort of embrace of purity ethics, I would suggest that Darlene's interest in reaching through the commodity chain for recognition while she labored at Delicious Foods finds itself expressed in her desire to reach out to other laborers. However, what is telling of the care with which she intends to treat people on the other end of the supply chain is that other members of the chain refuse to look backward and facilitate that care. The stock boys' running away only illuminates the lack of willingness to care for those trapped within spaces of exception.

One of the texts that Hannaham cites as central to shifting his thinking about agriculture and modern slavery is John Bowe's *Nobodies: Modern American Slave Labor and the Dark Side of the New Global Economy* (2007). In an earlier essay on topic of slave labor written for the *New Yorker*, Bowe (2003) writes the following:

Modern day slavery exists not because today's workers are immigrants or because some of them don't have papers but because agriculture has always managed to sidestep the labor rules that are imposed upon other industries. When the federal minimum-wage law was enacted, in 1938, farmworkers were excluded from its provisions, and remained so for nearly thirty years. Even today, farmworkers, unlike other hourly workers, are denied the right to overtime pay. In many states, they're excluded from workers' compensation and unemployment benefits. Farmworkers receive no medical insurance or sick leave, and are denied the right to organize.

Bowe's observations highlight that the plantation has historically refused its exception—from the conscription of Black convicts after emancipation to those marginalized by addiction, trauma, or a lack of documented citizenship rights, the plantation both structures and feeds the nation.

"Even in Death the Boys Were Trouble"

Colson Whitehead's *The Nickel Boys* opens with a discovery of bodies, much like the discovery of the "Sugar Land 95" in the Houston suburbs. The makeshift graveyard for the "Nickel boys" sets the novel off mysteriously, the way unburied bodies are wont to do. Like Hannaham's exploration of the plantation logics that inflect the labor practices on the Delicious Foods farm, Colson Whitehead considers the role of carcerality and memory within the transitional time between the Civil Rights and post–Civil Rights eras. Many would consider Whitehead's *Underground Railroad* (2016), which is set during the antebellum period and deals exclusively with the quest for freedom among enslaved peoples, a more traditional choice for discussing the genre of the neo–slave narrative.[5] However, *The Nickel Boys* serves as an example of the possibilities within the "plantation futures," significantly as the novel overlaps with expanding the neo–slave narrative. In other words, *Nickel Boys* tests the limits of the neo–slave narrative as it makes its way well into the post–Civil Rights moment, treating Black enclosure, dispossession, and forced labor not as historical remembrance but as a documentation of the long-lingering structures of enslavement that shape US life. I believe the neo-slave narrative is a genre capable of being renewed, a process that must take place through tracing and tracking enslavement outside of antebellum time. In fact, I would argue that the contemporary Black writer's capacity to renew the genre prompts us to think productively about the contemporary workings of racial capitalism and its antirelational logic. More than mere encounter with historic slavery and the way it shapes narratives and lives within the nation, the neo–slave narrative as Hannaham and Whitehead employ and expand it suggests the project of Black emancipation is ongoing and collectively battled every day.

So, in shifting to Whitehead's *Nickel Boys*, I am moving from the Gulf-South regions of Texas and Louisiana to the state of Florida, thereby extending and changing the forms of enslavement and carcerality under analysis. Moreover, whereas the characters of *Delicious Foods* are conscripted into extralegal peonage due in no small part to their poverty and addiction, the young men that populate and work Nickel grounds are marked by the state as "delinquents" for crimes that range from petty theft to being unhoused, being runaways from sexually abusive adults, living in poverty, or hailing from a nonnuclear family structure. Officially the boys were sent to Nickel for offenses they mostly did not understand: "malingering, mopery, incorrigibility" (Whitehead 2019: 74). However, what unites these texts is that they each engage a more extensive discussion of the impact of dispossession and the employment of spaces of exception to remove from public view the atrocities of the plantation in a nation formulated by Jim Crow modernity.

Whitehead's novel reads as a taxonomy of abuse and punishment doled out by actors imbued with the state's power. A fictionalized account of the Dozier School for Boys in Marianna, Florida, the Nickel Academy remains outside the prying eyes of the average Florida resident.[6] Readers follow two young Black men as they attempt to navigate, live, and imagine an escape from the space of exception that is Nickel: the wrongly accused and sentenced Elwood Curtis, who was college bound before his luckless run-in with the law, and Turner, a young man doing a second bid at the school and who is, thus, more seasoned. Billed as a reform school for young men who have committed what the state determines to be crimes, the remote location of Nickel Academy serves to hide the abuse the underaged residents, many of whom are Black, experience. As the professor whose student finds the unmarked graves remarks, "You can hide a lot in an acre, in the dirt" (5). Similar to Hannaham's Delicious Foods farm's remote location, Nickel Academy is a space of exception where agri-carcerality licenses the boys' physical and sexual abuse at the hands of their primarily white custodians and teachers. The most harrowing element of the novel's plotting is that the young people housed within the space are subject to death without legal recourse. They have already been sentenced by the State of Florida and found no longer worthy not just of their rights but of the protection usually reserved for minors. Instead of security, the Nickel boys find justice that is arbitrary, "a coin toss" (65).

While Nickel is called a reform school, the institution actually follows the prison logic of incapacitation. One of four rationales for maintaining prisons, incapacitation, Ruth Wilson Gilmore (2007: 14) notes, "doesn't pretend to change anything about people except where they are"; it "purports to solve social problems by extensively and repeatedly removing people from disordered, deindustrialized milieus and depositing them somewhere else." Nickel's objective to incapacitate the boys that end up on its grounds is carried out through the threat and delivery of punishment in what the Black boys call the White House; the white boys who are incarcerated in another part of Nickel's campus call the White House the Ice Cream Factory because one returns from the shed with "bruises in every color" (66). The minor distinction in naming around bruising is significant because it suggests that the white boys return from the White House beaten but merely bruised, while the Black boys often fail to return from a visit to the White House. The White House "delivered the law and everybody obeyed," while the Ice Cream Factory doled out bruises (66). It seems less than ironic that the site of rogue justice would carry the same name as the residence housing the president of the United States and the metonymic seat of power for the nation. Unlike the DC White House, the Nickel's White House is described as unassuming, previously a work shed, a building at which "you'd never look twice" but "why the school had no wall or fence or barbed wire around it, why so few boys ran: It was the wall that kept them in" (67). Beyond punishment, it is unclear what Nickel Academy offers its residents, especially its Black residents.

If indebtedness is the plantation logic used to enclose *Delicious Foods* laborers, then Whitehead's novel revolves around the misuse of consent and self-mastery to engender the plantation. The fabrication of sovereignty and personal responsibility are used to justify any violence experienced by the Black Nickel Boys. For instance, when he arrives at the reform school, Elwood is told by the school's white superintendent, Spencer Maynard, that "it's up to you how much time you spend with us," which depends on his mastery of the hierarchical system of ranked behavior. Nickel Boys are either a Grub, Explorer, Pioneer, or Ace based on merits and good behavior. Once a boy reaches Ace, he graduates and can leave Nickel, in theory. It appears to be a transparent and action-based system that results in release, should a Nickel Boy manage to "act right." Acting right involves the following: "listens to the housemen and his house father, does his work without shirking and malingering, and applies himself to his studies. An Ace does not roughhouse, he does not cuss, he does not blaspheme or carry on. He works to reform himself, from sunrise to sunset" (49). Saidiya Hartman is again helpful in thinking through the tenets of promised freedom when it is an encumbrance to freedom for Black people post-emancipation. She writes, "self-mastery was invariably defined as willing submission to the dictates of former master, the market, and the inquisitor within" (Hartman 1998: 134). She goes on to note that "the back bent joyfully to the burdens foisted upon it transformed the burdened individuality and encumbrances of freedom into an auspicious exercise of free will and self-making" (135). Hartman analyzes how Black freemen and women were held to servitude standards as markers of their freedom in such a way that liberty ends up looking nearly identical to enslavement. This dissonant relationship between freedom and enslavement resonates with the Nickel Academy's fabricated binary between "graduation" and punishment.

Within a system built by and maintaining plantation logics, there is a shortage of modes for Black people to access freedom within that system. We see this at play within *Nickel Boys* after Elwood receives a nearly deadly beating at the White House. Upon reflection, Elwood realizes that "there was no higher system guiding Nickel's brutality, merely an indiscriminate spite, one that had nothing to do with people" (Whitehead 2019: 85). This realization is both disheartening and freeing for him in that it allows him to see that there is no way to win fairly or "act right" enough to be set free from Nickel. As Turner tells Elwood while he is in the hospital recovering from his first White House beating, there is no graduating Nickel, "nobody else is going to get you out—just you" (82). Although Elwood continues to have faith in his capacity to act right, he also grows closer to Turner, who offers him a way to exist in the recesses within a system meant to extract his labor with little regard for his life.

Returning to both Tiffany Lethabo King's conceptualization of "Black Fungibility" and McKittrick's "plantation futures," I want to think through what it might mean to resist the death-bound subjectivity of Blackness through practices of dissemblance and hard choices. Both of these practices allow Black people an opportunity to reimagine the forms of sociality. In the case of *Nickel Boys*, through Turner's perspective, the novel provides a profound rumination on Black relationships and autonomy. Again, while Elwood is recovering from his beating, he is joined in the hospital by Turner. Unlike Elwood, Turner is a patient by choice, describing his stay as a form of vacation. He arrives by ingesting soap powders, which make him vomit and double over with severe stomach pain. Elwood worries that the hospital staff will discover Turner is "faking it" because Turner keeps whistling the theme music to *The Andy Griffith Show.* Turner quickly retorts Elwood's worries by saying, "I ain't faking it—that soap powder is awful" (79).

However, what is potent about Turner's hospital stay is that he delineates that he is there by his "choosing, not anyone else" (79). This exercise of free will and self-governing, while self-harming, provides a clear example of moving outside the system of enclosure and death Nickel Academy threatens its Black students with. When Elwood says Turner's whistling has embedded the TV theme music in his head, I would argue that what Turner has embedded is a possibility for self-will within the community. Though the theme song is for a show about an idealized, all-white community, Turner's manipulation reminds Elwood of what they are not, what they don't have access to, and, ultimately, what they must live against. Perhaps the blues might have been more appropriate to whistle, but I believe they are practicing the "plantation future blues," by living, acknowledging the trauma they experience at the hands of adults and a state that punishes them, and devising a mode of escape from Nickel.

The relationship between Turner and Elwood is progressively more complicated as the novel ends. One element of the novel that I have yet to mention is the temporal shifts it makes between a more contemporary time in New York City and Elwood's earlier days as a young man in Florida and a resident of Nickel. The narrative shifts between these two times and places to offer readers hope that Elwood could both survive and escape Nickel Academy. Juxtaposing the past with Elwood's present as an entrepreneur on the verge of a possible successful romantic relationship does offer a bit of respite from the disheartening and deadly narrative time spent in Florida. Yet, the twist of the novel reveals that Elwood of New York City is Turner. In a botched escape from Nickel, both Elwood and Turner make a run, but Elwood is murdered. Turner then takes Elwood's identity to start a new life. While this revelation is heartbreaking, I want to suggest that Turner's decision to take on Elwood's identity is the sort of refusal of fungibility that merely counts Black death. Instead, the lack of fixedness of Black identity is made possible in this shift of identity. It is not a perfect or seamless replacement but rather a replacement that incorporates the past into the present, which is at the heart of my configuration of plantation future blues. In other words, as Turner/Elwood readies to return to the home of his childhood trauma, the site of all the dead Nickel Boys, we might understand him returning to reclaim the life and living of his friend.

Conclusion

At some level, to write about modern slavery featuring African American protagonists is to invite considerations of the American postracial condition.

This is to say that postracial critiques of contemporary African American literary production fail to hold water in light of a plantation logic. Individualism as a racial politics does little to progress these characters' lives forward in a productive way. Such postracial politics are couched as reactionary in the novel. Darlene's response to the gruesome murder of her husband is to refuse racial solidarity and action; both failed to keep her husband alive, no doubt, but there is still work they might do for the living. Likewise, Elwood's naivety coupled with his faithful investment in the possibility of racial integration and individual uplift leave him vulnerable to the police state that targets young Black men. In contrast, Turner's taking up of Elwood Curtis's name and living "his" life after Elwood is killed trying to escape Nickel might be read as an offering toward life after death that the plantation cannot contain. By exploring the living plantation through and in excess of the neo–slave narrative tradition, each novel pushes not an abandonment of solidarity but an extension of those networks of understanding needed to resist a system that relies on anonymity and organizational failure and removal from sight to spaces of exception. Much like the remains of those held in peonage in Sugar Land, raising the dead reveals a history that refuses to stay buried. And rejecting the exception is a mode of participating in the plantation future blues—fingering the jagged edge of trauma, rejecting forgetting, and always remembering to care.

Notes

1   For more history on abolishing the convict leasing system in Texas, see Perkinson 2010.

2   For a detailed report on the historical, archeological, environmental, and political context surrounding the ninety-five bodies found in Sugar Land, Texas, see the Fort Bend Independent School District's report: Clark et al. 2020.

3   Here I am playing off of Giorgio Agamben's notion of the state of exception, which stands outside juridical rule, outside the confines of the law. Still, in that outside status, it ceases to be exceptional. Agamben focuses on the Nazi concentration camps of the Shoah as the ultimate space of exception producing "homo sacer," or the human being who lives and dies outside the state's protection. In "Necropolitics," Achille Mbembe calls into question Agamben's reification of "the camp" and the Holocaust as a singular modern example of the space of exception. Instead, Mbembe (2003: 12–13) posits that just as modernity engenders multiple concepts of sovereignty, so also does it engender multiple spaces of exception. Similarly questioning the uniqueness given over to Agamben's "camp," in *Habeas Viscus*, Alexander Weheliye (2014: 36–38) considers the enslaved person and the system of enslavement more apt examples of homo sacer, the state of exception, and the zone of indistinction. Weheliye posits that Hortense Spillers's distinction between the body and the flesh provides a more usable mode of assessing

bare life and the deprivation of personhood (body) experienced by those living within this zone of indistinction (flesh) (39).

4   Hannaham encountered this narrative in John Bowe's *Nobodies*. It encouraged him to think presently about modern-day slavery, not as a legacy but as an active present.

5   In a February 2021 taped interview for *60 Minutes*, Whitehead noted that writing *Underground Railroad* prepared him to encounter the contemporary "existential" terror of Jim Crow featured in *The Nickel Boys*. He links the two novels when discussing the bleak world that he's been creating in over the course of the past few years. See interview and transcript at www.cbsnews.com/news/colson-whitehead-profile-60–minutes-2021-02-28/.

6   In the acknowledgments that follow *The Nickel Boys*, Whitehead discusses his first encounter with the Dozier School story in 2014 after reading the *Tampa Bay Times*'s reporting on the discovery of the undocumented gravesites for the young men who died while housed at the school.

References

Bell, Bernard. 1987. *The Afro-American Novel and Its Tradition*. Amherst: University of Massachusetts Press.

Best, Stephen. 2016. "Code-Switching: An Interview with James Hannaham." *Public Books*, November 15. www.publicbooks.org/code-switching-an-interview-with-james-hannaham/.

Bowe, John. 2003. "Nobodies: Does Slavery Exist in America?" *New Yorker*, April 13.

Clark, Reign, Catrina Banks Whitley, Ron Ralph, Helen Graham, Theresa Jach, Abigail Eve Fisher, Valerie Tompkins, Emily van Zanten, and Karissa Basse. 2020. *Back to Bondage: Forced Labor in Post Reconstruction Era Texas*. Austin, TX: Goshawk Environmental Consulting.

Douglass, Frederick. 1845. *Narrative of the Life of Frederick Douglass, an American Slave*. Boston: Anti-Slavery Office. docsouth.unc.edu/neh/douglass/douglass.html.

Ellison, Ralph. 1945. "Richard Wright's Blues." *Antioch Review* 5, no. 2: 199.

Gilmore, Ruth Wilson. 2007. *Golden Gulag: Prisons, Surplus, Crisis, and Opposition in Globalizing California*. Berkeley: University of California Press.

Goyal, Yogita. 2019. *Runaway Genres: The Global Afterlives of Slavery*. New York: New York University Press.

Haley, Sarah. 2016. *No Mercy Here: Gender, Punishment, and the Making of Jim Crow Modernity*. Chapel Hill: University of North Carolina Press.

Hannaham, James. 2015. *Delicious Foods*. New York: Back Bay.

Hartman, Saidiya. 1998. *Scenes of Subjection: Terror, Slavery, and Self-Making in Nineteenth-Century America*. New York: Oxford University Press.

Holland, Sharon. 2000. *Raising the Dead: Readings of Death and (Black) Subjectivity*. Durham, NC: Duke University Press.

Keizer, Arlene. 2004. *Black Subjects: Identity Formation in the Contemporary Narrative of Slavery*. Ithaca, NY: Cornell University Press.

King, Tiffany Lethabo. 2016. "The Labor of (Re)reading Plantation Landscapes as Fungible(ly)." *Antipode* 48, no. 4: 1022–39.

Mbeme, Achille. 2003. "Necropolitics." *Public Culture* 15, no. 1: 11–40.

McKittrick, Katherine. 2013. "Plantation Futures." *Small Axe* 17, no. 3: 1–15.

Mervosh, Sarah. 2018. "Remains of Black People Forced into Labor after Slavery Are Discovered in Texas." *New York Times*, July 18. www.nytimes.com/2018/07/18/us/grave-convict-lease-texas.html?searchResultPosition=1.

Mitchell, Angelyn. 2002. *The Freedom to Remember: Narrative, Slavery, and Gender in Contemporary Black Women's Fiction*. Brunswick, NJ: Rutgers University Press.

Perkinson, Robert. 2010. *Texas Tough: The Rise of America's Prison Empire*. New York: Metropolitan.

Reese, Ashanté M. 2021. "Tarry with Me: Reclaiming Sweetness in an Anti-Black World." *Oxford American*, 112 (Spring). www.oxfordamerican.org/magazine/issue-112-spring-2021/tarry-with-me.

Rushdy, Ashraf. 1999. *Neo-Slave Narratives: Studies in the Social Logic of a Literary Form*. New York: Oxford University Press.

Sharpe, Christina. 2016. *In the Wake: On Blackness and Being*. Durham, NC: Duke University Press.

Sievers, Stephanie. 1999. *Liberating Narratives: The Authorization of Black Female Voices in African American Women Writers' Novels of Slavery*. Hamburg: Lit Verlag.

Weheliye, Alexander. 2014. *Habeas Viscus: Racializing Assemblages, Biopolitics, and Black Feminist Theories of the Human*. Durham, NC: Duke University Press.

Whitehead, Colson. 2019. *The Nickel Boys*. New York: Anchor.

Wood, Clyde. 1998. *Development Arrested: The Blues and Plantation Power in the Mississippi Delta*. New York: Verso.

Shaun Myers

Black Somatics:
Post–Civil Rights Movements
In and Out of Time

For all of its associations with flight, Toni Morrison's *Song of Solomon* ([1977] 2004) traffics heavily in suspension. From the novel's opening, with the suspended narration of Robert Smith's rooftop jump, to its closing still frame of Milkman's pendulous leap over Ryna's Gulch, this post–civil rights novel continually depicts stays of black motion. Suspension informs even the vernacular tongue in the novel. In chapter 2, the adolescent protagonist, Milkman, finally meets Pilate Dead, the "queer aunt" "his father had forbidden him to go near." Spellbound in her presence, Milkman becomes silent, prompting Pilate to playfully declare to him and his friend Guitar: "You all must be the dumbest unhung Negroes on earth" (36, 37). The appellation "unhung Negroes" discerns two possibilities for black life: hung and unhung. The past participle "unhung" implies the action has still to happen, meaning that the unhung are always already constituted by the potentiality of morbid suspension.

Pilate's everyday wisdom about the way lynching *hangs over* black life gives way to more abstract representations of how that life is held in suspension. In what is perhaps the novel's most poignant pendency, the adult vigilante Guitar has

The South Atlantic Quarterly 121:1, January 2022
DOI 10.1215/00382876-9561545 © 2022 Duke University Press

nocturnal visions of "little scraps of Sunday dresses" that "did not fly" but "hung in the air quietly, like the whole notes in the last measure of an Easter hymn." Evoking the "four little colored girls" killed in 1963 by the Klan bombing of the 16th Street Baptist Church in Birmingham, Alabama, Morrison depicts the state of black freedom as rent "bits" of "lace and voile, velvet and silk, cotton and satin, eyelet and grosgrain" (173). The narrator analogizes these hung shreds as the sustained, or held, notes of a hymn. The novel's other scenes of black suspension similarly reverberate rather than sound any final note of resolution. In 1977, after the movement for civil rights, Morrison thus figures black freedom as a *fermata*: a pause held beyond normal duration. A suspended note. An unfulfilled sound. The scene ultimately leaves us with the texture, color, and resonance of what I term *hung freedom*: the post–civil rights experience of prolonged unfreedom, a condition characterized by ostensible progress but also the past and potential of anti-blackness and its terrors. In this way, the unhung/hung binary graphically diagrams black life. The solidus depicts black freedom suspended between dyadic possibilities, only ever amounting to unfreedom. Morrison's images of hung scraps and "unhung Negroes," then, index how white supremacy dually structures time: as an external force unfolding toward untimely black extinction *and* as an anti-black atmosphere of suspense or precarity imposing on (our capacities to imagine) black being.

These mundane affects of hung freedom, sensations of hanging in the balance, are symptoms of what I call *imperative time*: the dominant construction of time as a demand or pressure exerted on black lives. Radiating from what Calvin Warren (2016: 59) describes as the transatlantic slave trade's "seismic force," this ongoing formation of time within Western racial order functions imperatively, warning, commanding, and compelling black life. In the system of racial capitalism, time serves as a powerful tool for racializing, extracting, and managing labor. I examine, in particular, how imperative time governs and constrains black mobility and comportment. Structured imperatively, phenomena as everyday as sunsets or routine as timetables hold black movement in abeyance and under pressure. On the one hand, this dominant temporal form dictates black motion through racialized mandates "compelling black people to wait" (Fleming 2019: 589). On the other hand, it conscripts black movement into chronologies of progress measuring our presumed distance from the ravages of transatlantic slavery. My emphasis on the imperative quality of dominant temporalities centers how black people experience the unevenness of "racial time," which Michael Hanchard (1999: 253) defines as the "structural effect" of temporal inequality arising "from power relations between racially dominant and subordinate groups." Imperative time names, in particular, the lived reality of racialization as a temporal pressure, a kind of clamp constructed to capture, hold, and compress black life. I draw on the capaciousness of imperative time to apprehend modernity's versatility in regulating the aim and pace of a variety of black movements.

In this essay, I examine how black cultural producers represent and contest the transhistorical phenomenon of imperative time, using the aid of a distinctly post–civil rights vantage. Whether portraying black "post–civil rights" experience as the afterlife of the black freedom movement or as a facet of the *long* life of the movement, their texts witness and engage the arresting copresence of progress and peril conditioning contemporary black life. This is to say, the contemporaneity of "juridical emancipation and civil rights" (Sharpe 2016: 14), on the one hand, and ongoing incarceral, educational, and economic structural inequity, on the other, have shaped the lens through which black writers understand imperative time as a through line of racial capitalism. In lieu of a chronology centering the Voting Rights Act of 1965 as the terminus of mid-century freedom dreams, these writers illumine the sheer porosity of the temporal border demarcating segregation and "post–civil rights." They aestheticize what I term *black somatics*: ways of moving outside national timelines, workplace time clocks, and protocols of linearity and resolution to refuse the impositions of imperative time. Writers such as Morrison, Claudia Rankine, and James Alan McPherson have used these rogue movements at times to buck racial capitalist temporalities, at others to ride them. In doing so, they spur movement within the stalled conditions of hung, or suspended, freedom by reclaiming black embodied experience from ascendant narratives of progress. Black somatics resist the prevailing post–civil rights imperative: render black movement as a sign of progress. Together, imperative time and black somatics converse and work in league with other concepts of black movement and pace variously forbidden or fostered by temporal imperatives. At one moment, imperative time works as a quickening agent outlawing the idle delays of Bruce's "loitering" (2019) and Adeyemi's "slowness" (2019). At another, in *Brown v. Board of Education* (1954), for example, it impedes freedom by decreeing that desegregation proceed "with all deliberate speed" (i.e., slowly), effectively mandating the stagnancy of Fleming's "black patience" (2019). I track black depictions of somatic stillness and motive flow that resist the competing but coproductive prescripts to "move along" and to "slow down." The rubric *black somatics* gathers together stances and fluid moves that blunt the full force of temporal oppression. These embodied interventions gesture to other temporal modes, suggesting alternative times.

To be clear, hung freedom is not a dysfunction but a function of the US racial project. A cognate of the "travestied freedom" ushered in by emancipation, the half-century of hung freedom we have experienced after civil rights reveals that the ongoing absence of fuller freedom including but "beyond individual rights and formal citizenship" (Hartman 1997: 10; Singh 2004: 132) is not an aberration but an inherent component of US national structure. Examining a range of texts produced after civil rights, I begin by studying Misha Green's television series *Lovecraft Country* (2020) and McPherson's essay "The Express" (2003) for their restagings of how imperative time detains blackness. I then turn to analyses of how McPherson's short story "A Solo Song: For Doc" (1968) and Rankine's prose poem *Citizen* (2014) and video-essay "Situation 5" (ca. 2011) figure black countermoves and postures challenging imperative time's demands for promptness and progression. I use the analytic of somatics to track how black writers rescript black movement in ways that might just, in Morrison's words, butt "time wide open" (Morrison 1997). In what follows, I map black cultural representations of the arresting power of imperative time, before analyzing imaginings of black somatics as acts of idleness, motive energy, and pointlessness. This essay's study of how black movement sets the clock and calendar otherwise offers ways to rethink black chronology—not as accretive sequences but as oscillating, irresolute transits of time.

Ordered by Time

The imperative "NIGGERS— DON'T LET THE SUN SET ON YOU HERE" functions as a potent grammar demanding black action in relation to time. The first episode of Misha Green's *Lovecraft Country*, an HBO series inspired by Matt Ruff's 2016 novel of the same name, presents this so-called sundown injunction on a billboard observed by a trio of black travelers driving from Chicago to Massachusetts in 1955. Posted at the limits of a white jurisdiction, the maxim appropriates the setting sun as a warning flag of racial terror and a catalyst of black flight. Restaging the historical formation of northern "sundown towns," the show illumines how this post-Reconstruction imperative form distressed the relation between temporality and blackness. In no uncertain terms, sundown ordinances commanded black people to enact their own expulsion by twilight each day, to detain themselves within zones of blackness. Sundown customs and laws, which peaked not during the Jim Crow era but *after* civil rights, inscribed white supremacy onto earthly rotation. In doing so, they harnessed the setting sun in the service of anti-blackness, rendering night an overseer of black mobility. Imperative time colonizes cosmic rhythms, then, but it also co-opts present time and time to come, directing the black subject to perpetually obey its command ("DON'T LET THE SUN SET ON YOU HERE [ever]"). The more familiar Jim Crow signage of "White" and "Colored" also issued imperatives, albeit tacitly. Even as these signs worked in tandem as "efficient shorthand for segregation," the "Colored" sign, in particular, functioned as a metonym, proxying the command that black people move into *this* designated space (Abel 2008: 10). Whereas the imperative form typically omits its implied subject "you," the "Colored" sign works inversely, explicating its ("Colored") subject and submerging its demand. The word *Colored*, then, works in multiple ways at once: it labels a space, names (and marks as abject) its addressee, and issues its command, summoning its subject to "colored" quarters.

The "Sundown" episode draws on other artifacts from the Jim Crow archive, including Gordon Parks's iconic photos of black life in Alabama in 1956, resuscitating them in ways that suggest their living trace in the twenty-first century. *Lovecraft Country* animates images that have long served as documentary evidence of the restraints of segregation. Bringing to life, as it were, the familiar still shot—of an elegantly dressed black woman and girl standing under the neon red "Colored" sign at a department store entrance or of a black man waiting with three children at the "Colored" window of an ice cream stand—the episode raises the question of the pastness or the historicalness of these archival documents. That is to say, the recasting *and* the mobilization of once-still figures suggest the contemporary or extant nature of the acts and affects of segregation, if not its material structures. For instance, the ice cream stand scene reconstructed emphasizes the black family's spent patience as they remain unserved while workers attend to white customers. The familiarity of this experience to black viewers in the twenty-first century speaks to a kind of affective and experiential continuity across time. Against the prevailing narrative of progress, the technicolor cinematizing of the iconic image appropriates and sets it in motion to express *ongoing* mundane feelings of blackness bearing, or enduring, imperative time. The "moving pictures" posit that these affects of the past, if not the past itself, are still alive.

Writer James Alan McPherson amplifies this temporal overlap or continuity in his portrayal of the impotency of spatial and temporal borders after the nation's transition toward de jure desegregation. Born in 1943, McPherson left the segregated South at the age of eighteen in June 1962. He traveled by rail from Atlanta to St. Paul, Minnesota, for a job as a dining-car waiter on the Great Northern Railway's Empire Builder route between Chicago and Seattle. Revisiting this critical journey out of the South in "The Express," a 2003 *Washington Post Magazine* essay, McPherson depicts the suspensions marking black experience in the emerging era of desegregation through the technology of the train. He recalls that first ride from Atlanta to St. Paul, when the train, having just crossed over the Georgia border, arrives in Chattanooga, Tennessee, a station remarkable for its location on an ever-shifting Mason-Dixon Line:

> There is no movement. Instead, there is a very long wait while additional cars are added to the train taking us from Atlanta to Chicago, and then to St. Paul for training. It is close to midnight and it is dark inside the "colored coach." The black man wheeling his food cart up and down the aisle, ostensibly selling soft drinks and sandwiches, is quietly subverting the established order. "Y'all don't have to sit back here no more," he whispers to those black passengers who are still awake. "This here's the Mason-Dixon line. Y'all can go on up to the other coaches." No one moves. Neither do I. Lifetimes spent conforming to the settled habits of segregation weigh heavily on us. We do not dare to move. (2003)

The borders of midnight and the Georgia-Tennessee line underscore other apparent divisions: between segregation and desegregation, the Deep South and the peripheral south, regional customs and federal law. These various divisions flow into the catchall of the Mason-Dixon, which in 1962 was no longer a fixed geographical feature but a moveable one, even after the Supreme Court had ruled it defunct in transit.[1]

By staging his initial departure from the South on the unofficial Mason-Dixon Line cutting through Chattanooga in 1962, McPherson fashions himself suspended over a line of contradiction determining black possibilities, a line signaling what Paul Gilroy terms the "antinomies of modernity" (1993: 115). The fact that McPherson and his fellow black passengers defer to a spatial, temporal, and psychic inertia signaled by the still train underscores the denial of autonomous mobility, a signature feature of liberal democratic selfhood. Experiencing integration as arrested development, the passengers sit detained at a Mason-Dixon Line that fails to transition into "free" territory. Instead, the customs of segregation illegally yet customarily extend or spill over into integration, compromising its time and terrain. Here, we glimpse Jim Crow's afterlife, its postmortem animations. The sole encouragement to address this failure of desegregation comes from the food-cart vendor's unheeded whispers to subversively move into the other coaches. The black man's to-and-fro movements, a pacing "up and down the aisle" defying the stillness, announce the ostensible arrival of the time-space of integration. McPherson and his fellow black passengers refuse the incitement to move, the call to an apparently new temporal order. The mobility promised by liberal democracy and newly protected by *Browder v. Gayle* (1956) remains suspended on both sides of the Georgia-Tennessee line and on either side of segregation's midnight. The "settled habits of segregation weigh[ing] heavily" on the passengers are, in part, temporal and embodied. Whether out of fear of repercussions, weariness, or discernment, they "do not dare to move," sensing the imperatives permeating borders. The hitching of "additional cars" to the "colored coach" after the train crosses out of Georgia suggests that these apparatuses of integration are mere appendages of segregation technologies, rather than overhauls or reconstructions. After all, the colored coach remains intact, leaving segregation to travel unchecked.

In Chattanooga, then, the greater outrage is not the unenforced desegregation at the Mason-Dixon Line but the shifting border's vigor and staying power. It lives on, remaining in and as time. Ostensibly a mark of division, it illumines here simultaneity. The eras of segregation and desegregation coexist, concurring to produce temporal conditions of hung freedom that compel and detain black people in a state of suspension. Magnifying this duality, McPherson uses a narrative strategy of anachronism he calls "remembering now," a form of recall or return perceptive to how the past not just erupts but more fully resides within the present (1998: 22). He describes this coincidence of the past and the present as the opening of "a portal into a finished past that has come alive again" (20). Constructed in this way, the narrative present of "The Express" operates as a constellation of epistemologies, ideologies, and, most important, imperatives that the era of integration has formed not after but *with* the era of segregation. This analeptic technique, in David Róman's words, "dilute[s] the binary between the contemporary and the past" (2005: 13). The time of segregation spills over, uncontained, in a way that, in Warren's words (2016: 56), "exceeds the frame of the historical event." Segregation's afterlife in the colored coach beyond Georgia refutes the linearity sustaining "the extant national narrative of racial progress" (Singh 2004: 8). As the train departs the Chattanooga station, it heads north spatially, but in terms of time, it turns back, stuck within a circular and oscillating transit of time that demands a reliving of the past.

Bucking Imperative Time

In the early years of the post–civil rights era, McPherson depicted this moment of apparent transition not so much as the presence of the durable past but as a remaking of imperative time into new forms. In his widely anthologized story, "A Solo Song: For Doc" (1968), set in 1965, a veteran rail waiter passes on to a young apprentice wisdom about dining car service, a Jim Crow art destined for extinction. The rail company's backlash against civil rights struggles, its loss of profits to the aviation industry, and black admission into the all-white rail workers' union takes shape as what the "Old School" waiter describes as the "big black bible," a handbook of rules governing every movement and minute of the black dining car waiters' workday (44). The dining car service manual demands that the black waiters "[live] by the book," meticulously managing even the finest details: "how the initials on the doily should always face the customer, and how the silver should be taken off the tables between meals" (45, 57). The black book distills imperative time into rules and memorandums regulating the black workers' movements and time, without pause. It prohibits them from "kill[ing] some time" between breakfast, lunch, and dinner service, instructing them to use these breaks instead to "polish the shakers or clean out the Pantry or squeeze oranges, or maybe change the linens on the tables" (45). The rail company reconstitutes its power lost to unionization and civil rights gains by codifying, in terms of time and movement, the black waiters' embodied art of service. Whereas "Colored" signs and the segregated order and layout of rail cars had once imposed subordinate status onto black laborers and passengers, the post–civil rights rule book "inflict[s] the stasis of social structure upon blacks in motion" (Stepto 1991: 75) through a transformed regulation of black workers' movements, from deportment all the way down to dexterity.

The Old School waiters' somatic subversions make them kin to the "black man wheeling his food cart," quietly urging disruptive movement, in "The Express." The unnamed veteran waiter who narrates "A Solo Song" conveys the embodied history of black rail-car work to the young trainee, whom we might imagine as McPherson himself fictionalized. The narrator schools the novice:

> So you want to know this business, youngblood? So you want to be a Waiter's Waiter? The Commissary gives you a book with all the rules and tells you to learn them. And you do, and think that is all there is to it. A big, thick black book. Poor youngblood.

> Look at me. I am a Waiter's Waiter. I know all the moves, all the
> pretty, fine moves that book will never teach you. I built this railroad with
> my moves. . . . That book they made you learn came from our moves and
> from our heads. (1968: 43)

The narrator constructs the bodily art of service as both source text and
counternarrative to the new book of rules. The regulations have been created
to "break up the Old School," undermining union protections by criminalizing unmediated, unauthorized movements in time (57). Distinguishing the
rote service elaborated in the "big, thick black book" from the virtuoso
improvisations of the Old School waiters who flowed, "mov[ing] with the roll
of the train," becoming "a part of the service," the aging waiter theorizes the
train as a disciplining structure but also as a performative site where its
black occupants might translate locomotion into a counterculture (43, 66,
67). Contrary to the book's regimenting of movement and keeping of time,
the exalted "Waiter's Waiter . . . got the rhythm of the wheels in him and
learned . . . how to roll with them and move with them" (47). The narrator
relates how the company finally "put to ground," or fired, Headwaiter Doc
Craft, a legendary Waiter's Waiter, because he had served a lemon wedge
with an oyster fork piercing its skin rather than its meat. He missed the
notice of this new rule because he had ignored the rule book's most important imperative: "Always check the book before each trip" (69). Even after
being "beaten . . . by a book" (71), Doc resists—not through movement but
through stillness. "Doc put his tray on the table and sat down in the seat
across from [the company inspector] Jerry. This was the first time we had
ever seen a waiter sit down with a customer, even an inspector." "Doc did not
move"; he "just continued to sit there" (70). Through his motionlessness,
Doc willfully "kills time," that is to say, he uses time unproductively and at
odds with the imperatives of promptness and progress weighting the black
rail workers' labor. In this way, Doc's performances of *both* locomotive flow
and resistant rest can be read as time-defying somatic forms that butt against
imperatives of nonstop advance.

Aestheticizing "the roll of the train," the Waiter's Waiters engage in
the blues practice of "reproducing or translating . . . locomotive energies"
(Baker 1984: 11). The Jim Crow car's spatial and social architectures are often
depicted as signs of white supremacy's absolute power, but blues aesthetic
theory turns our attention to the structural interstices, spaces where the
waiter-as-blues-performer is "absorbing and transforming discontinuous
experience into formal expressive instances" (8). The narrator of "A Solo

Song" recalls that when his mentor, Doc, "poured that pot of hot tea into that glass of crushed ice, it was like he was pouring it through his own fingers; it was like he and the tray and the pot and the glass and all of it was the same body. It was a beautiful move. It was fine service" (68). This embodiment of modern rail technology and its mechanical frictions threatens to dehumanize the laborer, but at the same time the laborer redirects the industrial rhythms of the locomotive machine, transforming "experiences of a durative (unceasingly oppressive) landscape" into the improvisational work: the rolls, tricks, and hustles of the Waiter's Waiters (Baker 1984: 7). In short, they ride time. The translation of locomotion, an embodying of (dis)location in and by time, offers a way to penetrate, if only briefly, imperative temporalities that shift shape but abide.

In Claudia Rankine's 2014 poem *Citizen: An American Lyric*, these mutable, enduring temporalities further convey a narrative of progress, mapping the call to advance onto the presumably liberatory velocities of automobility. The American myth of the "open road," a democratic thoroughfare of possibilities, often stalls for the black driver, a figure vulnerable to "stops" that could lead to deadly encounter or merely "the wrench and violence of everyday racial 'micro-aggressions'" (Hunt 2014). *Citizen* animates the clash of the progress narrative and stalled black mobility in its depictions of the black subject encountering the ceaseless unfolding of everyday social situations. The paradox of this form of imperative time—it demands advance even as it detains—is most poignantly and fully elaborated when the *Citizen* speaker situates the second-person "you," its black post–civil rights subject, behind the wheel of a car.

> You are in the dark,   in the car,   watching the black-tarred
> street being swallowed by speed; he tells you his dean
> is making him hire a person of color when there are so
> many great writers out there.
>
> You think maybe this is an experiment and you are being
> tested or retroactively insulted or you have done some-
> thing that communicates that this is an okay conversation to
> be having. (10)

The automobile, long associated with (in Gilroy's [2001] words) "escape, transcendence, and perhaps even resistance," here constitutes a private space subject to publicity, that is, the public-ness, of the racial mundane. Instead of secluding "you," the poem's subject, from unwanted social contact, the automobile's interior confines and exposes you. Here the presumed privacy and autonomy of automobility are rendered inoperable. Rather than signifying the car's liberatory velocities, "the black-tarred street being swallowed by speed" signals only the black subject's compliance with imperatives to progress that have become the protocol, the etiquette even, of black citizenship after civil rights: "Yes, and this is how you are a citizen: *Come on.* Let it go. *Move on*" (151; emphasis mine).

Impeded by "the go-along-to-get-along tongue pushing your [own] tongue aside" (154), the black subject finds escape from the post–civil rights consolidation of this *progressive* mode of imperative time in the chance possibility of an external interruption—a red light, a police siren going off:

> so you could slam on the brakes, slam into the car ahead
> of you, fly forward so quickly both your faces would sud-
> denly be exposed to the wind. (10)

The contemporary black subject longs for a visual or sonic cue to break the action, to suspend their own acquiescence to the linear, accretive time of automobility. But,

> As usual you drive straight through the moment with the
> expected backing off of what was previously said. (10)

The relentless advance of a progress narrative steadily marching toward an inevitable national racial redemption keeps the black subject from registering the moment's dissonance. The phantom "person of color" disparaged in the complaint settles and congeals within "you," the long-standing addressee of imperative time. Stillness offers a respite from or brief suspension of this injurious form of time:

> When you arrive in your driveway and turn off the car, you remain behind
> the wheel another ten minutes. . . . Sitting there staring at the closed garage
> door you are reminded that a friend once told you there exists the medical
> term—John Henryism—for people exposed to stresses stemming from rac-
> ism. They achieve themselves to death trying to dodge the buildup of era-
> sure. . . . You hope by sitting in silence you are bucking the trend. (11)

Juxtaposing the contemporary black driver and the folktale hero John Henry, the black steel driver who raced against a steam-powered hammer to construct a rail tunnel only to die after winning the contest, Rankine illuminates not only how black people have shaped technologies of movement but also how these technologies imbue racial experience. Automobility, rail, and other mechanical technologies here channel the demand that black people consign their endeavors to the logic of progress.

Like McPherson's Doc Craft "bucking" imperatives of productivity and forward motion, both the driver and car idle in the driveway, engaging in a restorative, resistant practice of inertia. In the black driver's lingering we detect a subtle refusal. Rankine's propertied black driver, ostensibly in control "behind the wheel," devises a strategy of stillness to avoid internalizing erasure. Sitting in stillness constitutes what Lauren Berlant calls a "citizen-action, . . . a weapon for resisting defeat and depletion in the face of the supremacist ordinary" (Berlant 2014: 45). Like a sigh, which momentarily suspends or interrupts the rhythm of the breath, sitting in silence constitutes a momentary refusal to continue racing forward to:

> a destination that doesn't include acting like this moment isn't inhabitable. (10)

Akin to the acts of arrest that Harvey Young defines as black performances of stillness, the driver's immobility in *Citizen* flouts the post–civil rights imperative to "move on" that sustains the dominant national narrative of inevitable racial progress. This call to advance demands our continual disavowal of the actual stasis inhering in what is understood as "progress." The *Citizen* driver avows this stasis through a still posture that (momentarily) resists the ever unfolding demand to advance. It is a moment to recollect, rather than to ceaselessly strive and "drive straight through the moment," like John Henry (10).

In the poetic video essay "Situation 5" (ca. 2011), Rankine attends not to rest but to sonic and visual depictions of aimlessness that resist progressive temporal imperatives. A work from the nine-part series Rankine created with her partner photographer/filmmaker John Lucas, "Situation 5" stages a stalled conversation that affectively registers how black life is held up between promise and precarity in the wake of civil rights. The video essay illuminates black cultural producers' attempts to express the felt experience of hung freedom, a slippery paradox whose affective complexity, to say nothing of its legal, political, and social unevenness, challenges representation. In the four-minute short, the poem's speaker imagines a phone call to a brother who has "been imprisoned, . . . though he has not been to prison":

> The sky is the silence of brothers all the days leading up to my call.

> If I called I'd say good-bye before I broke the good-bye. I say good-bye before anyone can hang up. Don't hang up. My brother hangs up though he's there on the phone. I keep talking . . . .

He won't hang up. He's there, he's there but he's hung up though he is there. Good-bye, I say. I break the good-bye. I say good-bye before anyone can hang up, don't hang up.

The brother's simultaneous presence and absence on the line parallels the speaker's own feelings of duality, of suspension between two places: the desire to call, only to "say good-bye." This ambivalence marking the black voice extends to the interplay of frictions among the sonic, the visual, and the linguistic. In depicting a perpetually postponed call, "Situation 5" apprehends the logic of suspension animating hung progress and governing contemporary black life. As the "Situation" speaker remarks, "We are all caught hanging."

Multimodal in form, "Situation 5" aestheticizes movement without aim, fashioning a poetics out of impasse. Even as the mise-en-scène of "Situation 5" evokes progress through its sonic and visual unfolding of spoken words and a motion picture unbroken by the still shot, its background track makes sounds void of direction. The forward motion conveyed by the rapid advance of Rankine's words spoken over unfolding footage of black men in vehicular transit works in tension with the affects of suspension imparted by the poem.[3] At the same time, the production techniques of sonic sampling set the poem's imprisoned, or pendent, brother in motion. Rankine's "moving poem," then, offers another object lesson in the way black writers represent even as they contest hung freedom and the imperative to advance, using black somatics to slip anchor.

"Situation 5" samples and rescripts the Miles Davis sextet's "So What," from the 1959 studio album *Kind of Blue*, in ways that repurpose the impasse created by the temporal imperative to relentlessly progress toward an inevitable racial denouement. A modal composition, "So What" launches with a piano and bass introduction played rubato, an off-tempo style whose "lack of rhythmic resolution . . . gives it an eerie, suspended feel" that contrasts with the melodic call-and-response that propels the remainder of the song (Kahn 2000: 113). Altered for "Situation 5," the opening measures float nearly indistinct at the lower registers of the audiovisual montage. Rankine and Lucas have cleaved the piano and bass's synchronized bars; each instrument is heard separately. The keys sound briefly and ethereally, making way for the bass to wander searchingly and then pluck a held note of discord. From that dissonant sound, the bass launches the familiar melody of the song's signature call, but instead of advancing to the expected response ("So what?"), the sample turns back twice to the vagrant bassline before looping back to the track's first note to start all over again. In this rearrangement, Davis's horn never sounds. In lieu of his anticipated reply, the sample turns back to dissonance. Shuttling between discord and melodic call, the "Situation 5" track enacts the sensation of being in between, of being just outside melodic time and order. The track continually loops back, out of tempo, to the site of impasse and the scene of discord.

Rather than rehearsing fictions of resolution, "Situation 5" turns back to digressive notes that might catalyze another call, a different question. While the notes sounding "So what?" in the sextet's original track fulfills the expectation of antiphonic sequencing by resolving the bass line's accruing tension, the "Situation 5" sample unhinges call from response, holding our desire for sonic and narrative resolution in abeyance. Through the technique of recursivity, the twenty-first-century reproduction cultivates a misty atmosphere of pendency, a feeling of indeterminacy created by "not knowing where the downbeat will fall" (Kahn 2000: 112). Placing spoken words and advancing landscapes against the sound of reversal and deferral, the video holds in tense relation black movement and suspensions of imperative time. If "So what?" was, in fact, "one of [Davis's] favorite expressions, a way of dismissing the grandiose" (Nisenson 2000: 153), then we might read "Situation 5" as eliminating the original song's two-note "So what?" theme and inserting in its place sonic loops whose digressions, recursivity, and aimlessness pose the question, "What's the point?" through technique and form. To the post–civil rights imperative to progress toward inevitable racial resolution, the rescripted sounds of "Situation 5" defiantly respond with a performance of pointlessness that is both interrogative and declarative. It asks and declares, "So what?" "What does it matter?" In this space outside normative structures of rhythm and melody, "Situation 5" offers a glimpse of black somatics as a form of counter-suspension. The techniques of isolating the found sonic object and altering its pace, direction, and heft—and thereby its relation to itself and the logics of linearity and resolution—give rise to an aesthetics of movement suggestive of an elusive affective experience, what Rankine (2011) calls "a different way to be": "If I knew a different way to be, I would call. . . ." This different way of being comes on the condition of knowing how to move differently in and out of imperative time.

Notes

1   The Supreme Court's 1956 ruling in *Browder v. Gayle* prompted many southern rail companies to desegregate their passengers, both interstate and intrastate, but because of pressure from Deep South communities and states, few companies publicized their elimination of Jim Crow seating. The result was a nebulous, ever-shifting

Jim Crow line that slowly and sporadically altered the South; the guarantee of desegregated travel was spotty, uncertain, and unreliable. After US attorney general Robert Kennedy warned the Interstate Commerce Commission (ICC) and rail industry representatives in 1957 that *Browder* had, indeed, outlawed *all* forms of Jim Crow transit, making the segregation of local and interstate travelers alike a crime, mandatory (but not always customary) segregation largely ended on southern trains. However, as McPherson's account corroborates, some interstate railroads, including the Central of Georgia, refused to desegregate their local passengers. By McPherson's first summer in St. Paul in 1962, the Central of Georgia, likely the line he rode from Atlanta to Chattanooga, was the sole railroad in the country ignoring ICC warnings and still segregating its passengers. See Barnes 1983: 129, 130, 182. See *Browder v. Gayle*, 352 U.S. 903 (1956).

2   Scripts of seven of the *Situations* video poems would come to comprise section 6 of Rankine's 2014 *Citizen*.

3   The images of black men in transit are drawn from Lucas's footage of Charlie Kelly's and Richard Roderick's releases from prison. "Situation 5" precedes Lucas' feature-length documentary film *The Cooler Bandits* (2014), which "follows the lives of Frankie [Porter], Donovan [Harris], Charlie [Kelly] and [Richard] Poochie [Roderick], four friends in Akron, Ohio, who as teens in 1991 committed a series of restaurant robberies and received stiff sentences of up to 500 years in prison" (Lucas 2012).

References

Abel, Elizabeth. 2008. "American Graffiti: The Social Life of Segregation Signs." *African American Review* 42, no. 1: 9–24.

Adeyemi, Kemi. 2019. "The Practice of Slowness: Black Queer Women and the Right to the City." *GLQ: A Journal of Lesbian and Gay Studies* 25, no. 4: 545–67.

Baker, Houston A. 1984. *Blues, Ideology, and Afro-American Literature: A Vernacular Theory.* Chicago: University of Chicago Press.

Barnes, Catherine A. 1983. *Journey from Jim Crow: The Desegregation of Southern Transit.* New York: Columbia University Press.

Berlant, Lauren. 2014. "Claudia Rankine." *BOMB* 129. bombmagazine.org/article/10096/claudia-rankine.

Bruce, La Marr Jurelle. 2019. "Shore, Unsure: Loitering as a Way of Life." *GLQ: A Journal of Lesbian and Gay Studies* 25, no. 2: 352–61.

Fleming, Julius B., Jr. 2019. "Transforming Geographies of Black Time: How the Free Southern Theater Used the Plantation for Civil Rights Activism." *American Literature* 91, no. 3: 587–617.

Gilroy, Paul. 1993. *The Black Atlantic: Modernity and Double Consciousness.* Cambridge, MA: Harvard University Press.

Gilroy, Paul. 2001. "Driving While Black." *Car Cultures*, edited by Daniel Miller, 81–104. Oxford: Berg.

Hanchard, Michael. 1999. "Afro-Modernity: Temporality, Politics, and the African Diaspora." *Public Culture* 11, no. 1: 245–68.

Hartman, Saidiya V. 1997. *Scenes of Subjection: Terror, Slavery, and Self-Making in Nineteenth-Century America.* New York: Oxford University Press.

Hunt, Erica. 2014. "All about You." *Los Angeles Review of Books*, December 8. lareviewofbooks
.org/article/all-about-you/.

Kahn, Ashley. 2000. *Kind of Blue: The Making of the Miles Davis Masterpiece*. New York: Da Capo Press.

Lucas, John. 2012. *The Cooler Bandits*. Trailer. Vimeo. https://vimeo.com/46061699.

McPherson, James Alan. 1968. "A Solo Song: For Doc." *Hue and Cry*. Boston: Little, Brown.

McPherson, James Alan. 1998. *Crabcakes*. New York: Simon & Schuster.

McPherson, James Alan. 2003. "The Express: A One-Way Ticket to a World He'd Never Known." *Washington Post Magazine*, July 6: W16.

Morrison, Toni. (1977) 2004. *Song of Solomon*. New York: Vintage.

Morrison, Toni. 1997. *Paradise*. New York: Knopf.

Nisenson, Eric. 2000. *The Making of Kind of Blue: Miles Davis and His Masterpiece*. New York: St. Martin's Griffin.

Rankine, Claudia, and John Lucas. ca. 2011. "Situation 5."

Rankine, Claudia. 2014. *Citizen: An American Lyric*. Minneapolis: MN: Graywolf Press.

Román, David. 2005. *Performance in America: Contemporary U.S. Culture and the Performing Arts*. Durham, NC: Duke University Press.

Sharpe, Christina. 2016. *In the Wake: On Blackness and Being*. Durham, NC: Duke University Press.

Singh, Nikhil Pal. 2004. *Black Is a Country: Race and the Unfinished Struggle for Democracy*. Cambridge, MA: Harvard University Press.

Stepto, Robert B. 1991. *From Behind the Veil: A Study of Afro-American Narrative*. 2nd ed. Urbana: University of Illinois Press.

Warren, Calvin. 2016. "Black Time: Slavery, Metaphysics, and the Logic of Wellness." In *The Psychic Hold of Slavery: Legacies in American Expressive Culture*, edited by Soyica Diggs Colbert, Robert J. Patterson, and Aida Levy-Hussen, 55–68. New Brunswick, NJ: Rutgers University Press.

Kaneesha Cherelle Parsard

Criticism as Proposition

In 1871, three decades after West Indian Emancipation, John Wodehouse, secretary of state for the colonies, wrote to Governor Rawson William Rawson of Barbados and the Windward Islands. Wodehouse had a question about the future of the plantation: he was "enquiring about the increasing disposition of Creole women to form connection with Chinese and Indian immigrants" (National Archives of the UK: CO 28/214/79: fol. 456). The sentence, stretching across nearly half of the folio, described not one relationship but a tendency. These were instructions to confirm a "disposition" and then to stop it. These were instructions to wrest control of the colonies from unruly subjects. That this question ended with a full stop, taking the form of an imperative, made this moment a decisive one—a crisis in which the present might give way to an undesirable future. Not an instance of absence and recovery, this document poses another archival quandary: one of British and West Indian officials breaking character and showing their uncertainty. But how to study moments in which imperial-colonial authority writes through what it doesn't know, what makes it uneasy and anxious?

This quandary underlies the title of this essay and its method, criticism as proposition

The South Atlantic Quarterly 121:1, January 2022
DOI 10.1215/00382876-9561559 © 2022 Duke University Press

(Scott and Laughlin 2008; Scott 2014).[1] It is a method of revisiting unsettled questions and posing alternative narratives about the legacies of slavery and emancipation. In analytic philosophy, proposition is two pronged, a truth claim that can be matched favorably or unfavorably to a question (Scott 2001). To make such a claim is to say, to quote one philosopher, "this is how things stand" (Wittgenstein [1921] 2001: 43). This approach challenges the epistemological and enunciative, as well as material, power of the colonial state (Derby 2014: 127).[2] As administrators fill the Colonial Office records with problems about race, family, and labor after Emancipation, criticism as proposition is a practice of calling into question Britain's narrative of its empire. If Wodehouse's question reveals that the project of freedom is faltering, we can generate new propositions about how West Indian subjects might have shaped their relations and tactics.

The end of chattel slavery had brought about a crisis for plantation capital (Taylor 2018). Three-quarters of a million African descendants became free subjects of the British Crown, and there would no longer be captive labor for the cane fields (Holt 1992). If the West Indian colonies were to revive their sugar industry, holding their own against European beet sugar and Brazil, they would need reliable, disciplined—and cheap—labor. Enter Asian contract labor. The British East India Company had facilitated the Trinidad Experiment decades earlier, during which small numbers of indentured Chinese workers migrated to Trinidad to work the sugar estates (Lowe 2015: 24; Jung 2006). Following Emancipation, the Company began to recruit greater numbers of workers from British India and from China (Look Lai 1998: 17; Roopnarine 2007: 27–28). The planters' need to sustain production rested on the hope that Indian and Chinese workers would not challenge their contracts like Black wage labor had (Lightfoot 2015: 130).

But indenture was also a means of modeling family life to the formerly enslaved. While both were thought industrious, Chinese labor was seen as even better suited to bourgeois family life than Indian labor (Sheller 2012: 93; Bahadur 2013: 87). From a captive existence, they would enter into a waged existence: a man who would support his wife and child with his pay, and in turn depend on his wife's unwaged work in the home so that he could continue to work.[3] *Creole*, at this moment, referred both to people of African descent and to anyone born in the West Indies (Burton 1997). Given the particular efforts of colonial administrators, churches, and aid groups to teach women of African descent to be chaste in the decades after West Indian Emancipation, it is more than likely that Earl Wodehouse is referring to Black women (Lightfoot 2015: 153–62). Rawson himself had lamented that women of African descent were giving birth without having married—or remarried, in the case of widowed women (Morton-Gittens 2017: 192). Under this logic, Creole women would be the worst possible partners for Indian and Chinese men if they were to understand the value of estate work.

While the first decades of the twenty-first century in the United States catalyze this issue, I want to look elsewhere in the hemisphere and to our past—not only for other examples of but also for lessons about Black temporality in times of crisis. Of late, Caribbean criticism has drawn on a long history of study in which crisis is "evidently a matter of life and death" (Jobson 2020: 71). But crisis is also a matter of discourse. Wodehouse and Rawson have "crisis talk" in the private space of bureaucratic correspondence. The meeting of these Creole, Chinese, and Indian subjects makes for an uncertain present, one that might be "stabilized" through making these subjects fit for liberal freedom (Masco 2016: S73). This crisis is thus one of empire's authority over temporality: that its ideal future would win out over the possible consequences of "connection" between "Creole women" and "Chinese and Indian immigrants." It is also a crisis of the archives in which it establishes and protects this authority.

Speculative methods have offered new temporalities to make sense of these crises of freedom and unfreedom (Fuentes 2016). Saidiya Hartman's critical fabulation takes up and reorganizes the "basic elements of the story" to identify the past conditional "what might have been" in conversation with Lisa Lowe (Hartman 2008: 11; Lowe 2015: 175). Looking ahead, Danielle Bainbridge offers the future perfect "what will have been" to underscore the urgency of continuing to reckon with the legacies of chattel slavery (Bainbridge 2020). And some temporal and conceptual problems are unresolved in their time. From my vantage, I could describe this "disposition of Creole women" in the simple past: it was and then it was no more. But it is multidimensional, occupying but also placing pressure on the same present in which Wodehouse and Rawson correspond. Proposition speaks back to questions like Wodehouse's to unveil a simultaneous, competing present, one in which these subjects challenge the unspoken terms of their labor and make freedom on different terms.

To untangle the "increasing disposition" after West Indian Emancipation, I offer proposition as a method for probing these officials' questions about the West Indian colonies. Returning to the correspondence between Wodehouse and Rawson, the "increasing disposition of Creole women" sheds new light on familiar narratives and figures of emancipation, Asian contract labor, and their legacies. I revisit the cultural milieu of the time— Michel Jean Cazabon's nineteenth-century Trinidadian landscapes and the travel writings of Edward Jenkins in British Guiana—to question the teleology that emancipation suggests, in which freedom follows slavery and is made possible through racialized labor and domesticity. In its place, I elevate ordinary scenes of encounter and ambivalence toward the plantation in order to suggest that this "disposition" toward "connection," far from mere rumor, might hasten the decline of empire.

On Proposition

Knowledge gives empire its heft. The verificationist style of Wodehouse and Rawson's correspondence seems to echo the eighteenth-century principle of "documentary governance," or "the concept of imperial commerce as knowable through the experience contained in reliable archival records" (Siddique 2020: 644–45, 662). I have been preoccupied with the truth claims that empire makes and then, in service of itself, confirms. The truth claims it seals tight, disallowing dissent. In turn, uncertainty is an epistemological and a temporal problem for empire. If uncertainty is the catalyst of anxiety, both are important to apprehending political presents and futures (Ngai 2005: 246; Thomas 2019; Sinha 1995; Grewal 2016).[4] What is Great Britain's worst nightmare after West Indian Emancipation? What is at stake for me is not a single answer but rather the potential catastrophes, the end of a panicked line of associations. And the two-pronged character of proposition—to be answered with a yes or no, and therefore to verify a claim—opens other possible timelines.

In this moment of crisis, proposition contends that another world, another order of things, could swallow up the fantasy of good labor and good subjecthood. The idea that discourse and cultural works offer other scenes of freedom to the "questions or problems" of Emancipation and its legacies, scenes that can then be tested (Scott and Laughlin 2008). It relies not on the imagination of the critic but the imagination of the moment under consideration. Proposition poses, if not a fully anarchic way of being, one that is quietly and persistently disruptive (Hartman 2019).[5] It is a method that intentionally looks beyond the familiar scenes of resistance and rebellion in favor of the mundane: here, "disposition" toward "connection."

Proposition picks up a recent thread of criticism that turns to analytic philosophy to make sense of Black temporality, either in whole or in part. Most recently, as Jonathan Kramnick argues, close reading itself becomes a "skilled practice," a "knowing how" that expresses itself through the seamless quotation of a text into the critic's prose (Kramnick 2021: 225). A key example for Kramnick is Christina Sharpe's *In the Wake*, in which her quotation and interpretation of the "branded mark" in Toni Morrison's *Beloved* makes the argument for what it means to live "in the wake" of Atlantic slavery (224). The time of *Beloved*, a neo–slave narrative, is collapsed with the time of interpretation, both commenting on the incomplete project of freedom (224). In Caribbean criticism, it is the interview form that has critical value: through question and answer, it puts on display the events that shaped the questions of postindependence Anglophone Caribbean figures (Scott 2014: 157). David Scott, as interviewer, reaches for "neither consensus nor critique, but clarification" (160). In so doing, rather than dismissing or overcoming, he models the study of earlier "problem-spaces" against one's own (Scott 2004: 4). In both cases, proposition hovers over but is not central to the argument. The in-text quotation facilitates the truth claim, while the interview seeks understanding instead of a resolution to another generation's questions. Proposition builds on these to instigate. It is a confrontation with—a stepping to, taking liberties with—colonial narratives to understand a bygone moment anew.

The unwieldiness of proposition makes it a fitting framework for the new imbrications of race, gender, sexuality, and labor after Emancipation (Haley 2020; Sweeney 2020). There are several senses of the term apart from its role in analytic philosophy. A rare, even obsolete sense of *proposition* is a legal or financial agreement prior to its signing, a proposed contract.[6] This submerged definition raises the contract at the heart of postemancipation labor—oft unspoken in the case of Black labor, and oft coerced in the case of Asian indenture—a liberal humanist contract (Lowe 2015: 39). This is a contract that allows people to sell their labor on the free market. It is a contract that also falsely envisions labor as a legal, economic, and moral pathway to full emancipation. Proposition, inversely, asks how postslavery subjects placed pressure on the labor contract and created freedom on different terms.

Emancipation as a moment of crisis brings up not just abstractions like proposition or capital but also matter like flesh (Spillers 1987). To ask about Great Britain's worst nightmare is also to ask for a glimpse of that fright, if not a full narrative. West Indian novels, travel accounts, landscapes and portraits, and photography create scenes that bring anxieties about the Negro or the "coolie" to life—or, try as they might, tamp them down (Thompson 2011). Who and what might be built, embraced, adorned, or abandoned? And, appropriately, proposition is also an overture, is suggestive. Imagine: an indentured man and a woman of African descent leave an estate, cut through brush, and in a new place nearby make a life and a legal claim on the very estate they had left (Gopaul Whittington and Pemberton 1986; Cordis 2019). Proposition, then, is an analytic that sketches worlds through encounter. It is concerned with form and politics, texts and discourses, and flesh bodies moving with and against one another (Macharia 2020).

Proposition is an act of building, too. I am interested in description and figuration: the networks of characters, space, objects that build out the time-space of another world. Literature and art reveal the terms of the debate, as they provide the shape of other worlds that West Indians imagined after Emancipation—an anti-imperial realism. While proposition as a critical gesture cannot upend the bureaucrat altogether, it draws attention to and foregrounds where governance falters. It shifts the weight of narration to that which does not enter the colonial archives, the everyday of its subjects. In all these ways, I consider how these scenes propose competing presents, parallel plots: the hypothetical "action-transpiring-in-time" ending not in the descendants of enslaved and indentured peoples as good subjects, toiling for the good of plantation and empire, but rather captured and coerced peoples making lives in all manner of relation (Kornbluh 2019: 38; Wynter 1971). And, in so doing, proposition shifts the dimensions of Black life in the Americas: time, space, and freedom. In this way, it loosens the dialogic structure that holds that only empire can provide an account of itself.

So—what if? What if the planters could not compel Black and Asian labor to remain in the cane fields without the lash? What if the prison, which comes to replace the lash, cannot contain them (Paton 2004)? What if they gather, carouse, organize? In this light, Wodehouse's question about "connection" frustrates the hope of an earlier moment: that Chinese contract labor would "occupy an intermediary position" (Lowe 2015: 27). The Trinidad Experiment with Asian "coolie" labor thus appears to be under threat by the late century, producing two modes of anticipation around the legacies of Emancipation: hope and dread. By inquiring into "connection," I question racial antipathy as a mode of discipline in the postemancipation West Indies. The possibilities encoded in "connection" need not lead to simple cross-racial solidarity or intimacy, though, but rather to a critique of the plantation and its domination over a multiracial labor force. My proposition: If colonial rhetoric bids them to labor and to live in opposition to one another, for the good of the plantation and the colony, what might be possible if they refuse (Mengesha and Padmanabhan 2019; Campt 2019)?

The Increasing Disposition . . . to Form Connection

Let us return to the Earl's letter, rumor without a source: "Enquiring about the increasing disposition of Creole women to form connection with Chinese and Indian immigrants." Rumor as a genre reveals the limits of colonial bureaucracy and, relatedly, the everyday lives and practices that frustrate it (Derby 2014: 126).[7] The letter contained no other news. These rumors were sufficiently disturbing to merit a memo all its own, the paper and envelope and seal making the long trip across the Atlantic. His recipient, Governor Rawson, mistakes the preposition "about" for the conditional "if" or "whether." Rawson appeals to the language of governance in a different way: to put the matter to rest. Rawson's rebuttal is, while servile, also clear: "I have the honor to report that as no such immigrants [Indian or Chinese] have been introduced into the island, I am unable to furnish any information on the subject" (National Archives of the UK: CO 28/214/79: fol. 456). There are no such Asian immigrants in Barbados, Rawson replies, so how could this be? He cannot "furnish" or supply information to the earl as the colonies would otherwise furnish its sugar to Britain.

Then, the correspondence opens again. One month after Rawson pens his reply, on July 21, 1871, a junior official comments on the exchange in a minute paper (Tough and Lihoma 2012: 193–94). This third party is loath to give up. Perhaps more aware of the political economy of the various West Indian colonies than Wodehouse is, he points out that Rawson is also an administrator of the Windward Islands—which at that time included Saint Lucia, Saint Vincent, the Grenadines, all of which also exploited indentured labor. This is a question, in other words, that still demands an answer.

But an answer is not to come. Less than one week after the minute paper, Wodehouse uses its exact language in a reply to Rawson. "I have to point out," he writes, "that my despatch was addressed to you, not as Gov. of Barbados alone, but as Gov. Gen'l of the Windward Islands, including the Coolie importing islands of Grenada and St. Vincent" (National Archives of the UK: CO 28/214/79: fol. 458). This "you" is an administrative plural. But Rawson sends no further response. The most plausible reasons for this are that Rawson has forgotten the scope of his duties, especially his jurisdiction, or that he is being evasive. If Rawson has forgotten his duties in their entirety, this would fit with the extant scholarship on his career as a British colonial administrator. Rawson would have many failures—among them, to integrate Barbados and the Windward Islands. And it would be gaffes and evasions like these that would eventually lead to Rawson's dismissal from the colonial service (Morton-Gittens 2017: 191). If he is being evasive, it suggests that this "disposition" did exist among Creole, or African-descended, women. His lack of response, however, is a sign that he wishes to conceal his lack of insight into the Windward Islands; the all-seeing colonial eye is not, in fact, all seeing. In moments like these, the British imperial state becomes frustrated in the face of this evasion—as it attempts to apprehend these new postemancipation subjects.

This is a frustration larger than either the earl or Rawson; it is a frustration of the British colonial archive itself, at a moment when freedom as a concept and as a status are yet undefined. British imperial authority is asking questions of itself. But as the Earl of Kimberley and Governor Rawson volley questions and evasions back and forth, they cannot answer each other. And though archival research is never complete or comprehensive, I have not found other documentation of such nineteenth-century "connection."

Connection, like proposition, is a concept that travels and links the various categories that are inaugurated by the modern world: race, gender, sexuality. In the late eighteenth and early nineteenth centuries, "connection" referred to "sexual relation or intercourse; a liaison," as in, "to have connection with."[8] While it always suggests illicit relations, "connection" is a troubling prospect in the Circular Despatch because of who is involved. The competing present, and the interplay of acceleration and deferral it conjures, is a Black temporality because it is catalyzed by Emancipation—even as Asian indenture follows it as a differently racialized labor regime.

Yet another kind of connection has been part of capital, and plantation capital in particular: it is "vampire-like," sinking its teeth into and consuming enslaved and then indentured labor in order to produce sugar (Marx 1887; Jobson 2021). These waged and indentured workers were profoundly alienated from their labor (Marx [1844] 1959; Robinson [1983] 2000). And, during Atlantic slavery, alienation was also a matter of gender and sexuality: proprietors exploited enslaved women's sexual and reproductive labor as well as physical labor (Morgan 2004; Weinbaum 2019). Inverting this sense, however, connection is a corrective to the alienation at the heart of racial capitalism. While the plantation is already in decline because of competition, issues of labor and agriculture, "connection" suggests that it is what laborers do away from the plantation or under the nose of overseers that hastens its decline.

On its own, Wodehouse's question begins to contest the postemancipation narrative of the British West Indies, and with it the idea that West Indian estates so successfully segregated Black and Asian labor as to entirely prevent any intimacies between peoples of African descent and Indian descent before the twentieth century (Diptee 2000). Instead of the grateful and dutiful emancipated, and Asian contract laborers joining them to save West Indian sugar, there are wanton Creole women and distracted Chinese and Indian immigrants. At least two figures are not present in the correspondence: one, the

Creole, or Black man; and, two, the "coolie" woman, who East India Company recruiters thought to vet extensively—who they would identify the "right kind of woman" for indenture, not a woman fleeing family duty or a sex worker (Reddock 1985). How might all these subjects be loosened from the figurative constraints of colonial governance? I wish to move beyond the familiar claims about these relations: that there are liberatory possibilities in cross-racial intimacy, or that there are uncrossable fault lines between these peoples. Connection or encounter exceeds tension, cooperation, solidarity—and, most importantly, is a threat to the order of the plantation.

For the Earl of Kimberley, his worst nightmare seems to be the figure of the Creole woman. The Creole woman is the colony's heat come to England's cold and damp. She is the source of the sweat dripping from the Earl's head as he dashes off yet another memorandum to Governor Rawson through the summer of 1871. If one's disposition is one's inherent character, how can these "Creole women" take on a new character? Under what circumstances might it develop? She is willful, taking advantage of the skewed sex ratios of Asian indenture. In both Chinese and Indian indenture, recruitment favored men. As a result, there was competition for and violence over the few available women (Bahadur 2013; Parsard 2016). In the imaginary of the plantation, the racial family made desire that flouted racial, gender, and sexual common-sense unthinkable: that men sought companionship with men or women with women or that Asian labor turned to Black women for companionship. It is Creole women who, seeing this weakness, initiate connection. If the Earl of Kimberley asks a question about Creole women and their interest in sex with Asian contract laborers, where might the answer lie? Certainly not with the shifty Governor Rawson.

If time is always geographic, this moment is unfolding at different paces at the level of the empire, the colony, and the plantation (Trouillot 1988; Thomas 2004; Carby 2019).[9] There is the time of the British Empire's decline and the decline of West Indian sugar. There is the time of wage labor, measured by workday and hour and task. Chopping the cane, gathering it, harvesting its juice in the mill. Beyond the fields, the time of social reproduction, too: the wife, who may herself work in the cane fields, who cooks and rears children so that the plantation will run another day. And then the time in excess of labor and reproduction, the time of mischief, of relation, of leisure (Fleming 2019). It is difficult to apprehend these tendencies across scales. In the late nineteenth century, the distance between the seat of the British Empire and a given West Indian colony or plantation meant that a given memo—even one of importance from the secretary of state of the colonies—could take two weeks or more to reach its destination by Royal Mail. This creates a lag between apprehending, reporting, and enforcing stops on wayward behavior. In this time, emancipated Black West Indians and indentured Indian workers could find the time to invent and test new relations and economies.

The question—of the "increasing disposition of Creole women to form connection with Chinese and Indian immigrants"—then becomes the proposition itself. It is as though the "Creole woman" is hastening this future, her "increasing disposition" an acceleration. Acceleration changes the relationship between the present and the future, bringing an unwanted future ever closer. As this "increasing disposition of . . . connection" picks up steam, it seems to grow larger, more powerful. It might yet overtake the liberal narrative of freedom. And the British colonial state might meet it with resistance: there was already residential segregation between Black and Asian labor on the plantations, and Wodehouse seems to desire greater surveillance. But there is nonetheless a kind of bureaucratic impotence in the face of connection.

But asking the question—Who or what is Great Britain's worst nightmare?—is not enough. As often as questions loosen our assumptions, they can also reify them by merely pointing to the absence. As though knowing there is a weak spot in colonial archives, colonial narratives, and colonial authority is enough. That the correspondence between Wodehouse and Rawson ultimately remains open invites proposition, an interrogation of the forms of imperial rule: its figures, networks, idioms. It allows an interrogation of our tightly held narratives of power, possibility, and impossibility, too. How does proposition invite us to pay closer attention to scenes that don't rely on familiar narratives?

The exchange between Wodehouse and Rawson also finds expression in West Indian painting and novelistic traditions—hidden in plain sight. The encounters between Black West Indians and West Indians of Indian descent seem to provide opportunity for disruptive "connection" because, unlike Chinese labor, Indian labor was not recruited as a bourgeois intermediary class. One scene of connection is in the painting tradition of the island at the end of the Windward chain: Trinidad. There, Michel Jean Cazabon painted not only portraits of racial types like the Creole woman or the "coolie" family, but also landscapes in which peoples of African descent and of Indian descent—and sometimes figures who were not identifiable as either—labored, gathered, and moved about the estates and Crown lands. Cazabon's depictions of nineteenth-century Trinidad are contested. Because he came from a family of Martinican free-coloreds, was educated in France, and commissioned by Governor Harris and notorious planters such as William Hardin Burnley, some critics see his paintings as an effort to "sanitize" the history of postemancipation Trinidad (Cudjoe 2003: 147–48; Raymond 2010). Others have seen parts of his body of work to be an expression of his tentative allegiance to the "Negroes" and "coolies" (Wahab 2010: 158). But there is something to be gleaned from Cazabon's painting beyond clear alliance with either the planters or labor.

There is ambivalence, particularly in Cazabon's surveying scenes. The moment of painting is the moment of crisis. Cazabon often painted *en plein air*, or outside. When he renders the landscape, it is as a palimpsest that makes visible the imperial-colonial past and its relationship to the present—historical and temporal "connection." The violence of enclosure and labor are not directly visualized but hinted at in the clearings and paths, traces of cultivation dating to the seventeenth century. In *Cedar Point, Mount Tamana* (1851), the painting evokes a surveying scene, common in the early modern Caribbean. It attempts to resuscitate visual mastery in the moment of emancipation. The weight of the burdens beside the laborer implies the lash and paltry wages. The painting figure in the background casts this work as a meditation on the act of painting itself. In this scene are simultaneous layers of history and possibility. And the white figures turn their back on the laborer, of unknown origin, and on the painter, confident that their eye is all-seeing. With eyes on the landscape, they miss the possible tactics of the laborer and the ambivalence of the painter. If the postemancipation period involves many timelines, unfolding at different levels, Cazabon is visualizing a present that might undo the seemingly picturesque scene before him (Thompson 2006: 18).

Another is in the travel writing of the late nineteenth century West Indies, which collapses the time-space and the racial logic of the plantation (Islam 2021).[10] Edward Jenkins's *Lutchmee and Dilloo: A Study of West Indian Life* (1877) is the product of his travels to British Guiana on behalf of the British Anti-Slavery Society. A Royal Commission of Enquiry had investigated claims of abuses against Indian contract labor and then dispatched Jenkins to further document the conditions. His first work, *The Coolie, His Rights and Wrongs* (1871), was a work of reportage, published in the same year that Wodehouse wrote to Rawson (Jenkins 1871). *Lutchmee and Dilloo* was a novel, the representational excess of Jenkins's time in Guiana. One scene in this latter narrative appears to be simply descriptive, tracing the idiosyncrasy of an L-shaped estate. But these odd dimensions also facilitate encounter: "For convenience['s] sake it was habitual for the Coolies of Hofman's Lust, who were working on their estate at the back of the longer line [of the estate], to take a shortcut to and from their work across the Negro village" (Jenkins [1877] 2003: 277). Here, the exposition—placing "Negroes" on the peripheries of scenes centered on poor so-called "coolies," or vice versa—places these two groups in much closer proximity than scholars have been led to believe. The Black West Indian ceases to be decoration, setting, in the plot of indenture. Despite its depiction as mere "convenience," as Indian contract labor goes to work, they also cross the civilizational line between themselves and the residents of the "Negro village"—that which had been the foundation of the Trinidad Experiment and which Jenkins would later uphold. There is something here about the incidental, the idea that Black and indentured Indian labor merely happen to live alongside one another—as though it were not the expansion of the West Indian plantation and an empire spanning oceans and continents that brought them together. The incidental as a mode of representation conceals the tactics that emerge against the modern plantation. But as the indentured workers become habituated to walking through the "Negro village," these encounters might nonetheless become the basis of a new "disposition" toward work and the plantation.

Cazabon's and Jenkins's scenes are a testing ground for connection. So, literary and visual cultures offer a possible answer to the question, albeit one that its asker—inert as it is, with John Wodehouse, Rawson, and the subjects of his letters long gone—would not expect or like. The "disposition of Creole women"—to answer, finally, the Earl of Kimberley's question—may indeed have been "to form connection": to thwart the agricultural and extractive industries, with the help of the new arrivals, and to steal and take pleasure in it all the while.

Proposition's Lessons

Empire gains its authority from the exchange among imperial officials, local administrators, and elites, from a closed system of questions and answers about the management of subjects, labor, economies. They are tautological conversations: the answer accepted to be true only shores up the authority of the British Empire. It is a form of persuasion oriented not only toward its objects—wage and contract labor, Black and Asian alike—but also toward colonial authority. It is, too, a form of persuasion that does not appear as such; its aim is to appear natural. But the increasing disposition, and the uncertainty it produces, punctures that imaginary.

Criticism as proposition presents a matrix of scenes of freedom made up of the other knowledges, moods, and temporalities that emerge from the Black and brown masses. Proposition questions the empirics of the archives and their investment in good governance. They can be found not only in colonial memoranda but also in novels, travel writing, portraits, landscapes, and photography. And, I have questioned how and why these small acts of "connection" inspire the same level of discourse, colonial correspondence, as work stoppage and rebellion.

Proposition reframes seemingly small questions as world-historical in nature. This is a malleable and interdisciplinary method: stretching both archives and cultural forms to seek new narratives, the possibilities for emancipated Africans, indentured Asians, and their descendants who shared the plantation and the colony. It asks how race, gender, sexuality, capital—rather than utterly separate categories of analysis, or merely intersectional—bear on one another in new and unexpected ways (Nash 2019). It looks also to the smallest of small places: here, moving with the currents of the Atlantic and Indian Ocean worlds, but in the corners of the colonies. Proposition sees refusal in place rather than in flight. It asks, Which tendencies—irritating, nagging—might be harnessed now in order to create a different future? But criticism as proposition goes beyond the teleology of progress and modernity, and even familiar counternarratives, to dally in the imagination. It is a what-if untethered to the lash, the wage, or the family. The "increasing disposition," the possibilities that emerge in the lag, are disruptive rather than resistive or invincible. But the uncertainty these scenes produced in their moment suggests that they might yet have another life.

While elaborated through the aesthetic and cultural history of the postemancipation West Indies, the care found here can be a lesson to feminist, queer, and minoritized communities at large. What we know as wages for housework or mutual aid today is in the Caribbean past: with people who sustained themselves by taking refuge in nonnuclear family relations, by sharing and hustling through the decline of the plantation industry, a global depression, and regional labor rebellions, and the attempt at postcolonial sovereignty. These are possibilities that flourished and then came to an end. Proposition makes possible a return to scenes of freedom that have been curtailed or extinguished or have run out of steam. So, when their propositions fail, they compel us to simply test them again! We should revisit these scenes, figures, objects—for the possibilities that make those in power sweat.

Notes

Thank you to Adrienne Brown, Allyson Nadia Field, and SJ Zhang for comments on the earliest version of this paper, which I presented at the Duke University Representing Migration Humanities Lab in 2019; to copresenters and audience members at the 2021 Modern Language Association meeting; and greatest thanks to the editors Badia Ahad and Habiba Ibrahim as well as to Chelsea Frazier, LaCharles Ward, and Tristram Wolff.

1   My formulation riffs on David Scott's "criticism as a question," which points to how the interview form illuminates the conjunctures that shaped Caribbean intellectuals.

2   As Lauren Derby (2014: 127) argues, "Local knowledge gleaned from hearsay can challenge received notions of historical causality and reveal alternative understandings of political authority."

3   But not just any wife for any man. What I call the *racial family* is an implied, but no less pervasive, nineteenth-century idea that African descendants should make lives only with other African descendants and that Asian contract labor should also form families only with one another. Because of the importance of the family to production, both in terms of physical and domestic labor, this indicates how racialized ideas about sexuality structure colonial capital.

4   To understand knowledge, feeling, and colonial bureaucratic masculinity in the West Indies, I look to the nexus of aesthetic theory, postcolonial theory, and transnational feminist theory. Sianne Ngai (2005: 246) argues in *Ugly Feelings* that anxiety is the province of continental theorists, often men, who experience anxiety as they work out conceptual problems—and therefore can be understood as a masculine disposition toward knowledge. I also think of Deborah Thomas's (2019: 1) stirring question in *Political Life in the Wake of the Plantation*: "What does modern sovereignty *feel* like?" See also Sinha 1995 and Grewal 2016 for accounts of how Indian colonial masculinity and postcolonial bureaucratic masculinity, respectively, managed and excluded Indians from the polity based on gender and ideas of racial difference.

5   See Saidiya Hartman's (2019) *Wayward Lives, Beautiful Experiments*, e.g., for a work of critical fabulation that rethinks anarchy from the position of the "colored girl" in the early twentieth-century United States.

6   *OED Online*, s.v. "Proposition, n." www.oed.com/view/Entry/152801 (accessed February 19, 2021).

7   Derby (2014: 126) critically shows us, "When rumor breaks into the public sphere it . . . can give rise to historical events." I am interested here in a related phenomenon: what happens when the imperial-colonial state attempts to conceal rumor in order to shape a narrative about the present and future.

8   *OED Online*, s.v. "Connection, n." www.oed.com/view/Entry/39356 (accessed February 19, 2021).

9   Michel-Rolph Trouillot's (1988) *Peasants and Capital*, Deborah Thomas's (2004) *Modern Blackness*, and Hazel V. Carby's (2019) *Imperial Intimacies* are works of Caribbean and Caribbean diaspora scholarship that critically theorize across scale in the following contexts: the Dominican peasantry, Blackness in transnational Jamaica, and the intertwined histories of Great Britain and Jamaica, respectively.

10   Najnin Islam importantly points to how contemporary novels like David Dabydeen's *The Counting House* (1996) have a similar capacity to question the organizing logics of the postemancipation West Indies in "Racial Capitalism and Racial Intimacies" (Islam 2021).

References

Bahadur, Gaiutra. 2013. *Coolie Woman: The Odyssey of Indenture.* Chicago: University of Chicago Press.

Bainbridge, Danielle. 2020. "The Future Perfect, Autopsy, and Enfreakment on the Nineteenth-Century Stage." *TDR: The Drama Review* 64, no. 3: 100–117.

Burton, Richard D. E. 1997. *Afro-Creole: Power, Opposition, and Play in the Caribbean.* Ithaca, NY: Cornell University Press.

Campt, Tina Marie. 2019. "Black Visuality and the Practice of Refusal." *Women and Performance: A Journal of Feminist Theory* 29, no. 1: 79–87. doi.org/10.1080/0740770X.2019.1573625.

Carby, Hazel V. 2019. *Imperial Intimacies: A Tale of Two Islands.* New York: Verso.

Cordis, Shanya. 2019. "Forging Relational Difference: Racial Gendered Violence and Dispossession in Guyana." *Small Axe: A Caribbean Journal of Criticism* 23, no. 3: 18–33. doi.org/10.1215/07990537-7912298.

Cudjoe, Selwyn R. 2003. *Beyond Boundaries: The Intellectual Tradition of Trinidad and Tobago in the Nineteenth Century.* Wellesley, MA: Calaloux; distributed by University of Massachusetts Press.

Derby, Lauren. 2014. "Beyond Fugitive Speech: Rumor and Affect in Caribbean History." *Small Axe: A Caribbean Journal of Criticism* 18, no. 2: 123–40. doi.org/10.1215/07990537-2739893.

Diptee, Audra A. 2000. "Indian Men, Afro-Creole Women: 'Casting' Doubt on Interracial Sexual Relationships in the Late Nineteenth-Century Caribbean." *Immigrants and Minorities* 19, no. 3: 1–24. doi.org/10.1080/02619288.2000.9974997.

Fleming, Julius B., Jr. 2019. "Transforming Geographies of Black Time: How the Free Southern Theater Used the Plantation for Civil Rights Activism." *American Literature* 91, no. 3: 587–617. doi.org/10.1215/00029831-7722140.

Fuentes, Marisa J. 2016. *Dispossessed Lives: Enslaved Women, Violence, and the Archive.* Early American Studies. Philadelphia: University of Pennsylvania Press.

Gopaul Whittington, Viola, and Rita Pemberton. 1986. Oral and Pictorial Records Programme. The University of the West Indies-St. Augustine, Alma Jordan Library.

Grewal, Inderpal. 2016. "The Masculinities of Post-Colonial Governance: Bureaucratic Memoirs of the Indian Civil Service." *Modern Asian Studies* 50, no. 2: 602–35. doi.org/10.1017/S0026749X13000772.

Haley, Sarah. 2020. "Racial Capitalism's Gendered Fabric." In *Saturation: Race, Art, and the Circulation of Value,* edited by C. Riley Snorton and Hentyle Yapp, 15–24. Cambridge, MA: MIT Press.

Hartman, Saidiya. 2008. "Venus in Two Acts." *Small Axe* 12, no. 2: 1–14.

Hartman, Saidiya. 2019. *Wayward Lives, Beautiful Experiments: Intimate Histories of Social Upheaval.* 1st ed. New York: W. W. Norton.

Holt, Thomas C. 1992. *The Problem of Freedom: Race, Labor, and Politics in Jamaica and Britain, 1832–1938.* Baltimore, MD: Johns Hopkins University Press.

Islam, Najnin. 2021. "Racial Capitalism and Racial Intimacies: Post-Emancipation British Guiana in David Dabydeen's *The Counting House.*" *Interventions,* April 4. doi.org/10.1080/1369801X.2021.1892516.

Jenkins, Edward. 1871. *The Coolie, His Rights and Wrongs. Notes of a Journey to British Guiana, with a Review of the System and of the Recent Commission of Inquiry.* London: Strahan. catalog.hathitrust.org/Record/006627012 (accessed March 3, 2021).

Jenkins, Edward. (1877) 2003. *Lutchmee and Dilloo: A Study of West Indian Life*. Oxford: Macmillan Education.

Jobson, Ryan Cecil. 2020. "States of Crisis, Flags of Convenience: An Introduction." *Small Axe: A Caribbean Journal of Criticism* 24, no. 2: 67–77. doi.org/10.1215/07990537 -8604490.

Jobson, Ryan Cecil. 2021. "Dead Labor: On Racial Capital and Fossil Capital." In *Histories of Racial Capitalism*, edited by Destin Jenkins and Justin Leroy, 215–30. New York: Columbia University Press.

Jung, Moon-Ho. 2006. *Coolies and Cane: Race, Labor, and Sugar in the Age of Emancipation*. Baltimore, MD: Johns Hopkins University Press.

Kornbluh, Anna. 2019. *The Order of Forms: Realism, Formalism, and Social Space*. Chicago: University of Chicago Press.

Kramnick, Jonathan. 2021. "Criticism and Truth." *Critical Inquiry* 47, no. 2: 218–40.

Lightfoot, Natasha. 2015. *Troubling Freedom: Antigua and the Aftermath of British Emancipation*. Durham, NC: Duke University Press.

Look Lai, Walton. 1998. *The Chinese in the West Indies, 1806–1995: A Documentary History*. Kingston, Jamaica: University of the West Indies Press.

Lowe, Lisa. 2015. *The Intimacies of Four Continents*. Durham, NC: Duke University Press.

Macharia, Keguro. 2020. *Frottage: Frictions of Intimacy across the Black Diaspora*. Sexual Cultures. New York: New York University Press.

Marx, Karl. 1887. "The Working-Day." In *Capital, Volume I*, edited by Frederick Engels, translated by Samuel Moore and Edward Aveling. Moscow: Progress. www.marxists.org /archive/marx/works/1867-c1/ch10.htm.

Marx, Karl. (1844) 1959. "Estranged Labour." In *Economic and Philosophical Manuscripts of 1844*, edited by Andy Blunden and Matthew Carmody, translated by Martin Milligan. Moscow: Progress. www.marxists.org/archive/marx/works/1844/manuscripts/labour.htm.

Masco, Joseph. 2016. "The Crisis in Crisis." *Current Anthropology* 58, no. S15: S65–76. doi .org/10.1086/688695.

Mengesha, Lilian G., and Lakshmi Padmanabhan. 2019. "Introduction to Performing Refusal/Refusing to Perform." *Women and Performance: A Journal of Feminist Theory* 29, no. 1: 1–8. doi.org/10.1080/0740770X.2019.1574527.

Morgan, Jennifer L. 2004. *Laboring Women: Reproduction and Gender in New World Slavery*. Philadelphia: University of Pennsylvania Press.

Morton-Gittens, Dane. 2017. "Sir Rawson William Rawson: Governor of Barbados, 1869–1875." In *Ideology, Regionalism, and Society in Caribbean History*, edited by Shane J. Pantin and Jerome Teelucksingh, 179–205. Cham, Switzerland: Springer Nature.

Nash, Jennifer C. 2019. *Black Feminism Reimagined: After Intersectionality*. Next Wave: New Directions in Women's Studies. Durham, NC: Duke University Press.

National Archives of the UK: CO 28/214/79, no. 65, fols. 456–58.

Ngai, Sianne. 2005. *Ugly Feelings*. Cambridge, MA: Harvard University Press.

Parsard, Kaneesha Cherelle. 2016. "Cutlass: Objects toward a Theory of Representation." In *Indo-Caribbean Feminist Thought: Genealogies, Theories, Enactments*, edited by Gabrielle Jamela Hosein and Lisa Outar, 241–60. New Caribbean Studies. New York: Palgrave Macmillan US. doi.org/10.1057/978-1-137-55937-1_15.

Paton, Diana. 2004. *No Bond but the Law: Punishment, Race, and Gender in Jamaican State Formation, 1780–1870*. Durham, NC: Duke University Press.

Raymond, Judy. 2010. "Out of Sight." *Caribbean Review of Books*, November 2010. caribbean reviewofbooks.com/crb-archive/24-november-2010/out-of-sight/.

Reddock, Rhoda. 1985. "Freedom Denied: Indian Women and Indentureship in Trinidad and Tobago, 1845–1917." *Economic and Political Weekly* 20, no. 43: WS79–87.

Robinson, Cedric J. (1983) 2000. *Black Marxism: The Making of the Black Radical Tradition.* Chapel Hill: University of North Carolina Press.

Roopnarine, Lomarsh. 2007. *Indo-Caribbean Indenture: Resistance and Accommodation, 1838–1920.* Kingston, Jamaica: University of the West Indies Press.

Scott, David. 2001. *Refashioning Futures: Criticism after Postcoloniality.* Princeton, NJ: Princeton University Press.

Scott, David. 2004. *Conscripts of Modernity: The Tragedy of Colonial Enlightenment.* Durham, NC: Duke University Press.

Scott, David. 2014. "The Temporality of Generations: Dialogue, Tradition, Criticism." *New Literary History* 45, no. 2: 157–81.

Scott, David, and Nicholas Laughlin. 2008. "Criticism as a Question." *Caribbean Review of Books*, November 18, 2008. caribbeanreviewofbooks.com/crb-archive/18-november -2008/%E2%80%9Ccriticism-as-a-question%E2%80%9D/.

Sheller, Mimi. 2012. *Citizenship from Below: Erotic Agency and Caribbean Freedom.* Durham, NC: Duke University Press.

Siddique, Asheesh Kapur. 2020. "The Archival Epistemology of Political Economy in the Early Modern British Atlantic World." *William and Mary Quarterly* 77, no. 4: 641–74.

Sinha, Mrinalini. 1995. *Colonial Masculinity: The "Manly Englishman" and the "Effeminate Bengali" in the Late Nineteenth Century.* Studies in Imperialism. Manchester: Manchester University Press.

Spillers, Hortense J. 1987. "Mama's Baby, Papa's Maybe: An American Grammar Book." *Diacritics* 17, no. 2: 65–81. doi.org/10.2307/464747.

Sweeney, Shauna J. 2020. "Black Women in Slavery and Freedom: Gendering the History of Racial Capitalism." *American Quarterly* 72, no. 1: 277–89. doi.org/10.1353/aq.2020.0014.

Taylor, Christopher. 2018. *Empire of Neglect: The West Indies in the Wake of British Liberalism.* Radical Américas. Durham, NC: Duke University Press.

Thomas, Deborah A. 2004. *Modern Blackness: Nationalism, Globalization, and the Politics of Culture in Jamaica.* Durham, NC: Duke University Press.

Thomas, Deborah A. 2019. *Political Life in the Wake of the Plantation: Sovereignty, Witnessing, Repair.* Durham, NC: Duke University Press.

Thompson, Krista. 2006. *An Eye for the Tropics: Tourism, Photography, and Framing the Caribbean Picturesque.* Durham, NC: Duke University Press.

Thompson, Krista. 2011. "The Evidence of Things Not Photographed: Slavery and Historical Memory in the British West Indies." *Representations* 113, no. 1: 39–71. doi.org/10.1525 /rep.2011.113.1.39.

Tough, Alistair, and Paul Lihoma. 2012. "The Development of Recordkeeping Systems in the British Empire and Commonwealth, 1870s–1960s." *Archives and Manuscripts* 40, no. 3: 191–216. doi.org/10.1080/01576895.2012.738786.

Trouillot, Michel-Rolph. 1988. *Peasants and Capital: Dominica in the World Economy.* Baltimore, MD: Johns Hopkins University Press.

Wahab, Amar. 2010. *Colonial Inventions: Landscape, Power, and Representation in Nineteenth-Century Trinidad.* Newcastle upon Tyne, UK: Cambridge Scholars.

Weinbaum, Alys Eve. 2019. *The Afterlife of Reproductive Slavery: Biocapitalism and Black Feminism's Philosophy of History.* Durham, NC: Duke University Press.

Wittgenstein, Ludwig. (1921) 2001. *Tractatus Logico-Philosophicus.* Translated by D. F. Pears and B. F. McGuinness. London: Routledge.

Wynter, Sylvia. 1971. "Novel and History, Plot, and Plantation." *Savacou,* no. 5 (June): 95–102.

Tao Leigh Goffe

Stolen Life, Stolen Time:
Black Temporality, Speculation,
and Racial Capitalism

Black life has always existed on the other side of
time. In the film *Space Is the Place,* Afro-futurist
maestro Sun Ra (Coney 1972) recommends, "The
first thing to do would be to consider time as officially ended. We work on the other side of time."
Blackness inaugurates possibility because it is, in
part, defined by being exiled from history. Sun Ra
describes abolishing time as a liberatory act for
Black people. "With the official end of time comes
the end of a history that includes African slavery
and all the miseries of the dead," he says. Put
another way, blackness, understood as a certain
set of politics, necessarily critiques time itself,
because Black being poses a challenge to the fixity
of history. Racial slavery attempted to steal African
life by fixing time and thus history. Western or
colonial modernity's notion of history then forms
an enclosure or limited world. In this essay, I
explore how fixed notions of history foreclose
potential fictional worlds, whereas speculative
modes of storytelling informed by Afro-futurism
inaugurate and birth possibility, new worlds. With
an interest in how blackness was inaugurated and
what it inaugurates, or what blackness is the conditions of possibility for, I examine a series of contemporary texts: Chang-rae Lee's *On Such a Full*

The South Atlantic Quarterly 121:1, January 2022
DOI 10.1215/00382876-9561573 © 2022 Duke University Press

Sea, Mohsin Hamid's *Exit West,* the HBO series *Watchmen,* Bong Joon-ho's *Parasite,* and Khalik Allah's *Black Mother.* Reading moments from these contemporary apocalyptic stories against each other, I track how entangled temporality is Black temporality whether Black characters are present or central or not to the plot. Black temporality is deeply antagonistic to the way European colonialisms attempt to organize and enclose the world.

Building on Sun Ra's words, Black temporality is a refusal to labor within the limits of history. It exists on the other side, not simply outside or excluded from time, but on the B-side of time and thus history. In spite of more than four centuries of racial exclusion and theft of the body, Black time does not demand inclusion within European colonial timelines. Instead, Black time continues to be stolen away by Black people, accumulating on the other side of history and the edges of the plantation as a resource for Black futures. Maroons across the hemisphere understood this intimately. The prehistory of Afro-futurism is evidence of the power of the speculative and how playing with time has been definitive of Black storytelling across the diaspora. I posit the way Black people have deployed the speculative then as a praxis of *stealing away* colonial time in order to unravel it. Black speculation claims time back from capitalist regimes of colonial extractivism that attempted to steal life itself through the mechanisms of racial slavery.

W. E. B. Du Bois's (1900) color line is then a temporal line as much as a prophecy because he speculated on what the future would hold, knowing the fate of Black people would determine the fate of the world. Not so much an oracle as he was acutely attuned to the definition of race and mechanics of racialization, the color line remains the vexing question of the twenty-first century. The avoidance of race in most sci-fi and speculative fiction, genres that often stage the future, is not a neutral act. Ignoring the future color line reinforces white supremacy because avoiding race does not solve racism. The limited capacity to imagine people of color in the future always has ethical underpinnings regarding genocide and who will exist in the future. The novels, films, and TV shows I examine here provide different answers to the question of who will exist in the future and the potential plot of the undoing of colonialism. The desire for race to not exist in the future is always coupled with a genocidal logic of multiracialist dilution of blackness and other people of color.

Ethnic studies offers numerous critiques of such raceless storytelling. Techno-orientalism has emerged as an Asian Americanist critique (2015) of white sci-fi narratives often located in ultramodern cities that look like Tokyo or Hong Kong, while Asians, if present, are depicted as "technologically advanced and intellectually primitive" (Rutgers University Press, n.d.), often as robots (see Roh, Huang, and Niu 2015). Non-Western Indigenous practices of dreaming and nonlinear storytelling form a type of "scientific literacy," Anishinaabe cultural critic Grace L. Dillon (2007) tells us in her definition of Indigenous futurisms. Indeed, modern capitalism inaugurated multiple apocalypses, foreclosing worlds for Indigenous peoples and Black people across the Americas. Because it depends not only on engineering fixed inequality but also uncertainty, I define capitalism as speculation in its purest and most raw form. The stock market depends on a series of bets and gambles. Speculative finance, which is to say all finance, depends on the accumulation of stolen time from laborers converted into surplus value. Profit is possible and unevenly distributed because of the uncertainty of how stocks will perform. Speculative storytelling, now, poses a challenge to the fixity or inevitability of capitalism as it allows us to create worlds beyond coloniality (Kamugisha 2019). The speculative mode has been critical to the Black radical tradition because it carries the potential to undo speculation in its purest form, capitalism.

Speculative fiction forms a critique of the present (see Lim 2009). Racial capitalism requires history, race, and time—three constructed variables—to be fixed as an ongoing dynamic. In moments of crisis, all three of these categories become called into question and are rescripted and redefined. I explore various narrative strategies for staging race and racialization in moments of global crisis. Each narrative confronts the terrain of the same country that we all live in that Bong Joon-ho aptly called *capitalism*. Countless reviews have done the work of analyzing thematic or biographical angles of these contemporary speculative novels, television series, and films; however, in reading them against one another here, I attend to what is encoded in contemporary literary and popular culture. I am led by philosopher Sylvia Wynter's (2010) comments on the value of storytelling: "Culture is for me, primarily, the societal machinery with which a particular society or group symbolically codes its sense of self." The extent to which the architecture of these filmic, TV, and literary worlds encodes a timeline of racial capitalism or not determines the ethical stakes about the future of race and racial formation.

As a form of escape, the prophetic worlding of the conquest, what cultural critic Tiffany Lethabo King identifies as Black and entangled Native apocalypse, in particular translates present anxieties into future dystopias. Between the narrative strands of these texts, I limn the capacity of contemporary storytellers to reckon with the contours of how political theorist Cedric Robinson defined *racial capitalism*.[1] In the realm of speculative fiction, race is written and rewritten in moments of global crisis where premature death looms unevenly. Race itself is speculative, as a concept it is simultaneously reinforced and undone in these historical moments of crisis. The speculative has the potential to reorder the conditions of existence beyond coloniality. Organized in three parts, this essay begins by defining Black time as a stolen resource, in contrast to standard or colonial time. Next, I examine how storytellers deploy *the future* as either an alibi or as a resource in the cultural texts mentioned. Put differently, to some *the future* is merely an excuse to not have to be historically accurate, to others it is a narrative device full of possibility. Ultimately, I propose Maroon time as blackness working on the other side of time, as a cultivated resource stolen away across the Black diaspora often in coalition with peoples native to the Americas from the Great Dismal Swamp of Virginia to the Quilombos of Brazil (see also Hanchard 1999). Reading across contemporary and racialized modes of storytelling, a certain set of ethics regarding the racial politics of who has the right to occupy the future becomes apparent.

The Syncopation of Keeping Black Time

Black time is not-yet-standardized time. Drawing from Martinican theorist Édouard Glissant's (1999) poetic definition of Creole as "not-yet-standardized language," the power of the "not-yet" is a resource located in both Black language and time. Polyrhythmic and often syncopated, Black time orders Black music (jazz, dub, reggae). It is anchored in, and mutated from, the multiplicity of precapitalist African temporalities (Russell 2009). My aim in defining Black time is not to essentialize time or racialize it, but to understand it as a philosophical critique of standardization as an imperial impulse. After all, race too is an imperial process of standardization. The very undoing of race is critical to the philosophy of Black temporality, central to a certain set of politics enacted by Black people across the ages. Cultural theorist Saidiya Hartman (2002) refers to the "time of slavery" as disjointing all forms of relation, including time. On the plantation, time became a violent metric of colonial management stolen from Black people. As much as time was stolen from enslaved Africans, Black people *stole away* and stole away time as a resource.

Black time, then, stands in contrast to imperial time, quite literally "standard time," the standardization of Greenwich Mean Time (GMT). The very opposite of the "not-yet" of Black time, GMT arbitrarily centers the world clock and time, thus the universe, as beginning in London. GMT orders time in order to secure and underwrite the power of coloniality. A convenient fiction of standardization, GMT or Coordinated Universal Time

(CUT) is fairly recent, beginning in 1884 when the Greenwich meridian became universally recognized as 0° at the International Meridian Conference. This moment of standardization unsurprisingly coincides with the period of abolition in Brazil, not seeing full emancipation until 1888. The Berlin Conference (1884–85) is another example of European colonial statecraft as a violent attempt to organize space and avoid interimperial conflict. The British attempt to standardize and segregate time into zones was a tactic of imperial statecraft and management that is rarely questioned.

The Middle Passage is a time zone not only of racialization and gender differentiation but also of other transfigurations of the flesh (Spillers 1987). This oceanic zone simultaneously inaugurates and also throws into crisis a multitude of categories. The "not-yet-standardized" threatens to undo imperial power of time and space (geography) through variance (other worlds). Cartesian lines of longitude and latitude dissect the globe into infinitesimally small quadrants, that is, coordinates. The time zone of the Black diaspora, for many thinkers, begins in the undifferentiated space of the Middle Passage (Gilroy 1992; Spillers 1987). The space is almost unrepresentable, but some draw imaginatively on the unspeakable horror and multiplicity of the Middle Passage racialized as a zone of the suspension of time and space. Black time accumulates over the generations in the intervals of time in which Black being emerges: abolition, independence, rebellion, refusal.

Cultural critic Stuart Hall (Hall 2017) describes Black time as a resource when discussing the anticolonial Black labor uprisings that swept across the Caribbean in 1938. He writes, "What had seemed like the premonition of imminent social collapse turned out, as I subsequently came to see things, as inaugurating a world of new possibilities, a world in which blackness itself came to function as a resource for the future" (47). Whose future? Black, here, functions not merely as epidermal or as a socioeconomic designation of class in Jamaica's pigmentocracy, but rather as a certain set of radical politics of refusal to labor, to have one's time stolen. Black temporality (time) is blackness itself as a resource for (Black) futurity. The very conditions of extended genocide of the transatlantic slave trade mean that a future inhabited by Black people has never been certain. The conspicuous absence of people of color from speculative fiction is an ethical determination on who is imagined to exist in the future, "epistemic genocide."

Speculative genres allow for psychic doomsday prepping. Some storytellers unwittingly recast past atrocities in the timeless far future not as a critique but as a limit of imagination. Man as a fabulist species, theorized by Wynter and others as *homo narrans*, lives because of the desire to create a story.[2] What if there is no plot? Black thinkers have known these narratives of climate and financial crisis are entangled and inseparable because blackness continues to disrupt colonial history's periodicity. Speculative fiction then is a political battleground for the future existence of people of color. Speculation is also always an act of valuation. Speculative writing is not the antonym of "well-documented" history. It is not easier because it is "made up." Often much, if not more, archival research informs the writing of demolishing the world, in order to build new futures. Toni Morrison, for instance, understands the detail of horror required to build a world anchored by the time zone of the Middle Passage in *Beloved*. A radical tradition, Black feminism centers generation itself (*poesis*) as universe building. In opposition to competition and militarism, Black feminisms conceive beyond the margins. Speculative worlds need not reproduce the asymmetry of violent systems of valuation of the present, and yet they often do.

The Future as Alibi: *On Such a Full Sea* and *Exit West*

Beginning with the ways the future becomes deployed as an alibi or excuse, two novels, *Exit West* (2017) and *On Such a Full Sea* (2013), are bound by the coloniality of time. Both are written by authors, Mohsin Hamid and Chang-rae Lee, respectively, who have been socialized by the West as a political project as much as they are rooted in the location of Asia (Pakistan and South Korea).[3] Attempting to restructure the limits of the "immigrant novel," often the only genre Asian and Asian American authors are allowed to exist in by commercial publishers of contemporary fiction, Lee and Hamid build worlds animated by the urgency of the "migrant crisis." *Exit West* and *On Such a Full Sea* presciently forecast global crisis, centering characters of color. Both optimistically cast romance between Afro-diasporic and Asian-diasporic characters in the future toward a happy ending of racial reconciliation. In the ruins of global crisis, the authors reinvent the immigrant novel using the speculative in many ways informed by Afro-futurism. Missing though from the future worlds of *Exit West* and *On Such a Full Sea* is a reckoning with the timeline of racial capitalism. Asian identity chafes against defining who is considered native and who is an immigrant. In doing so, the failure to confront the long history of US militarism as ongoing warfare in the narratives becomes a missed opportunity of critique.

Lee amalgamates African American and Asian worlds some two hundred years into the future, where Chinese people have relocated to Baltimore. *On Such a Full Sea*'s hypercapitalist Shenzhen as warzone translocated to

Lee's invented B-Mor, riffing on the African American Vernacular English nickname B-More for the city. A mid-Atlantic dystopic port city, it is haunted by HBO's *The Wire* (2006), having already colonized the world's imagination as a postapocalyptic Black foreclosure, a city ruined by Black-on-Black crime and drug trafficking. What makes it so easy to substitute the hyperdrive of industrialization of the Shenzhen borderlands with the deindustrialized peril of Black Baltimore? Lee describes his fieldwork, traveling voyeuristically to the Hong Kong–China border as an American intending to pen a critique of labor exploitation. He said, "Well, I had gone over to China to Shenzhen, to the villages there, where there are lots of factories, and visited a factory, and had this—you know, big idea to write this broad social novel about workers, owners, you know, all their struggles."[4] While in other novels Lee has portrayed the detailed texture of the Korean American experience, the afterlife of World War II, and ongoing carnage of Japanese imperialism, his attention to China and Baltimore is not as keen in *On Such a Full Sea*. Not wanting to get stuck narratively by the burden of a realist proletariat tale of Chinese labor rights, Lee (Leyshon 2014) continues,

> I felt as if I didn't have a special angle on the material, that it was going to be good journalism. But I think, for novels, you need the extra perspective or other layers of approach that make the story, you know, come alive in a different way. And so I dropped that novel. And, at the same time, you know, looking for something else, I came upon a premise about setting a novel in the future. And I had to set the novel in the future, because the premise involved bringing over en masse Chinese laborers to the United States, which I knew couldn't happen now, but perhaps could in a very different future.

I quote at length here to track Lee's narrative decisions for "a very different future" as a device that I identify as an *alibi*. The future as *alibi* allows Lee narrative possibility of what he thinks is a loophole but becomes a trap. The future as setting allows him to not be beholden to what Asian Americanist literary critic David Eng (2008) has aptly named the unfair requirement of ethnic American literature to *accurately* fill the gap of history. However, in not rigorously accounting for the teleology of racial capitalism, Lee off-handedly references blackness and Indigenous presence in ways that reproduce erasure of Black and Indigenous people of color. He gives the name Seneca to the first Charter Village where the main character, Fan, a Chinese American girl, arrives. Considering the Haudenosaunee presence and dispossession of Seneca sovereignty in the Northeast US, this is a loaded choice to not unpack. Furthermore, it conjures Seneca Village, a nineteenth-century free African American independent settlement in present-day Central Park, and beckons a missed opportunity to consider US practices of naming stolen land (Central Park Conservancy 2021).

In a future world ravaged by a mysterious C-disease, Lee champions "hybrid vigor" by creating characters who are immune to the disease because they are of mixed heritage. He signals their "hybridity" with names such as James Beltran Ho and Pei Pie Xu-Tidewater, representing a chimeric multiracial Chinese American future. He does not say it in as many words, but the Black DNA of the so-called "originals" is potentially the antidote to the C-disease. In the moments where Lee provides the backstory of postapocalyptic B-Mor, he oversimplifies US history. He indigenizes and romanticizes African Americans and Latin American, Central American, and Latinx people, erasing US Native people:

> We should concede that unlike the experience of most immigrants, there was very little to encounter by way of an indigenous population. There were smatterings of them, to be sure, pockets of residents on the outskirts of what is now the heart of B-Mor, these descendants of nineteenth-century African slaves and twentieth-century laborers from Central America and even bands of twenty-first-century urban-nostalgics, all of whom settled the intimate grid of these blocks and thrived for a time and, for reasons that history can confidently trace and identify but never quite seem to solve, inexorably declined and finally disappeared. (Lee 2013)

The characterization romantically and tragically fetishizes Black Baltimore as only beginning in the nineteenth century, disregarding Native Americans. Lee often describes the racial marker of Reg's "Afro-type hair" and "genetic filaments woven through genes." In the future New China, people wear bronzer and "tease their hair" to look like "originals." What Lee describes as "native blood," or African descent, is desired. His attempt to critique anti-blackness reifies race. Lee obliquely references that history cannot solve the problem of the extinction of certain groups. Setting the stage for Chinese futurity becomes complicated by not problematizing the category of "immigrant." Lee does not see the speculative potential to imagine the clandestine itineraries of Black and Lumbee, Piscataway, and Cherokee people in nineteenth-century Maryland.

Even as Lee does better than most contemporary white authors, guilty of avoiding race, this clumsy racialization and Afro-Asian romance at the end of the world between Reg and Fan serves a triumphant narrative of multiracialism. Genetic essentialism creates race in the future as a sorting tool that determines who is biologically predetermined to be worthy of living and dying. Though Lee presents a compelling futuristic Chinese American her-oine in Fan, and her love story with Reg, who is of African and Asian mixed heritage, is convincing, the novel falls short of a true critique of ruination of capitalism. In *On Such a Full Sea*, race becomes reproduced as a biological fact because Lee's universe aspires to a postracial future that inherently fetishizes diluted blackness as a horizon of aspiration.

Among mixed reviews, famed US sci-fi writer Ursula Le Guin (2014) chided Chang-rae Lee for dabbling in this futuristic genre of the postapoca-lypse, though not for the reasons I outline here. An NPR review by literature professor Maureen Corrigan (2014), who like Le Guin is white, declared that Katniss Everdeen of *The Hunger Games* "is a much more genial companion to have along on a trek through dystopia than the monochromatic Fan turns out to be." Corrigan's use of "monochromatic" is an example of techno-orientalism, seeing Asian characters that are not robots as robotic. It is this orientalism that Lee is pushing against by making a space in contemporary literature for fully fleshed-out Asian futuristic characters. Readers struggled with the experimental form of Lee's narration of the novel, a collective con-sciousness of "we" that almost feels like an all-knowing chorus of the future narrating. In conversation with author Susan Choi, who is Asian American, Lee was asked to say more about the question of vantage in the novel. Choi (Korea Society 2014) identified the narrative technique of the book as poten-tially being Asian or Confucian in the way it denies a singular individualistic American "I." Lee had not considered this but agreed when it was posed to him by Choi as an experimental choice.

Published a few years later, Mohsin Hamid's novel *Exit West* (2017) fea-tures similar narrative choices as a futuristic love story. Coinciding with the crisis of the Brexit referendum, it was accordingly dubbed by press and pub-lishers as a post-Brexit novel. The title signals a futuristic exit toward the West through magic portals that do not require the danger of the passage or the red tape and bureaucracy of asylum testimonials. As Glissant (1999) reminds us, "The West is not in the West. It is a political project, not a place." To exit the West as political project requires a critique of history. Understanding the necessity of Black capital and racial slavery to the political project of the West requires acknowledging modernity was always already failed. Many now, I believe, would opt to exit the West for the so-called Global South, and Brexit presents an interminable crisis, the result of unresolved colonial afterlives. The main characters of *Exit West*, Nadia and Saeed, who are South Asian, inhabit Dark London and Light London with Nigerian characters as squatters in abandoned houses in Kensington.

Hamid (2014) is asked often about his choice to live in his native Lahore with family and has written on the topic. Though as a part of Pakistan's socio-economically elite class he was educated in Ivy League institutions, Hamid's choice to live in South Asia is deliberate and political. Hamid's literary choices also are often are a negotiation between two worlds. In an interview, Hamid (2017) explains, "[*Exit West*] begins in a city which is a lot like Lahore, where I live. And the city is beginning to be rocked by these militants and terrorists. But partly, I just couldn't bring myself to write the collapse of a city like Lahore, where I live. I just didn't have the heart to write it." Hamid illustrates the power of naming, and the texture of crisis and racialization. Beyond Lahore and Pakistan, he specifically names other places and ethnicities: Mykonos, Mexicans, London, Nigerians. The novel concludes in Marin in what could have been a critique of Manifest Destiny and the violence of westward expansion, but he falls short. Hamid presents future California as a promised land representing futurity for Black and Asian characters without adequately historicizing the deep past of dispossession of Native sovereignty.

As a device, Hamid's magic doors become an *alibi* just like Lee uses *the future*. Hamid explains he wanted to experiment with skipping the narrative work of the trauma of the refugee journey the West requires for asylum, for instance. He refuses to perform the harrowing immigrant novel. The magic doors shrouded in darkness allow his hero and heroine, lovers Nadia and Saeed, to hop westward across continents, desperately seeking refuge, eventually building a new community with African American characters in Marin. The Bay Area, where real estate has continued to inflate exponentially since the dot-com bubble, is a racialized backdrop that Hamid does not problematize. With a Black population of two percent, Marin County has been portrayed as the end of the world in the pointed filmic critique *The Last Black Man in San Francisco* (2019). Black displacement, ecological disaster, and nuclear contamination are underscored by the echo of Native dispossession. Marin County was created in 1850, but Hamid does not tell the story of its recent Mexican past, the geography of the Treaty of Guadalupe Hidalgo (1848), or further back beyond the colonial Spanish timeline. The toponymy speaks even if Hamid does not in the missed opportunity to explain that Marin is not named for being seaside or marine, but for the chief of Licatiut (Coast Miwok) tribe Huicmuse who became baptized and renamed as Marino (see Goerke 2007).

As for Lee, indigeneity is an afterthought for Hamid. The project of the United States is romanticized in ways that repeat the conquest. Hamid (2017) writes,

> In Marin there were almost no natives, these people having died out or been
> exterminated long ago, and one would see them only occasionally, at
> impromptu trading posts—or perhaps more often, but wrapped in clothes
> and guises and behaviors indistinguishable from anyone else. . . . And yet it
> was not quite true to say that there were almost no natives, nativeness being
> a relative matter, and many others considered themselves native to this
> country, by which they meant that they or their parents or their grandpar-
> ents . . . had been born on the strip of land that stretched from the mid-north-
> ern-Pacific to the mid-northern-Atlantic, and their existence here did not
> owe anything to a physical migration that had occurred in their lifetimes.
>
>   A third layer of nativeness was composed of those who others thought
> directly descended, even in the tiniest fraction of their genes, from the
> human beings who had been brought from Africa to this continent as slaves.

Biology and genetics come into play here as they do in *On Such a Full Sea*. Few
narrate the conquest as the ongoing catastrophe that is what US cultural critic
Alyosha Goldstein (2014) identifies as the "colonial present." Romantic histories repeat "discovery" like Columbus, uncritically rehearsing Manifest Destiny. To say the United States is a nation of immigrants erases a world built
through the entangled dispossession of Native sovereignty and African
enslavement. Black American characters are romanticized as "originals," erasing Native American presence by omission, much as in *On Such a Full Sea*.
Again, human extinction is gestured to. Shorthand history makes the future
into an alibi, an excuse to not be held accountable for ethical narrative choices.
Periodizing the ongoing refugee crisis through an understanding of racial
capitalism would illuminate how the United States became inaugurated as a
gatekeeping nation. US imperialism invades, foreclosing and occluding.

The Future as Resource: *Watchmen* and *Parasite*

The speculative worlds of *Watchmen*, the HBO limited series, and *Parasite*
are not anticolonial by design but are attuned to the ongoing psychic trauma of
US colonialism that uses the future as a resource. Without centering the
United States, both stories form pertinent critiques of it. Black temporality, as
I have defined it here, poses a disruption to time itself, and while *Watchmen*
and *Parasite* are not produced by Black artists, they are informed by Black temporality in their engagement with the conditions of the creation of the United
States that necessarily include racial slavery. Blackness emerges in phantasmic
and material forms that disrupt the plot of racial capitalism, the speculative,

for a critique of the colonial present. Creator and writer of *Watchmen* Damon Lindelof (HBO 2019), who is a white man, admits and emphasizes that the production was truly a collaboration with Black writers and other writers of color in his writer's room, in which he was pushed to confront his whiteness and the white masculinity of comic books.

The South Korean production of *Parasite* may not seem racialized because everyone is Korean, and yet Bong Joon-ho touches on many layers of South Korea's colonial racialization by the United States and Japan that haunt. We hear echoes of Japanese colonialism in *Parasite* in the reference to tables for a garden party to be arranged in the crane formation of Admiral Yi defeating the Japanese navy during the Imjin Wars of 1592. The Academy Award–winning film has been celebrated for being at once a critique of Korean class warfare and also deeply universal. Whether by intention or not, both Lindelof and Bong build worlds attentive to the contours of racial capitalism to differing degrees. Engaging the timeline of US militarism and the Cold War—the Korean War and the Vietnam War—charts a protracted and urgent critique of US colonial time. US military bases in East and Southeast Asia form the haunted architecture and infrastructure of colonialism. The border of North and South is a scar similar to the scar that divided the North and South in the US Civil War, and that divided Vietnam. *Parasite* and *Watchmen* are steeped in a US colonial time, military time. According to the counterhistorical premise of the *Watchmen* comic, the Watergate scandal was never exposed, and Richard Nixon wins the Vietnam War by calling on superhero Dr. Manhattan. Vietnam becomes annexed as the 51st state of the United States.[5]

Though not intended by *Watchmen* comic book creator Alan Moore, a white British man from the north of England, the name Dr. Manhattan carries the phantasmatic presence of race in the way Marin does in *Exit West*. The blue-skinned superhero, Dr. Manhattan, is the masculine immortal embodiment of nuclear modernity. He is the entangled temporality of US settler-colonial histories. Each time the name Dr. Manhattan is uttered as a signal to nuclear possibilities of mutually assured destruction and US might, it also necessarily conjures Lenape people. The citation of Native presence in place-names is also already an erasure for Indigenous futures, without invoking the referent histories or possible survivance (Vizenor 2008). The Manhattan Project was a genocide project in multiple ways. The Manhattan Project too does this work as a secret weapon of military technology developed at Columbia University, an institution built on stolen land that also poisoned the land, ecocide. The toxicity of the true Manhattan Project is an ongoing one of theft. The blue nuclear glow of Dr. Manhattan as counterhistorical figure is doubly haunted symbolically by the shadow of the human racialized nuclear toll of Japanese life in Hiroshima and Nagasaki, though it is not named. Asian life and Native life are disposable life to the US military complex.

Angela Abar represents quintessential blackness and Black womanness in the way that Toni Morrison defines it as creating choice amid choicelessness. Angela is a new world woman *and* is new world Black in her sense of intersectionality (Morrison 1988). Beyond the epidermal schema of what it means to be Black, as a girl orphaned by the shrapnel of the Vietnam War, Angela makes choice out of choicelessness. Angela literarily experiences the pain of her time-traveling grandfather—a man who survives the 1921 Tulsa Race Massacre as a young boy—threefold. She inherits his pain almost epigenetically as "blood memory," a concept that resonates in both Black and Native epistemologies. Angela literally ingests her grandfather's pain by overdosing on his memories of white supremacist violence in the form of his Nostalgia pills. In this future world, dementia medicine comes in the form of capsules that trigger memory, but they are only prescribed to the person they belong to. Angela is pulled into the historical memory of an entangled temporality of blackness in Oklahoma, the place of her ancestral roots, and Vietnam, the place of her birth. The fictional Nostalgia pills are the resource of blackness. She affectively comes to understand the pain of directly experiencing what her grandfather did as the sole survivor of the Black Wall Street Massacre as a little boy. *Watchmen* has been critiqued for shedding light on "Black Wall Street" but also occluding the intimacy and overlap between Black Native life and the history of freedmen, critical to any true depiction of Oklahoma. The disruption forms its own set of elisions, but it importantly challenges the US colonial timeline. While the depiction of the colonial present is not perfect, and Viet Than Nguyen (2019) has also critiqued the show's portrayal of Vietnam, there are important reckonings with US colonialism the TV series stages.

The HBO adaptation does not shy away from the narrative challenge of the comic book. The epidermally blue Black Dr. Manhattan in the series deploys blackness and time as a resource in his vessel, the corpse of a recently deceased Black soldier that Angela selects. It is important that his embodiment as Black is Angela's choice. Extracting choice out of choicelessness, she chooses a Black husband, and they choose to adopt children who happen to be white. Choosing family is important also because she is orphaned at a young age in Vietnam. The promotional posters play with a visual effect of blue blackness with a filter of blue light on actress Regina King's skin to foreshadow the godly glow of what Angela Abar has the potential to become in relation to Dr. Manhattan, a superhero. The yellow clock icon, the classic

Watchmen symbol, forms a golden halo of time framing the Black heroine. The blue glow suggests something transformative other than the often-imagined green glow of toxic sludge. Another nod to entangled temporality, the motif of eggs stands in for the proverbial temporal quandary of "the chicken or the egg," signifying Black time as a resource. A choice is given to Angela by Dr. Manhattan in the form of an egg she can ingest to gain his powers and in the form of her grandfather's Nostalgia pills, which she ingests so they do not end up in the wrong hands. To ingest or not the racial injury of our ancestors is often not a choice for Black people.

Entangled temporality is the premise that makes *Watchmen* the series such a poignant love story. It is inevitable to Dr. Manhattan that he and Angela will fall in love, because he experiences all time all of the time. As a plot device he embodies entangled temporality. Yet as Lindelof (HBO 2019) explains, Dr. Manhattan does not experience the emotionality of the multiple futures he sees. Angela's love makes Dr. Manhattan vulnerable. The demiurge chooses mortality in order to save Angela's life. Marked by the phantasmatic presence of race, indigeneity in his name and living in a Black man's body (Yahya Abdul-Mahteen II), Dr. Manhattan disrupts the original raceless universe of *Watchmen* that like other DC comics valorizes white masculine power as superpowers. The biological fact of Dr. Manhattan's blue and Black body is a powerful statement of Black love and thus futurity, though epidermally blue.

Dr. Manhattan's final act of love is transferring his power to Angela, should she choose to accept it. The egg grants her consent, whether to receive the superpowers bestowed on her by her lover or not. Consent or choice here is significant because of the precondition of lack of sexual consent that prefigured Black women's choice under racial slavery. It is important then that the TV series that will not have a second season ends with Angela barefoot taking a step to potentially walk on water. Will she, or won't she? The viewer does not know in this speculative future for the DC Universe, and it almost does not matter. In some sense, from a Black feminist lens, for Angela to simply inherit the power of Dr. Manhattan like a first lady later becoming president is not the point. The significance is in the leap, the Fanonian leap of potentiality for inaugurating a new world of possibility beyond masked white-supremacist avengers. The power lies in the uncertainty of the speculative. Fanon (1967: 229) writes, "The real leap consists in introducing invention into existence." For Angela, the water of the swimming pool suggests temporal fluidity and oceanic potentiality. It not only signifies the miraculous, of Jesus walking on water, but also Black Atlantic amniotic potentiality. Abar's Black futurity is importantly not premised on having biological children, though it is significant that she is a Black mother with a chosen family amid choicelessness.

Like *Watchmen, Parasite* received almost universal critical acclaim. The film's hyperpresent representation of hypercapitalism is a filmic critique of the cult of meritocracy and consumerism in contemporary South Korea. Undercurrents of US conquest of Indigenous people emerge symbolically at moments that explicitly permeate the diegesis. The young boy Da-Song's cosplay obsession with "playing Indian" subtly marks US imperialism in Korea. Da-Song does not play "Cowboys and Indians," only the Indian, which is concerning to his mother. This racial performance is echoed by the foundational US theatricality of "playing Indian" during the Boston Tea Party. As Ralph Ellison (1953) wrote of the defining racial performativity of redface, "When American life is most American it is apt to be most theatrical" (see also Deloria 1999). Toy suction-cup arrows shoot across the house. A teepee is erected in the backyard, and Bong consistently returns the viewer's attention to subtle haunting of US warfare and the dispossession of Native sovereignty as child's play.

While Bong does not touch on blackness in any explicit way, the social and labor arrangement he stages is choreographed by a logic familiar to that of the US colonial plantation. It is the architecture of occupation. The proximity between the Kims and the Parks is the spatial logic of the plantation, where smell becomes a dividing socioeconomic line that often threatens to betray the Kims. Because they all smell the same, the stench of their semi-basement subterranean dwelling almost gives them away. Desire and disavowal of bourgeois intimacy structures the Park household. The Kims are not merely their house servants but an echo of the subversive cakewalking of enslaved Africans who play house as soon as the Parks are away on a weekend camping trip. The subterranean tunnels of the ornate Park residence represent a hidden architecture—not simply of Cold War bunkers designed for fears of nuclear proliferation, but also, it is stated embarrassingly that the tunnels were designed to hide from debt collectors and from North Koreans. Labyrinthine bunkers are the architecture of both civil wars, the Korean War and the impending collapse of capitalism facilitated by an unpayable debt. The tunnels are an insurance plan, a house hidden with the house as refuge, in case the have-nots should one day return and want to collect on the debt of South Korea living in the sun. In this way we might imagine that every South Korean has their tethered resentful North Korean twin—tethered economies and worlds—diametrically opposed. The architecture is Black and of the US plantation. The hypercapitalist regime means that they need not cross the border to locate their body doubles. A servant underclass of subterranean semi-basement dwellers is ready to take their place. Cold War carnage carves a divided architecture—communism or democracy (capitalism).

To see *Parasite* for the con movie that it is means to understand how South Korean cinema inherits the tropes of US confidence games, race, and theatricality. The originally American genre of "faking it till you make it" is what the Kims perform like a vaudevillian family of actors. The impossible proximity and cramped architecture of their impoverished subterranean living quarters is akin to the proletariat intimacy of Tin Pan Alley tenements. Korea is postbellum, and the art that surfaces after war, like Vaudeville, reflects this racial phantasmatic unreckoning. Wars within wars, the afterlife of the Korean War is haunted by the afterlife of the US Civil War. After these wars of secession and attrition, unresolved betrayals shape the inequal architecture, dividing the peninsula and the nation in two. The long history of US militarism as part of the project of US conquest entangles the temporality of Bong Joon-ho's hyperpresent speculative critique of a multiplicity of Korean colonial occupations.

Bong (2020) says, "I tried to express a sentiment specific to Korean culture, [but] all the responses from different audiences were pretty much the same. Essentially, we all live in the same country, called Capitalism." *Parasite* is necessarily site specific to South Korea and demands an international audience. Yet Bong notes the universal appeal of the film is experienced by viewers the world over because of the conditions created by capitalism. Whether Bong is aware of the academic valence of "racial capitalism," *Parasite* belies an understanding of its temporality in the way the colonial present of US militarism haunts contemporary Seoul.

South Korean economic success since the Korean War casts it as the exemplar republic for Cold War US exportation of democracy. Bong's critique of US militarism is also mediated through US military standardized language made intimate. The film ends on a tragic epistolary note of Morse Code, a US military language, the code of dots and dashes, of letters repeatedly performed through blinking lights from a distance. *Parasite* ends in a speculative future where the son who learned Morse Code as a Boy Scout is possibly able to free his father who has been trapped in the subterranean tunnels of the wealthy house for decades. There is power in waiting and dreaming otherwise than the genocidal dreaming of the "American Dream." Ki-woo works his way up toward the social ladder or capitalist success in order to buy the house to free his father Ki-taek, who has become a ghost in the basement, a fungible replacement for another poor man who inhabited the substructure of the house decades before. The submerged human secrets of the colonial basement haunt the suburban South Korean house, much like the Great House of the plantation.

Trimesters of Becoming: Black Waiting and Maroon Time

A better understanding of history does not guarantee a more just future. Speculative worlding reveals the ethics and codes of society. Every hundred years or so we see cycles of forgetting and cycles of liberation in Jamaica, in 1736 (the Maroon Wars), in 1838 (Sam Sharpe's Christmas rebellion leading to Emancipation in the British West Indies), and in 1938 (anticolonial labor uprisings across the Caribbean). What could 2038 hold? *Black Mother* (2018) by director Khalik Allah gestures toward a possible answer. Another nonlinear engagement with Black time as a resource for the future, the film centers becoming and the *not-yet* I have identified as the signature of Black time. The promise of the future, or futurity, is a resource not an alibi for Khalik Allah. A film without a plot, *Black Mother* is nondiegetic. If the plot represents enclosure—a linear beginning and end—*Black Mother* exists beyond narrative, free of any timeline. The filmmaker rewrites history through Black time and storytelling directly by Maroons and Rastas he interviewed in Jamaica. Maroon indigeneity and what Wynter calls "indigenization" are doubly significant because many Maroons are also of Indigenous Amerindian heritage in Jamaica. Coalitions exist and survive in the blood and reflect who the Spanish attempted to exterminate and subjugate in the sixteenth century before being supplanted by the English. Black time accumulates as a resource stolen away and handed down for the future that Hall described. *Black Mother* is out of time and out of place, working on what Sun Ra describes as "the other side of time."

Sonically (disjointed audio) and visually (light leaks), the film ruptures expectations of visuality by intentionally disorienting the viewer. Enveloped in the darkness, the viewer is immersed in the underside of the Caribbean as vacation paradise. Khalik Allah's Kingston Noir of sex workers and other people considered "indigent" or houseless are central to the order of his diasporic return to his grandfather's native Jamaica. Like Angela Abar, Khalik Allah is in dialogue with a Black past of spirituality with his grandfather, a deacon. The film stages the personal yet universal inheritance of trauma with the climactic event of the emergence of the blackness, the birthing of a Black baby. Shocking as this may or may not be as a filmic trope, the miracle of life unsettles inasmuch as it centers emergency and emergence, cutting the cord of colonial modernity.

Khalik Allah stages the Black womb and the literal crowning as a theater to show how the edict of the Americas of racial slavery as hereditary slavery *partus sequitur ventrum*, that which is brought forth follows the womb. The curse of original sin across the hemisphere, blackness has long been narrowly defined as slave status inherited from the mother. Following the womb need not represent the enclosure of "natal alienation" in the filmic world of Khalik Allah. He celebrates the universality of birthing and the specificity of what comes forth from the Black Madonna, new worlds. The concealed means of production, the labor power of Black women's reproductive work, are revealed (see Morgan 2018).

The imagery of water spilling down stairs is amniotic and poignant in both *Black Mother* and *Parasite*, which also features a flood. The water breaks, cascading down stairs. Khalik Allah reminds the viewer of the precarity of climate crisis and the increasing frequency and strength of hurricanes for an island nation like Jamaica. Water signals the natural disaster of cleansing too in *Parasite*. The imagery of flooding signifies the shared fate of climate crisis for us all, albeit uneven. The Kims are climate refugees after the flood, taking refuge in a high school gymnasium, forced to evacuate their semi-basement dwelling, recalling Black climate refugees seeking shelter in the Louisiana Superdome. The trajectory of racial capitalism is the pressure that broke the levees of New Orleans, and Hurricane Katrina, the catastrophe of failed infrastructure for the have-nots of US colonialism, which the Koreans are too.

There are perhaps as many forms of Black time as there are Black people. The time zone extends across the multiplicity of geographies and ecologies of Black life. One vital form of Black time is found across the Black diaspora, Maroon time. The Maroon clock is centuries old, anchored in a deep sense of history. Frantz Fanon (1968: 120) described such waiting as definitive of who he was: "If I were asked for a definition of myself, I would say that I am one who waits; I investigate my surroundings, I interpret everything in terms of what I discover, I become sensitive." Black waiting then is defined by an acute sensitivity to environment, and to observational praxis, that is determined by investigation. Maroon philosophy, grand and petit, can be traced across the hemisphere from Brazil to Suriname to Haiti to Jamaica to Virginia to Florida (see Roberts 2015). The speculative has always then been a mode of power, because the word's etymology is rooted in "seeing" as "spying," looking with a purpose—not necessarily for surveillance but for observation, for information before acting.[6] Seeing here also resonates with the prophetic and the ability to foresee what has yet to arrive. Thus, Black speculation is a horizon of radical possibility celebrating the power of uncertainty in uncertain times of crisis.

The speculative carries the potential to undo speculation itself, or capitalism. Race is one of capitalism's stories or fictions. Black feminist speculative modes, in particular, are essential to the plot of undoing. Hartman (2019) poetically defines "the plot of her undoing" as capitalism. She deploys the speculative power of critical fabulation to attempt to undo the violence of the plot. If, as historian Vincent Brown (2020) urges us to reconsider, the Haitian Revolution and other Black rebellions are inflection points in an ongoing state of warfare between West Africa and Western Europe, then the emergence of blackness itself is a resource for Black futures. Brown's elegant reperiodization reframes *marronage*, and the Maroon Wars in Jamaica in particular, as an ongoing series of acts of global proportion and strategy. Just as the Haitian Revolution was a thirteen-year interruption to the space-time of coloniality, Black freedom threatens to abolish the very notion of time itself. Blackness is not fixed and thus it continues to redefine historiography by restructuring structure itself, as a trickster, redefining *form*. A politics and aesthetics of shapeshifting and mutability, defying genre, Black temporality cyclically emerges as a resource for Black people but also influences the fate and story of the world, as Du Bois prophesied. So though the stories examined here are not all Black stories, they are impacted by Black time and storytelling.

"There are years that ask questions and years that answer," wrote Zora Neale Hurston (1937), speaking in the register of Black time as critique. Black grammarians understand this intimately when they deploy Black time, stolen away over the generations. The conquest was not inevitable, nor is it over.[7] The power of the Black grammarian resides in the patience and precision of the storyteller, the power of observation and narration. The Black grammarian *watches, sees, reads, waits,* and *prophesies.* Keeping the Maroon clock, waiting is his or her decisive act, a military tactic. Maroon time, lying in wait, is as critical to the guerrilla nature of Maroon warcraft as it is to Maroon cooking, like jerk, that requires many days of low smoking.[8] Maroon settlements continue to show the world that another world beyond racial capitalism is possible. Waiting and camouflaged in nature, intimate inhabited knowledge of the earth and sea, is the Maroon strategy. The quiet patience, persistence, and fortitude of *marronage* is in the not-yet standardized potentiality of Black time. Ongoing, *marronage* is then not a metaphor but an urgent tactic of survival that depends on stealing back stolen time. Accumulating Black time as a resource toward imagining Black futures, the speculative nature of Black storytelling is a radical act. Always drawing attention to the speculation that is the very uncertainty which capitalism is founded upon, blackness continues to work on the other side of time, the B-side of radical possibility.

Notes

Many of the ideas on contemporary apocalyptic storytelling congealed here began their formation at the Global Condition workshop held at the Performing Arts Forum in France, organized
by Denise Ferreira da Silva, Mark Harris, and Alyosha Goldstein. I am thankful for the feed-
back from organizers and participants. In addition, I thank Alyosha Goldstein for his insights
into the development of this essay. Many thanks to Habiba Ibrahim and Badia Ahad for their
insight and their cowritten words calling to action and inspiration for the occasion of this issue
to write through and with the shifting meaning of race and how it informs the ongoing crisis.

1   For a genealogy of the usage of the term *racial capitalism* beginning in South Africa to
     Cedric Robinson's deployment of the phrase to its present revival, see the introduction
     to Jenkins and Leroy 2021.
2   Sylvia Wynter (2010) extends *homo narrans*, or the binomial nomenclature for man as
     storyteller, also theorized by Kurt Ranke and Walter Fisher in the 1960s, to theorize
     what defines Man as genus distinct from other hominids.
3   Lee grew up as the son of a doctor in Westchester, migrating from South Korea at age
     three with his family.
4   For Chang-rae Lee on the fun of writing the future for *On Such a Full Sea*, see PBS
     Newshour 2014.
5   Lindelof notes that he was inspired by the ongoing nature of the dispossession of
     Hawaiian sovereignty as a model of the colonial present.
6   OED Online, "speculative, n." Oxford University Press (accessed March 2021)
7   Sylvia Wynter's (2010) usage of the term "Black grammarians" alerts us to the ways in
     which time is located in language, both the grammar of speaking and the historicity of
     writing. Tiffany Lethabo King casts Wynter as a "Black grammarian," with a cohort of
     others, including Toni Morrison, Junot Díaz, Hortense Spillers, and graffiti artists who
     vandalize Columbus statues because of their refusal to accept the conquest is complete.
8   Tactics of warcraft and cooking are equally necessary modes of Black survival. See
     Goffe 2020.

References

Brown, Vincent. 2020. *Tacky's Revolt: The Story of an Atlantic Slave War.* Cambridge, MA: Har-
     vard University Press.
Central Park Conservancy. 2021. "The Story of Seneca Village." *Central Park Conservancy Mag-
     azine*, January 18. www.centralparknyc.org/articles/seneca-village.
Coney, John, dir. *Space Is the Place.* New York: Plexifilm, 1972.
Corrigan, Maureen. 2014. "Chang-rae Lee Stretches for Dystopic Drama, but Doesn't Quite
     Reach." *Fresh Air*, January 13. wwno.org/2014-01-14/chang-rae-lee-stretches-for-dystopic
     -drama-but-doesnt-quite-reach.
Deloria, Philip. 1999. *Playing Indian.* New Haven, CT: Yale University Press.
Dillon, Grace L. 2007. "Indigenous Scientific Literacies in Nalo Hopkinson's Ceremonial
     Worlds." *Journal of the Fantastic in the Arts* 18, no. 1: 23–41.
Du Bois, W. E. B. 1900. "To the Nations of the World." BlackPast.org. https://www.blackpast.
     org/african-american-history/1900-w-e-b-du-bois-nations-world/.
Ellison, Ralph. 1953. *Shadow and Act.* New York: Vintage International.

Eng, David. 2008. "The End(s) of Race." *PMLA* 123: 1479–93.

Fanon, Frantz. 1967. *Black Skin, White Masks*. Translated by Charles Lam Markmann. New York: Grove Press.

Gilroy, Paul. 1992. *The Black Atlantic: Modernity and Double Consciousness*. New York: Verso.

Glissant, Édouard. 1999. *Caribbean Discourse*. Charlottesville, VA: University of Virginia Press.

Goerke, Betty. 2007. *Chief Marin: Leader, Rebel, and Legend*. Berkeley, CA: Heyday Books.

Goffe, Tao Leigh. 2020. "Kitchen Marronage." *Funambulist*, August 27. https://thefunambulist .net/magazine/politics-of-food/kitchen-marronage-a-genealogy-of-jerk-tao-leigh-goffe.

Goldstein, Alyosha. 2014. *Formations of United States Colonialism*. Durham, NC: Duke University Press.

Hall, Stuart. 2017. *Familiar Stranger: A Life between Two Islands*. Durham, NC: Duke University Press.

Hamid, Mohsin. 2014. *Discontent and Its Civilizations: Dispatches from Lahore, New York, and London*. New York: Riverhead.

Hamid, Mohsin. 2017. "Mohsin Hamid's Novel 'Exit West' Raises Immigration Issues." NPR. March 6. https://www.npr.org/2017/03/06/518743041/mohsin-hamids-novel-exit -west-raises-immigration-issues.

Hanchard, Michael. 1999. "Afro-Modernity: Temporality, Politics, and the African Diaspora." *Public Cultures* 11, no. 1: 245–68.

Hartman, Saidiya. 2002. "The Time of Slavery." *South Atlantic Quarterly* 101, no. 4: 757–77.

Hartman, Saidiya. 2019. "The Plot of Her Undoing." Notes on Feminism. Feminist Art Coalition. https://static1.squarespace.com/static/5c805bf0d86cc90a02b81cdc/t/5db 8b219a910fa05afo5dbf4/1572385305368/NotesOnFeminism-2_SaidiyaHartman.pdf.

HBO. 2019. "The Official Watchmen Podcast." https://www.hbo.com/watchmen/watch men-listen-to-official-podcast.

Hurston, Zora Neale. 1937. *Their Eyes Were Watching God*. New York: J. B. Lippincott, Inc.

Jenkins, Destin, and Justin Leroy, eds. 2021. *Histories of Racial Capitalism*. New York: Columbia University Press.

Kamugisha, Aaron. 2019. *Beyond Coloniality: Citizenship and Freedom in the Caribbean Intellectual Tradition*. Bloomington: Indiana University Press.

Korea Society. "Chang-rae Lee: On Such a Full Sea." Podcast. https://koreasociety.org/education /item/642.

Lee, Chang-rae. 2013. *On Such a Full Sea*. New York: Riverhead.

Le Guin, Ursula. 2014. "*On Such a Full Sea* by Chang-Rae Lee Review." *Guardian*, January 30. https://www.theguardian.com/books/2014/jan/30/on-such-full-sea-chang-rae-lee -review.

Leyshon, Cressida. 2014. "The Chorus of 'We': An Interview with Chang-Rae Lee." *New Yorker*, January 6. https://www.newyorker.com/books/page-turner/the-chorus-of-we-an-interview -with-chang-rae-lee.

Lim, Bliss Cua. 2009. *Translating Time: Cinema, the Fantastic, and Temporal Critique*. Durham, NC: Duke University Press.

Morgan, Jennifer. 2018. "*Partus sequitur ventrum*: Law, Race, and Reproduction in Colonial Slavery." *Small Axe* 22, no. 1: 1–17.

Morrison, Toni. 1988. "Unspeakable Things Unspoken: The Afro-American Presence in American Literature." Paper presented at the Tanner Lectures on Human Values,

University of Michigan, October 7, 1988. quod.lib.umich.edu/m/mqrarchive/act2080
.0028.001/14?page=root;size=175;view=text.

Nguyen, Viet Tanh. 2019. "How 'Watchmen's Misunderstanding of Vietnam Undercuts it
Vision of Racism." *Washington Post*, December 18. www.washingtonpost.com/outlook
/2019/12/18/how-watchmens-misunderstanding-vietnam-undercuts-its-vision-racism/.

PBS Newshour. 2014. "Chang-Rae Lee on the Fun of Writing the Future for *On Such a Full
Sea*." March 11. www.pbs.org/newshour/show/chang-rae-lee-fun-frustration-writing
-future-full-sea.

Roberts, Neil. 2015. *Freedom as Marronage*. Chicago: University of Chicago Press.

Roh, David S., Betsy Huang, and Greta A. Niu, eds. 2015. *Techno-Orientalism: Imagining Asia in
Speculative Fiction, History, and Media*. New Brunswick, NJ: Rutgers University Press.

Russell, Heather. 2009. *Legba's Crossing: Narratology in the African Atlantic*. Athens: University of Georgia Press.

Rutgers University Press. n.d. "Techno-Orientalism: Imagining Asia in Speculative Fiction,
History, and Media." https://www.rutgersuniversitypress.org/techno-orientalism
/9780813570631.

Spillers, Hortense. 1987."Mama's Baby, Papa's Maybe: An American Grammar Book." *Diacritics* 17: 64–81.

Vizenor, Gerald. 2008. *Survivance: Narratives of Native Presence*. Lincoln: University of
Nebraska Press.

Wynter, Sylvia. 2010. *Hills of Hebron*. Kingston, Jamaica: Ian Randle.

Julius B. Fleming Jr.

Anticipating Blackness:
Nina Simone, Lorraine Hansberry,
and the Time of Black Ontology

Anticipation is a slippery act that unfolds between
the known and the unknown worlds of time.
Staged at the crossroads of times that have come
and times that are yet to come, anticipation mar-
shals knowledges of pasts and presents to specu-
late about, imagine, and forge relationships to the
future. Within the field of black studies, the repetition of anti-black violence across the historical
expanse of modernity has rendered anticipation
an increasingly powerful conceptual and theoretical tool. Alert to the historical and contemporary
dynamics of black life—and their striking overlaps and continuities—black studies scholarship
has seen an outpouring of methods that use the
realities of pasts and presents to theorize what
blackness is and what blackness will be. To be sure,
the violent histories of transatlantic slavery and its
afterlives enable a certain precision in mapping the
nature of black ontology as well as in anticipating
its futures. Still, anticipation is not a perfect science. What are we to make of those moments
when the anticipated outcome fails to arrive? And
how do we develop modes of analysis that refrain
from ceding anticipatory logic the authority to
frame black ontology as the always already given
rather than as matter that is open to wonder and

The South Atlantic Quarterly 121:1, January 2022
DOI 10.1215/00382876-9561587   © 2022 Duke University Press

surprise, to the contingent and the unanticipated. This, after all, is the character of blackness.

In this essay, I argue that black ontology is usefully approached as a temporal entity whose movements through time help to define the nature of its constitution. Attending more specifically to what I call *the time of black ontology*, I am interested in the complex, shifting, and multiscalar relationship between time and black ontology, and in how this symbiotic relationship is vital to the formation and analysis of the ontological conditions of blackness. This call to conceptualize black ontology as a temporal entity builds on literary theorist Fred Moten's claim that blackness is the "irreparable disturbance of ontology's time and space" (Moten 2013: 739). Blackness, Moten contends, "is ontologically prior to the logistic and regulative power that is supposed to have brought it into existence . . . blackness is prior to ontology" (739). Here Moten frames black ontology as "products of time" (Moten 2008: 192). He is interested, more specifically, in the priorness of blackness in relation to ontology as a discursive category of the West. His concern with "ontology's time," then, is a matter of history and historicity, namely as it relates to the long and deep time of Western modernity and thought.

I am invested in this essay in a smaller-scale analysis that prioritizes the more local, everyday time of black ontology: the fleeting and ephemeral moments, the slippages, the sudden shifts in black being. I contend that alongside those large-scale structures of time that inflect and help to constitute black ontology (e.g., past and present), we must also attend to the small-scale temporalities—like the moment or the instant—that are just as pivotal to the production and understanding of black ontology. These discrete structures of ontological time, and the feelings and experiences that generate and drive them, are as important to the formation of black ontology as the epochal temporalities that often serve as the conceptual foundations of black studies theorizing. Without question, the long view of black being is necessary and illuminating, and has cultivated a useful critical approach that I call *anticipatory logic*, or the critical practice of using the historical record of modernity to forecast the weather of blackness.[1] But as we know, forecasts have their limits; the weather often surprises.

Though most widely remembered as an architect of the cultural and intellectual life of the Harlem Renaissance, black philosopher Alain Locke was also an astute theorist of anticipation and, as I discuss later, affect and feeling. Seeking to provide a theoretical alternative to what he understood as totalizing conceptions of value—that is, the ideals, standards, and actions that we use to evaluate our worlds—Locke argued for methods of analysis that would foreground "immediate context of valuation" rather than "anticipation of experience." Absolutism, Locke laments, had "come forward again in new and formidable guise" (Locke [1935] 1989: 53). It had "made truth too exclusively a matter of the correct anticipation of experience, of the confirmation of fact" (37). But truth, he submits, can also be "the sustaining of an attitude, the satisfaction of a way of feeling" (37). These observations from Locke are important for my thinking about black ontology for two reasons. First, Locke's philosophy of value exposes the limits of granting anticipatory logic—however tried and tested it be—unbridled power to overdetermine what constitutes truth, and, for my purposes, the truth of black ontology. In this way, Locke offers a point of departure to more carefully consider the time of black ontology, specifically by helping us to understand how "immediate context" is just as pivotal to black ontology as the more enduring systems of anti-blackness that form the conceptual foundations of structural analysis. Second, in claiming that "truth" can be "an attitude" or a "way of feeling," Locke highlights the critical relationship between feeling and value, even suggesting that value itself is "an emotionally mediated form of experience" (45). Putting forth what he calls "an affective theory of valuation," Locke turns to affect to challenge rigid attachments to the anticipation of experience—to facts and absolutes—by demonstrating that the shifting terrains of our affects and feelings also inform truth. It is my contention that this outlook is clarifying for understanding the truth, or the nature, of black ontology.

At stake in analyzing this interrelationship of time, affect, and black ontology is an effort to grapple with the intricate workings of structural critique and to ponder what, in fact, rises to the level of a structure that is significant enough to function as a building block of structural analysis. There is no question that racism, patriarchy, homophobia, capitalism, and other large-scale experiments in modern violence should be at the center of our paradigms for structurally assessing our self- and world-making practices. But we cannot allow the sheer violences of these world systems to so overdetermine our methods of analysis that we miss those moments where the archive and its objects, where black people, index a narrative of relation that moves in excess, though not outside, of these violences. To be sure, the regularity of this gratuitous violence must figure into any calculus that aims to assess the structure of the modern world. But we must stop short of authorizing the force of these systems to cultivate an anticipatory logic that frames black ontology as an unvarying variable, as a priori knowledge that is given rather than explored. We should instead open black ontology up to methods of analysis that carve out space for the unknown, for the unanticipated. This is not a call to unthink the structural history of anti-black violence but instead to engage in practices of deep listening to black people, to their thinking, to their feelings. In this way, our investigations of black ontology will not be primed to prioritize the workings of the oppressor but will be oriented toward the legitimate feelings, experiences, and complex conditions of the object itself.

With this in mind, this essay seeks to contribute to recent scholarship in the field of black studies that explores the nature of black ontology. Afro-pessimism, an intellectual orientation within these discourses, has been at the forefront of these efforts to analyze the fraught constitution of black being. Attuned to the transhistorical nature and singularity of anti-black violence, Afro-pessimism has persuasively challenged triumphalist narratives of racial progress, disrupting their propensity to cleave contemporary anti-black violence from the *longue durée* of anti-black terror. It has shown how this terrorizing enterprise has engineered a network of world systems that can seem to orient the trajectory of black being toward an ostensibly inevitable fate: social death. Largely rooted in the seminal work of black writer, activist, and psychiatrist Franz Fanon, this school of thinking often forwards a negative theory of blackness that urges "the black" to "fully [accept] the definition of himself as pathological"—to live, in other words, in social death (Sexton 2011: 27). For film critic Frank Wilderson, this admonition is rooted in the claim that black people's relationship to the world is structured by an "antagonism" rather than a "conflict" (Wilderson 2010: 5). Whereas conflicts can be resolved, antagonisms, Wilderson contends, are irreconcilable, eclipsing the possibility of a dialectical resolution. The result of this impossibility is a transhistorical structure of anti-black oppression, one that was inaugurated in and through New World slavery.

The necro-political enterprise of destroying black life is a centuries-old project that spans from transatlantic slavery to contemporary police brutality, from redlining to medical injustice and mass incarceration. As Afro-pessimism makes clear, such structures and practices of oppression have been ductile in their capacities for change, resilient in their duties of fortifying whiteness, and steadfast in their commitments to their own reproductive futurity. For people of African descent who bear the weight of these violent assemblages, social death has been a paradigmatic condition of their being. It makes sense, then, that the reach and prevalence of these structures of racial oppression can seem to enclose the entirety of black being.

And yet, as literary critic Kevin Quashie observes, "the racist thing is not the beginning or the end of being, and what matters is not only what is done to the subject but also *how* the subject is. Antiblackness is part of blackness but not all of how or what blackness is" (Quashie 2021: 5; emphasis mine). In a similar tenor, literary critic Christina Sharpe contends that even as black people have "experienced, recognized, and lived subjection," they do not *"simply or only* live *in* subjection and *as* the subjected" (Sharpe 2016: 4). They make "livable moments . . . in the midst of all that [is] unlivable" (4). In addition to their illuminating arguments about the nature of black life (or, as Quashie puts it, "black aliveness") and its relational proximities to black death, I am struck by how both scholars rely on temporal grammars (i.e., "not the beginning or the end of being" and "livable moments") to articulate the complex and dynamic geographies of black being, which are bound to, but not wholly bounded by, the death machine of anti-blackness. If anti-blackness is not the beginning or the end of black being, if there are "livable moments" within black being, then it is necessary that we pay attention to the *time of black ontology.* Because black ontology is, in part, a question of when, and because the "when" of black being encompasses both the long view of structural analysis and the fleeting and ephemeral moment, our use of anticipatory logic must unfold in relation to a critical consciousness that is conditioned to recognize, analyze, and center not only the predictable violences that inflect black ontology but also the unanticipated moments that rub up against and explode—however briefly—the constraints of anti-blackness and its imperative of black death.

To better understand this layered approach to black ontology and its timing, I turn to the work of black singer Nina Simone and her dear friend and fellow civil rights activist, black playwright Lorraine Hansberry. On the one hand, I argue that Hansberry and Simone used theater and performance to engage in structural critique, and to signal the productive possibilities of anticipatory logic in black art, politics, and thought. On the other hand, I argue that both artists and activists also exposed the limitations of anticipatory logic, spotlighting the power of the unanticipated by foregrounding the role of affect in the production of black ontology. As affects are prone to be, these moments are often unanticipated, surprising, and fleeting. Even so, they are no less real and meaningful to the making and analysis of black ontology. Inviting a closer look into how affect and feeling function as building blocks of black ontology, and relatedly of structural analysis, Simone and Hansberry help us to understand how ways of feeling, as Locke observes, can ignite shifts in black being and in black people's relationships to freedom.

In the sections that follow, I develop this argument by turning first to Nina Simone. Through live performances of songs like "I Wish I Knew How

It Would Feel to Be Free," Simone captures the blunt force of anti-blackness. But in the moment of live performance, she reveals how black people's feelings and affects—which are often unanticipated—are pivotal to their relationships to being and freedom. I then read Lorraine Hansberry's canonical, award-winning play *A Raisin in the Sun* (1959) alongside one of her grossly underexamined plays from the 1960s, *The Arrival of Mr. Todog*—a riveting parody of Samuel Beckett's modernist classic *Waiting for Godot* (1952). Like Simone, Hansberry uses performance to engage in modes of structural critique that highlight the profundity of anti-black violence but stops short of allowing that violence to overdetermine the shape of black ontology. In framing black ontology as a "tussle of being" rather than a totalized, always predictable configuration, she, too, challenges the conceptual and theoretical grip of absolutism when engaging questions of black ontology and ideas of black freedom (Quashie 2021: 1). For both Simone and Hansberry (and for me), black ontology is ultimately a flexible and shifting configuration of moments—moments of freedom and oppression, of social life and social death, of being and nothingness—that make it futile to anchor this fraught but fugitive category of being to any fixed paradigm of existence. By paying attention to these moments and, more broadly, to the time of black ontology, we arrive at a more complex and nuanced understanding of the ontological conditions of blackness.

Nina Simone and the Feeling of Freedom

In a rousing 1976 performance at Switzerland's Montreux Jazz Festival, legendary black artist and activist Nina Simone posited freedom as a feeling. Performing an extended version of her classic anthem "I Wish I Knew How It Would Feel to Be Free," she opened the song in this way:

> Wish I knew how it would feel to be free.
> I wish I could break all the chains that still binding me, yea.
> Wish I could say all the things that I can say *when I'm relaxed*.
> I'd be starting anew (emphasis mine)

Repeating the verb *wish* and the modal verbs *would* and *could*, Simone yearns to know and to feel freedom, to know freedom through feeling. Each line extends and reelaborates this grammar of desire, installing a hopeful but conditional mood that highlights the precarious grounds on which her freedom dreams are perched. This evocative language of desire pervades and colors the song's lyrical architecture. In this opening instance, the audience is left to wonder if Simone's dreams will ever come to fruition, or if the object of her desire—that is to say, freedom—will remain elusive, hanging in the balance of the hoped-for-but-not-yet-here.

But as the performance unfolds, Simone, in a somewhat surprising gesture, claims to know the feeling of freedom and to thereby know precisely how it feels *to be* free. In a striking grammatical shift from the conditional to the declarative, she sings:

> How sweet it would be,
> If I could find that I could fly.
> Soar to the sun,
> Look down at the sea,
> Then I'd know,
> Yes I'd know,
> Aw yea, the spirit's moving now
> Mmmmmmmmmmm
> I know,
> Got news for you,
> I already know,
> Jonathan Livingston Segal ain't got nothing on me.
> Free
> Free
> Free
> Free
> I'm Free
> And I know it.

Uttering desires to fly like a "bird in the sky," Simone lifts her right arm from the piano. Though initially suspended in the air, she soon sets this arm in motion, maneuvering it up and then down like a "bird in the sky." Subtle finger snaps accord with slight twists of the body, producing an assemblage of embodied rhythms that moves to the tempo of the song. Singing in a near whisper, crooning indeed, Simone offers the first and only smile while performing this number. "The spirit's moving now," she exclaims, as she appears to become increasingly more—to use her word—"*relaxed*." This spiritual and physical kinesthesia, this locomotion of black flesh and black feeling, inaugurates a striking transformation from desire to possession, from wish to fulfillment, from unfreedom to freedom. In this moment of live performance, Simone stakes an ontological claim to freedom, one forged in and through black feeling. "I'm free," she tells the audience. "And I know it."

Simone's performance highlights the significance of black feelings to black freedom. It shows how structures of black feeling—like modernity's more often regarded structures of anti-blackness—are critical to the production of black ontology. At no point in the six minutes of Simone's performance does news of improved social structures arrive, are more equitable political practices instituted, are economic policies radically transformed, is the material world created anew. But Simone begins to feel free. And insofar as she felt free, I would argue that she was free.[2] Unfolding within the domain of feeling, Simone's sudden, or unanticipated, access to freedom in the moment of live performance marks an important ontological shift. What makes this claim to freedom vis-à-vis feeling ontological is that it is one fundamentally about being, and more specifically about the condition of being free. Anchored by the being verb *am* (i.e., "I'm free"), Simone's forceful declaration of freedom in the moment of live performance leads her to speak with a different grammar (moving from the conditional to the declarative), to alter the temporality of black freedom (from future to present, from wish to fulfillment), and to enter a new mode of being ("I'm free / And I know it," she sings).

Commuting between freedom and its absence, the dynamic movements of Simone's black feelings, and the shifts that they trigger in her relationship to freedom, allow us to better understand how affect and feeling inflect the shape of black ontology—often in the time that separates a single stroke of the piano key from the next. In other words, not only are Simone's black feelings on the move, but this movement of feeling through time sparks a similar movement in her relationship to being and freedom. These movements demonstrate how structures of black feeling are pivotal to the making and the study of black ontology as well as to the critical enterprise of structural analysis. Seen this way, black ontology is not solely a product of the external structures that strive to forge an indestructible relationship between black being and death. It emerges also from practices of self, of self-making, of self-possession. By inviting us to consider the time of black ontology, Simone's performance shows that black ontology is not only composed of "facts and absolutes," or the truths of anti-black violence. But it is also produced in and through the surprise, fugitive, and unanticipated moments of feeling and being free, whatever the timescales of those events.

My conception of black feeling is not intended to invoke a reductive paradigm of racialized feeling. Instead, I offer this term as a particular iteration of what the late cultural theorist José Esteban Muñoz refers to as the "affective particularity" of minoritarian peoples. "How," Muñoz asks, "does the subaltern feel?" Muñoz finds depression a productive category for pondering this question. Using depression as a conceptual point of departure, he coins the phrase "feeling brown, feeling down" as a way to theorize an affective particularity "coded to specific historical subjects who can provisionally be recognized by the term *Latina*" (Muñoz 2006: 675–79). Muñoz's intellectual project is famously shaped by a radical commitment to hope and possibility for minoritarian subjects as well as minoritarian futures. But, in this instance, there is a curious affinity between Muñoz's theory of minoritarian feeling and Afro-pessimism. Both schools of thought traffic in the negative order of things as a way of formulating concepts of minoritarian being that acknowledge the distinctive violences aimed at specific racial groups. Whereas Afro-pessimism often constrains black being to social death, Muñoz's framework confines the feelings of the subaltern to depression. But paying attention to Nina Simone's black feelings highlights the dynamic character of minoritarian feelings. It shows how they emanate from various times and spaces, histories and memories, discourses and experiences, thus rendering them irreducible to the low, the high, or any absolute position between.

I am interested in the itinerant character that defines the "archive of [black] feelings," and in how this itinerancy contributes to the shape of black ontology (Cvetkovich: 2003). It is certainly the case that slavery and its afterlives have collaborated across time to restrict black people and their feelings to the territory of the low. But as Simone's performance demonstrates, black feelings often escape the depths of depression, taking routes that disturb tendencies to understand black feeling as always already subjacent, or blackness as eternally tethered to social death. Blackness and black feeling must necessarily be thought both at and beyond the site of the low and outside the walls of social death. To cede sovereignty to the depressive or the socially dead would constrain the fugitive force of blackness and black feeling, in the same way that underestimating the ubiquity of depression and social death would enact a similar foreclosure. It is therefore important to engage black ontology as a matter of feeling and experience as well as a matter of "timed history rather than timeless eternity" (Locke [1935] 1989: 37).

When Nina Simone exclaims, "I'm free. And I know it," I believe her— in the same way that I believe her when she registers an absence of freedom within the same performance. Hardly contradictory, her shifting relationships to freedom and being highlight the centrality of black feeling to black being and index how the time of black ontology is vital to understanding the nature of black being in all of its fundamental irreducibility. To be sure, my aim in redirecting ontological thought away from absolutist logic is not to replace the anticipation of experience with what Locke calls a "Protagorean relativism" that would make "each man the measure and each situation the gauge of value" (38). Nor is my argument that Simone's sudden experience of freedom indexes a totalized ontological state of freedom. Rather, it is that her feelings and experiences of freedom are as important to the composition of her being as are the structures of anti-black violence that strive to mediate the totality of her existence. This relational analysis of feeling, experience, and social structures renders the intellectual undertaking of theorizing black ontology, social life and social death, a more complex and situated enterprise. It demonstrates that no singular structure or network of structural relations (political, economic, racial, or otherwise) can fully contain, anticipate, or explain away black being.

In a probing meditation on the process of cutting a border, literary theorist Hortense Spillers offers a series of instructive queries that help to put a finer point on this claim. "Who," Spillers asks, "cuts the border?" "By what finalities of various historico-cultural situations are we *frozen forever* in precisely defined portions of culture content? There are days when her household cuts the border, then there are days when someone else's does" (emphasis mine) (Spillers 2003: 335). Spillers chronicles a dynamic act of border cutting that is helpful for conceptualizing the itinerant motions of black feelings and the time of black ontology. If we linger on Spillers's metaphor for a moment to grapple with the question of black ontology, we might say that the border that divides black life and black death—which is also to say the border that joins them—is hardly a static or impervious terrain. Further, the agents that "cut" the border are numerous and diverse. Here perhaps the agent is politics; there it is a feeling; elsewhere a combination of both. The point, then, is that black people are not "frozen forever" in a single territory of social life or social death, of freedom or oppression. Further, how they navigate these borders is as inclusive of black feelings as it is of any other structure that conspires to compromise black people's access to life itself. As Simone put it while performing another piece from her repertoire of feeling songs, this one titled "Feelings," "I will always have my feelings. Nothing can destroy that."

A Note on Performance and Black Ontology

In addition to unfurling the relationship between black feelings and black ontology, Simone's live performance signals how performance itself functions as a route to existence and freedom, and thus as a building block of black ontology. Like black feelings, black performance manifests as being and reality.[3] In some areas of recent scholarship that engages the question of black ontology, scholars have sometimes drawn a troubling dichotomy between culture and politics, taking aim at black performance in particular. For instance, Frank Wilderson (2010: 57) advocates for a "conceptual framework, predicated not on the subject-effect of cultural performance but on the structure of political ontology, a framework that allows us to substitute a culture of politics for a politics of culture." This call for a substitution of politics for culture belies and obscures the formidable intimacies between culture and politics across the long black freedom struggle.[4] In fact, during watershed black social and political movements—from the Abolition movement to the Civil Rights and Black Power movements to the Black Lives Matter movement—black cultural experiments in performance have functioned as forms of political expression and mechanisms for altering black political ontology. As such, rather than cloud our understanding of the vicissitudes of black being, these modes of black cultural production lend clearer insights into the textures of black (political) ontology.

This recognition of the interrelation of black ontology and black performance clarifies an important historical fact: black people have been sophisticated theorists and architects of their own ontology, rather than passive receivers or repositories for the ontological manufacturings of Western humanism. Seen this way, black performance is more than a form of cultural production, or genre of embodied political expression. It is also an embodied framework through which black artists, activists, and everyday people have shaped and theorized black ontology. These embodied acts both inflect black being and produce critical knowledge about it. Reading black performance in this way reveals how the production and analysis of black ontology has not been restricted to writing, but has also been a performance-based practice that is both critical and creative, cultural and political, and hardly restricted to the agents of Western humanism and their exercises in anti-black violence. In addition to building a stronger bridge between the fields of black performance studies and black intellectual history, this conception of performance stresses that black people and black bodies are not solely objects of analysis, nor are they simply the playgrounds of modernity's racialized paradigms of oppression. They are vectors of intellectual expression; they are shapers and theorists of black political ontology. This is nowhere more apparent than in the work of black playwright Lorraine Hansberry.

Lorraine Hansberry: On Social Life and Social Death

Few artists have wrestled with the intricacies of black ontology and black freedom more poignantly and beautifully than Lorraine Hansberry. The daughter of a successful real-estate broker and educator, Hansberry was born into a life of relative privilege in 1930s Chicago. Though growing up in the thick of the Great Depression, she continued to enjoy the spoils of her parents' affluence—even donning a white ermine fur coat to school while the Depression raged. Hansberry would go on, furthermore, to become the first black woman to have a play produced on Broadway, and the first black playwright, and youngest woman, to win the coveted New York Drama Critics' Circle Award for Best Play of the Year. A rising star with an international reputation, it would seem that Hansberry had every reason to inhabit and to advocate for the seemingly blind optimism constantly pegged to her art and her career. But Hansberry was black, a woman, and queer, and was thus vulnerable to the costs incurred by those who occupy these historically devalued categories of social being. Whether dodging bricks and spit hurled from the mouths and hands of "howling mobs"—livid because the Hansberrys dared to integrate their neighborhood—or being forced by a matrix of racism, sexism, and homophobia to tactically calibrate the queer dimensions of her life, Hansberry had compelling reason to capitulate to the external structures that endeavored to enfold the totality of her being—to decimate, in fact, the possibility that she could be (Nemiroff 1995: 51).

But even as Hansberry lay dying at the young age of 34, reeling from the pain of pancreatic cancer, she continued to embrace and create life, and to demonstrate that black people could feel and be free in a world that demands otherwise. It is this delicate and fraught wrestling with life and death—in her art, her activism, and her movements throughout the world—that makes Lorraine Hansberry chiefly important to recent critical theories of black ontology. It is my contention that Hansberry is a major theorist of black ontology whose work should be read with and against the grain of these discourses, in the same way that the work of her distinguished contemporary Frantz Fanon has rightly been. Whereas Fanon has been the consistent point of departure within this body of scholarship, Lorraine Hansberry's contributions to black cultural production and intellectual thought belong at the center of these critical dialogues.

It is hard to imagine the 1950s and 1960s without the sheer intellect and political courage of Lorraine Hansberry and Frantz Fanon. The similarities that link the two are arresting, even uncanny. In their short but prolific careers, Hansberry and Fanon grappled with heady questions of race and oppression, colonialism and economics, politics and culture; both of them experienced relatively privileged upbringings; they both died in their mid-thirties, each suffering from cancer. But whereas Fanon has been central to recent discourses surrounding black ontology, Lorraine Hansberry has received far less attention. If Fanon accepts the definition of himself and black people as pathological, Hansberry acknowledges the social invention of black pathology without invariably embracing the terms and assumptions of this creative fiction. For her, black ontology is a mode of being that shifts through time rather than an absolute anticipation of experience. At stake here is not a claim about which thinker was right or wrong, better or worse, but rather an opportunity to expand the cast of black thinkers, and the arc of black intellectual thought, that inform contemporary conversations regarding the nature of black ontology.

To be sure, Lorraine Hansberry was keenly aware of the stark exigencies of being black in a world of anti-blackness; she knew all too well that the price of this ticket was often death. The playwright's consciousness of the interrelationship between blackness and death surfaces throughout *A Raisin in the Sun* (1959)—the award-winning play that catapulted Hansberry onto the international stage. From its opening stage directions to its denouement, *A Raisin in the Sun* orbits around black death. When the play opens, the family patriarch is dead. The living room that he leaves behind is dying. And when the curtains close, his family stands gazing at the proximity of their own deaths. Having decided to integrate a white neighborhood (just as the Hansberrys had), the Younger family is plagued by the terror of bomb threats, not from the Soviet Union—for which duck-and-cover drills in this era of Cold War angst might have prepared them—but rather from white supremacists. In a rather wry fashion, Miss Johnson, the family's tastefully jealous neighbor, illuminates the cloud of death hovering over the family. "I bet this time next month," she exclaims, "y'all's names will have been in the papers plenty—*(Holding up her hands to mark off each word of the headline she can see in front of her)* 'NEGROES INVADE CLYBOURNE PARK—BOMBED'" (Hansberry [1959] 1995: 102).

Even offstage, Hansberry's lived experiences were an object lesson in the precarity of black life and the seemingly eternal proximity of black death. As she came of age, for example, she witnessed her father's exhausting struggle to secure the rights and protections that US citizenship ostensibly affords. In her estimation, this fight led to his "early death," not unlike Mr. Younger, whose exploited labor was to blame for his own early death (Nemiroff [1969]

1995: 51). In a similar tenor, Hansberry's friend, black writer and activist James Baldwin, suggested that Hansberry suffered a comparable fate. "It is not at all farfetched," Baldwin suggests, "to suspect that what [Hansberry] saw contributed to the strain which killed her, for the effort to which Lorraine was dedicated is more than enough to kill a man." Taken together, Hansberry's art and lived experiences reflect her critical consciousness of a stark historical reality: that is, the wage of blackness is often death. And yet, despite her cognizance of the institutional structures and procedures that instantiate black death, she refused to grant to these forces unbridled power over the sum of black life. In her own words, Lorraine Hansberry was "determined to live" (45).

The thick tension that moves between black life and black death is manifest in the set that Hansberry imagines for *A Raisin in the Sun*. This is especially true of the living room, in which most of the dramatic action unfolds. Everything about the room and its contents signify the impending arrival of an end, an approaching finality that mimics the black death encircling the fringes of the Youngers' existence. But Hansberry interjects a telling remark, a significant philosophical provocation, that rubs up against the web of deathly imagery that pervades the play: "All pretenses but living itself have long since vanished from the very atmosphere of this room" (Hansberry [1959] 1995: 102). Hansberry frames the act of living as a pretense among a wider field of pretense; the only pretense, in fact, that has survived. On the one hand, this notion of living-as-pretense suggests that those who claim to "live" while occupying dying territory are merely pretending toward life, clinging to an artifice that conceals a more realistic death. In this way, the charge of pretense functions as a claim about the truth and authenticity of life and death, and it hinges on a rigid set of evidentiary standards.

While it is certainly not difficult to detect the formidable presence of black death throughout the play, what if the characters in *A Raisin in the Sun* occasionally feel alive and outside the walls of death? Who, then, can claim to be the arbiter of truth and authenticity in this instance, the judge of pretense? Considering the plot of Hansberry's play, and the broader bend of her extensive corpus of work, I would argue that for Hansberry the pretense of living is an occasional mode of experiencing rather than feigning black life. Living in a dark and cramped tenement, and suffering the weight of capitalism, sexism, and racism, there are several moments throughout the play that can be said to index feelings of social death. I am no more interested in denying these moments than I am in ignoring the voices of those who sometimes feel wretched, but at other times don't. Who has the power to frame as eternally dead those who in no uncertain terms claim, I am free, I am alive?

Much like Simone, Lorraine Hansberry understood the affective utility and the rhetorical power of the wish, especially when mobilized to will black life into being. "I wish to live," Hansberry exclaimed, "because life has within it that which is good, that which is beautiful, and that which is love. . . . Since I have known all of these things, I have found them to be reason enough and—I wish to live. . . . I wish others to live for generations and generations and generations" (Nemiroff [1969] 1995: 40–41). It could seem, perhaps, that Hansberry's wish is steeped in the deceptive logics of what literary theorist Lauren Berlant has called "cruel optimism" (Berlant 2011). In other words, Hansberry's wish for (the good) life potentially signifies an attachment to a "significantly problematic object" (24). Perpetually elusive, the object instigates a strenuous pursuit that eventually "wears out" the subject who chases it to no avail. For Hansberry, the problematic object, which is to say (the good) life, was made even more problematic by the fraught confluence of her race, gender, and sexuality. This alchemy was enough to render the struggle for life itself—emptied of the modifier *good*—an utterly taxing enterprise that succeeded, according to Baldwin, in wearing Hansberry out.

But Hansberry understood that black subjection was never infinite in its capacity to anticipate and shape black ontology. She recognized that as gratuitously violent as structures of anti-black oppression are they do not highjack the totality of black being. Throughout her work, Hansberry challenges absolutist logic and exposes the limitations of tethering black being to the anticipation of experience. One of her most stark and creative works in this vein is her little-known 1960s unpublished and unproduced playlet *The Arrival of Mr. Todog*—a parody of Samuel Beckett's *Waiting for Godot*.

"As It Were": Hansberry's Aesthetics of the Contingent

In *The Arrival of Mister Todog*, Hansberry's challenge to absolutist logic commences before the action of the play begins, namely, through repeated uses of the phrase "as it were" in the stage directions. Describing the play's setting, she writes,

> AT RISE: We are exposed to a great plain, *a wasteland, as it were*. A few hills rise in the background. Wending through it all is *a road which disappears, as it were*, into the horizon in either direction. Stage that as you will. At right or left of no place in particular—there is *a tree. Barren, as it were*.
>   There is nothing else." (Hansberry 1966: 1)

By definition, "as it were" denotes a relation that is not formally exact though practically right. Slight but significant, this distinction indexes a relation of proximity rather than one of total alignment. Put another way, Hansberry's stage directions call attention to the importance of the interstitial space that separates the formally exact and the practically right. The very existence of this break—however narrow it might be—pressures the enclosing logics of absolutist frames. In this way, things are not always and totally what they might appear or have been commissioned to be, even as they tread dangerously close.

Hansberry situates the line "as it were" after her descriptions of the geography and landscape that constitute the play's setting. Separated by a comma, this idiomatic expression modifies those elements of the setting that precede each of its appearances: the wasteland, the road, and the tree. This gesture reconfigures and destabilizes a range of meanings that audiences, performers, and directors might be inclined to graft onto such familiar and highly symbolic dimensions of the setting. Consider, for instance, the wasteland: a metaphor that is habitually associated with plaguing deficits and surpluses, death and decay, ugliness and neglect. Hansberry's rendering of a "barren" tree signals her awareness of the negative metaphoricity often attached to wastelands. But in attaching the phrase "as it were," she not only destabilizes the conventional meanings of the wasteland but also shows how the wasteland comes to exist as a negative metaphor because its identity as such is consistently repeated and rehearsed in the realms of language and cultural imagination. This performative repetition comes to naturalize as truth, fact, and absolute that which is in reality far more contingent.

This performative constitution of being is as relevant to Hansberry's depiction of the road and the far more positive metaphoricity that it evokes. Like the wasteland and the barren tree, the road is a product of the discursive economies of language and cultural imagination. According to the stage directions, both of the road's outer extremities disappear into the horizon, seeming to afford some prospect of escaping the desolate territory of the wasteland. A potentially transcendent voyage, movement along the road can perhaps lead to a place where the wasteland encounters the sky, where a dismal space of aborted futures transitions into an *empyrean* site of openness, possibility, and freedom. The particular contexts of black experience make difficult any reading of the road—or of black ontology—as unfettered freedom, but also challenge any static interpretations of these entities as total oppression. From New World slavery to Jim Crowism to anti-black Apartheid, black people's ability to move unencumbered along the "road" has been compromised at every turn—figuratively, of course, but also quite literally in and through legal measures like the Black Codes and racial spatial segregation. Yet, this same history bears witness to how people of African descent have transformed the very shape and meanings of the wasteland, how they have converted these allegedly wasted sites—including black ontology itself—into places of home, pleasure, possibility, and even freedom. This tension, complexity, and ambiguity of meaning highlight the conceptual and theoretical import of Hansberry's use of "as it were" in the stage directions. Emphasizing the interstitial space between the formally exact and the practically right, the playwright acknowledges a slipperiness of meaning, a fungibility of experience, in her subtle and playful challenges to the stability of metaphorical meaning itself.

One of the chief tensions that moves between Locke's affective theory of valuation and much of Afro-pessimist thought is how they envision the relationship between experience and ontology. According to Frank Wilderson, black freedom is "an ontological, rather than experiential, question" (Wilderson 2010: 23). "There is no philosophically credible way," he contends, to "attach an experiential, a contingent, rider onto the notion of freedom when one considers the black" (23). But, for Locke, to evacuate the "contingent" from philosophical discourse would be to cultivate the seeds of absolutism, and to negate the value of experiential perspective. He contends, in fact, that the "gravest problem" of contemporary philosophy is the absence of the contingent—a void that, in his estimation, produces narratives of value that are rooted in "dogmatism." Philosophies, he posits, are "products of time, place and situation, and thus systems of timed history rather than timeless eternity" (Locke [1935] 1989: 37). Hansberry and Simone show how experience is not antithetical to black ontology but is rather constitutive of it. As black ontology moves through time, and as the pendulum of black being swings from freedom to unfreedom, from social life to social death, it is in the contingent and interstitial spaces of black being that we can locate the true nature of black ontology. As *The Arrival of Mr. Todog* proceeds, Hansberry urges a more careful attention to the metaphysics of the wasteland, encouraging a questioning of its ontology that accounts, as Locke urges, as much for the contingent and the specific context as for the anticipation of experience. Throughout *The Arrival of Mr. Todog*, Hansberry suggests that time matters to ontology insofar as specific engagements with the wasteland potentially challenge its very existence as such. Reading the play with this symbolic grammar in mind uncovers interpretations of the play—its characters, settings, props, and themes—that exceed customary (metaphorical) meaning. In doing so, it also spotlights the limits of reducing black experience to a singular, paradigmatic modality. A barren tree and a wasteland, Hansberry shows, no more signify *total* ruin than a wending road on the horizon signifies *complete* freedom.

When *The Arrival of Mr. Todog* opens, the audience meets Mary and POOPOO, two protagonists who enter the stage dressed as "indigents," toting bundles usually lugged by "tramps in the comic strips and in modern drama" (Hansberry 1966: 1). Samuel Beckett's *Waiting for Godot* is obviously one of these dramas that Hansberry has in mind. Mary and POOPOO bear an uncanny resemblance to Vladimir and Estragon, Beckett's own hopeless "tramps"-turned-protagonists. But Hansberry revises the script and the characterization significantly, namely by replacing Beckett's pessimistic ethos with a spirit of hope, optimism, and freedom. Especially notable in this regard is how Hansberry recasts two of the most notable props/costume items in the play: one of the tramp's boots and a rope. When Beckett opens his version of events, the audience finds Estragon weary, out of breath, struggling to remove a boot from his foot. After a cycle of failing and trying again, he gives up, concluding that there was "[n]othing to be done" (Beckett [1952] 1954: 1). Vladimir agrees: "I'm beginning to come round to that opinion. All my life I've tried to put it from me, saying Vladimir, be reasonable, you haven't yet tried everything. And I resumed the struggle. (*He broods, musing on the struggle. Turning to Estragon.*) So there you are again" (1). Counter to Beckett's pessimistic and absolutist narrative of doom, in Hansberry's parodic version of events "Mary puts down his bundle and sits on it and takes off his shoe and smells it and puts it back on again and then takes it off again and then puts it on and then takes it off and then puts it on and then takes it off. This goes on until the action is, as it were, established" (Hansberry 1966: 1). Rather than a fatal and unachievable mission, removing the boot is not only possible but the repetition of the removal suggests that it is seamless and without complication.

Similarly, another of the most iconic props in Beckett's *Waiting for Godot* is a rope that defines the relation between Lucky and Pozzo, two characters who play a master/slave duo. Not only does Lucky, the slave, have the rope fastened around his neck, but Pozzo, his master, holds the rope in his hand, thus controlling it. The rope also surfaces in Beckett's play as a prop to aid in the commission of suicide. Navigating an environment that is thick with doom and terror, Vladimir and Estragon contemplate suicide. They abandon this journey toward death when they discover that they have no rope. In *The Arrival of Mister Todog*, Hansberry radically reimagines the meaning of the rope, framing it as an instrument of joy and pleasure rather than a tool of self-imposed death. When POOPOO asks Mary for a "bit of rope," Mary responds by asking if POOPOO planned to hang them. POOPOO not only answers "no" but asks what motivated the question. Mary's answer is telling: "I don't know. I simply think it's the sort of thing that would occur to anyone in this desolate setting." "It isn't desolate because you're here," POOPOO retorts, before clarifying what sparked a desire for the rope: "Because it is an extraordinarily nice day and I thought we might skip it a bit." Finding this "divine," Mary pulls out a rope and they start to skip together, "smiling heavenly at one another" (4).

Perhaps the starkest revision that Hansberry makes to Beckett's pessimistic and absolutist narrative is altering the meaning of Godot himself, who reappears in Hansberry's satirical reimagining as TODOG: literally a reverse spelling of GODOT. This inversion is carried out in the plot. Whereas Beckett's protagonists are trapped in a cycle of waiting for the arrival of one Mr. Godot, someone who has made no promises to come, Hansberry's characters decide to abandon the wait, and conclude in fact, "We are he. All of us—on this barren landscape. We are TODOG!" (9).

MARY:

You mean there isn't anyone to make up the rules?

POOPOO:

No one to make up the rules!

MARY:

No one to say yes when you think you feel no?

POOPOO:

No one to say yes when you think you feel no.

MARY:

No one to say no when you think you feel yes?

POOPOO:

No one to say no when you think you feel yes.

MARY:

You mean—utterly?

POOPOO:

UTTERLY

MARY:

No upstairs and downstairs?

BOTH:

No upstairs and downstairs!

MARY:

You mean that we are really and truly completely and in all ways free—and that, moreover,

(gesturing)

ALL of this belongs to us—not to him?

BOTH:

We ARE him—it all belongs to us— (10)

"[H]ow MAH-VAH-LOUS," Mary replies. Pulling out party favors, balloons, and streamers, they decide to celebrate, having "an absolute ball" as the joyful tune of "Auld Lang Syne" plays in the background. "Oh, the habits you get into on this road!" (11). In effect, rather than continue waiting for some abstract, invisible entity who exerts control over their worlds, Hansberry's protagonists decide to reorient their relationship to this figure as well as to the territory of what once existed as a wasteland. By the time the play reaches its denouement, in fact, the wasteland is no longer a place of incessant waiting, terror, slavery, and uncertain futures, but is rather a site of joy and pleasure—a party thriving with sociality.[5]

It is worth pointing out that in her efforts to resist the pessimistic and absolutist enclosures of Beckett's *Waiting for Godot*, and the general air of pessimism that defined so much modern literature in the postwar modern world, Hansberry risks falling into an absolutist trap of her own. That is, in her resistance to the absolutism of pessimistic art and philosophy, she could seem to nearly make invisible the structures of oppression that continue to shape the wasteland, even as its subjects recalibrate their relationship to it, which is hardly the case in works like *Raisin*. But instead of reading Hansberry's alternative plot and resolution as absolutism, I would posit that they function in a way similar to Nina Simone's sudden feelings of freedom.

Rather than serve as an indicator of a stable paradigm of black freedom and ontology, they are moments along a continuum—points in time that must be read alongside other points. This is why it is important to think about the time of black ontology, its specific contexts and interrelationships. It is through a comparative analysis of all of these moments that we can best grapple with and understand black ontology and engage in the practice of structural critique. Doing so reveals how, rather than a fixed or absolutist entity that can always be anticipated, black ontology is a dynamic mode of being that is always on the run through time.

Notes

1   For a brilliant discussion of the conditions of (anti-)blackness as weather and climate, see Sharpe 2016. Sharpe theorizes weather as predictable "death" and "disaster," an environment in which "anti-blackness is pervasive as climate." But, importantly, she points out that weather is also "possibility," that it "necessitates changeability and improvisation" and is the "condition of time and place" (105–6).

2   Here, I am not encouraging an ahistorical, feel-good, socio-politically irreflective framework for analyzing the exigencies of black being. What I am suggesting is that Simone's experience in this performance of knowing and feeling freedom, however fleeting this experience might be, indexes the centrality of black feeling to conceptions of black freedom.

3   This point has been elaborated in the work of performance studies scholars like E. Patrick Johnson (2003), Daphne Brooks (2006), Harvey Young (2010), Stephanie Batiste (2011), Jayna Brown (2008), Koritha Mitchell (2011), Soyica Colbert (2011), and Uri McMillan (2015), for example.

4   Jared Sexton (2011: 40), a theorist of Afro-pessimism who describes this intellectual orientation as a "complication of the assumptive logic" of black cultural and performance studies, contends that Wilderson's position "has been misconstrued as a negation of the agency of black performance." According to Sexton (2011: 33–34), Wilderson "is indicating not so much that ontology is not performative, but rather more so that performativity does not, in fact, have disruptive power at the level or in the way that it has been theorized to date." In this essay, my goal is not to overestimate the transformative potential of black performance but to insist that black performance contains the capacity to shape black ontology in ways that Afro-pessimist discourses often downplay and negate.

5   This transformation of oppressive geographies into sites of black political possibility has been theorized in detail by scholars like Katherine McKittrick, Thadious M. Davis, Rashad Shabazz, and Judith Madera.

References

Batiste, Stephanie. 2011. *Darkening Mirrors: Imperial Representation in Depression-Era African American Performance.* Durham, NC: Duke University Press.

Beckett, Samuel. (1952) 1954. *Waiting for Godot.* New York: Grove Press.

Berlant, Lauren. 2011. *Cruel Optimism.* Durham, NC: Duke University Press.

Brooks, Daphne. 2006. *Bodies in Dissent: Spectacular Performances of Race and Freedom, 1850–1910*. Durham, NC: Duke University Press.

Brown, Jayna. 2008. *Babylon Girls: Black Women Performers and the Shaping of the Modern*. Durham, NC: Duke University Press.

Colbert, Soyica Diggs. 2011. *The African American Theatrical Body: Reception, Performance, and the Stage*. New York: Cambridge University Press.

Cvetkovich, Ann. 2003. *Archive of Feelings*. Durham, NC: Duke University Press.

Hansberry, Lorraine. (1959) 1995. *A Raisin in the Sun*. New York: Vintage.

Hansberry, Lorraine. 1966. *The Arrival of Mr. Todog*. Lorraine Hansberry Papers. The Schomburg Center for Research in Black Culture, New York.

Johnson, E. Patrick. 2003. *Appropriating Blackness: Performance and the Politics of Authenticity*. Durham, NC: Duke University Press.

Locke, Alain. (1935) 1989. *The Philosophy of Alain Locke: Harlem Renaissance and Beyond*. Edited by Leonard Harris. Philadelphia: Temple University Press.

McMillan, Uri. 2015. *Embodied Avatars: Genealogies of Black Feminist Art and Performance*. New York: New York University Press.

Mitchell, Koritha. 2011. *Living with Lynching: African American Lynching Plays, Performance, and Citizenship, 1890–1930*. Urbana: University of Illinois Press.

Moten, Fred. 2008. "The Case of Blackness." *Criticism* 50, no. 2: 177–218.

Moten, Fred. 2013. "Blackness and Nothingness (Mysticism in the Flesh)." *South Atlantic Quarterly* 112, no. 4: 737–80.

Muñoz, José Esteban. 2006. "Feeling Brown, Feeling Down: Latina Affect, the Performativity of Race, and the Depressive Position." *Signs: Journal of Women in Culture and Society* 31, no. 3: 675–88.

Nemiroff, Robert. (1969) 1995. *To Be Young, Gifted, and Black: Lorraine Hansberry in Her Own Words*. New York: Vintage.

Quashie, Kevin. 2021. *Black Aliveness or a Poetics of Being*. Durham, NC: Duke University Press.

Sexton, Jared. 2011. "The Social Life of Social Death: On Afro-Pessimism and Black Optimism." *InTensions* 5, no. 1: 1–47.

Sharpe, Christina. 2016. *In the Wake: On Blackness and Being*. Durham, NC: Duke University Press.

Spillers, Hortense J. 2003. "Who Cuts the Border? Some Readings on America." *Black, White, and in Color: Essays on American Literature and Culture*. Chicago: University of Chicago Press.

Young, Harvey. 2010. *Embodying Black Experience: Stillness, Critical Memory, and the Black Body*. Ann Arbor: University of Michigan Press.

Wilderson, Frank B., III. 2010. *Red, White, and Black: Cinema and the Structure of US Antagonisms*. Durham, NC: Duke University Press.

Margo Natalie Crawford

What Time Is It When You're Black?

What *time is it when you're black?* In the poetry volume *Finna*, Nate Marshall (2020) offers "finna" as an answer to this question. Marshall defines *finna* as

1. going to; intending to [rooted in African American Vernacular English]
2. eye dialect spelling of "fixing to"
3. black possibility; black futurity; blackness as tomorrow (back cover)

The everyday use of *finna*, in the interiority of black community, reshapes a universal feeling into a state of anticipation that is specifically black. *Finna* is the feeling of urgency and expectancy produced by what Michael Sawyer (2018: vii) describes as black fractured temporality—"Be(ing) Out of Time." Sawyer argues that black "be(ing) out of time" is created by the "time-fracturing technologies" that have shaped black subjects, technologies such as the transatlantic slave trade, slavery, white supremacy, police brutality, and so on (2018: vii). The Ellisonian "different sense of time" created by these shattering technologies is being reimagined, in the first decades of twenty-first century African American literature, through new frames. Claudia Rankine's *time of the sigh*, in *Citizen: An American Lyric* (2014) and *The White Card* (2019), and

The South Atlantic Quarterly 121:1, January 2022
DOI 10.1215/00382876-9561601 © 2022 Duke University Press

Toni Morrison's *time of the open body* and the *anticipation of second skin*, in *Five Poems* (2002) and *God Help the Child* (2015), are twenty-first-century recalibrations of Frantz Fanon's theory of the "slow composition of my *self* as a body in the middle of a spatial and temporal world" (Fanon 1967: 111). Reading Rankine alongside Morrison makes us rehear this iconic Fanonian premise as the "slow composition of my *flesh* as a body in the middle of a spatial and temporal world." Twenty-first-century African American literature is opening up new dimensions of the liminal space where black flesh *never* quite consolidates into the black body. Black flesh is always "finna" be contained and always subverting the forces of containment. The black radical imagination is set in motion by the liminality and openness of black flesh.

Toward a Theory of *Finna*

The liminality of the black vernacular "finna" is the old, black vernacular grammar that continues to sound too new to be assimilated into standard English. Suspended between shattering historical trauma and a present that is marked and not marked by that historical trauma, blackened people live in a state of *finna*. The liminality of the past deeply shaping the present, even as the present begins to move away from that past, is the feeling of *finna*. "Finna" is the sound of the "immediate future" and it is also a "preparatory activity between the speech act and the action to which it refers" (Zanuttini et al. 2018). Marshall's *finna* is an aesthetics of black temporality that makes the everyday experience of anticipation feel like the immediacy of futurity, the touching of what is almost here. The black *finna* is the "already here" of the "not yet here." José Muñoz, in *Cruising Utopia*, rethinks queer aesthetics as the art of what is "not yet here" (2009). In *The Sense of Brown*, Muñoz separates brownness from the not yet here of queerness: "I suggest queerness is in the horizon, forward dawning and not-yet-here. Brownness diverges from my definition of queerness. Brownness is already here" (Muñoz 2020: 121–22). The space that Muñoz gives "brown," the way he allows it to be amorphous and a collective feeling, is similar to the lowercase "blackness" that moves in and out of the settled identity of "Black." When Marshall, in the poem "Finna," slides from capitalized blackness to lowercase brownness ("it's Black / & it's brown & it's alive"), the settled identity of "black" (the only capitalized word in the poem) is wonderfully undone as the lowercase brownness makes the capitalized blackness lose the aura of the definitive and gain the rhythm of *finna* (the repetition of the ampersand).

The feeling of blackness as *finna* is steadily erased when the past overdetermines the black present and makes black life the afterlife of trauma that has already happened. As the already here of the not yet here, black *finna* is the tingle that can only be felt by the person living the already here of the not yet here. The 2020 move to standardize the capitalization of the word *black* cancels out black *finna*. In the summer of 2020, during the national and transnational Black Lives Matter protests, the *New York Times* decided to begin capitalizing "black." W. E. B. Du Bois, in 1926, started a movement to push the *New York Times* and other publications to capitalize the word *negro*. In 1930, the *New York Times* agreed to begin capitalizing "negro." This *New York Times* mainstream media shift to "Black" has motivated many other publishers, academics, journalists, and people in social media to shift to capitalizing "black" with consistency as if lowercase blackness is an inability to understand what blackness signifies. But lowercase blackness is the already here of the not yet here; capitalized Blackness is simply already here.

When the *New York Times* framed their 2020 decision to capitalize *black* by invoking Du Bois's 1926 campaign for the capitalization of *Negro*, the difference between "Negro" and "Black" was effaced. But lowercase *negro* never had the signifying power tied to lower- or uppercase blackness. During the 1960s global Black Power Movement, people of African descent rejected the name "negro" and mobilized "black" as a way of naming and hailing a new collective consciousness, a new way of thinking, appearing, and feeling—what A. B. Spellman (1998: 52–53) described as the "sensuality of a collective consciousness that declared itself on sight." The Black Arts and Black Power movements mobilized "black" as an identity and as a world. The words "Black World" are omnipresent during the Black Arts and Black Power movements. These liberation movements created space for the *world* of unsettled lowercase blackness that is much more complex than a fixed identity. In the fall semester of 2020, one of my students included the following footnote as she explained her use of capitalized "Black" throughout her essay: "My capitalization of the word 'Black' is a reclamation, a resistance to Blackness and Black people being relegated to un-proper categories. 'Black' is a color. 'Black' is an identity, proper." This student wants "black" to signal a "proper" identity. Her reference to the "un-proper categories" (embedded in lowercase blackness) reveals a lack of interest in the black space and time of *disorder* that the 2020 widespread move to standardize the capitalization of "black" is shutting down. The impulse to fix black disorder and standardize what cannot be standardized cannot crush the impulse to create the nonstandard English aesthetic possibilities of *finna*.

The temporality of lowercase blackness animates the wave of twenty-first-century black art that gestures, in many different ways, to the unmarking of "the black past equals the black present" and the scenes of loosening what Toni Morrison, in "The Slavebody and the Blackbody" (2019), describes as the equation of "slavebody" and the "blackbody" (2019: 74–78). When Morrison, in *A Mercy*, writes, "You say I am wilderness. I am," we hear the state of being possessed by dispossession, the state of lowercase blackness (2008: 184). Fred Moten, in *Black and Blur*, develops this idea of being possessed by dispossession. Moten calls for "acknowledging what it is to own dispossession, which cannot be owned but by which one can be possessed" (Moten 2017: 85). In *A Mercy*, the poetics of dispossession becomes the poetics of *finna* when Morrison gives us the most tender line in the novel: "I need Lina to say how to shelter in wilderness" (Morrison 2008: 49). When Florens delivers these words, she is in the colonial America, pre-consolidation of "slave equals black" zone. She is in what Morrison describes as "ad hoc territory" (15). Florens needs Lina "to say how" to live in the in-between zone of being marked and not marked. She needs Lina "to say how" to live her blackness as shelter and wilderness, as marked and unmarked. Once Lina "says how," Florens is *finna* be her own shelter in her own wilderness. *Finna* is the only verb tense that expresses what is black about what she needs from Lina, what is black about this desire, this need, to "shelter in wilderness."

Finna is the verb tense that captures the lower frequencies of Morrison's famous words "we do language" (as opposed to being done by language). Florens *finna do language*, at the end of *A Mercy*, when Morrison imagines her writing on the walls of the master's house and learning "to say how" on her own terms, once she reaches the point of claiming the wilderness as her shelter. Moten's way of thinking about the "possessed by dispossession" lived experience of blackness has a temporality—the temporality that Hortense Spillers describes as the latent movement in the still being. Spillers's words "Something still is about to move" express the feeling of *black finna* (Spillers 2010). This non-gap between black stillness and black motion is felt in Claudia Rankine's *Citizen* when she makes the black sigh express a type of melancholic hope that is the time of the "pathway to breath" (Rankine 2014: 60).

The Time of the Sigh

The "pathway to breath" is, in *Citizen*, the state of stillness "about to move" and become the release of outbreath. In many parts of *Citizen*, Rankine makes the sigh signal what it feels like to be a black person who is trapped because she is both inside and outside of the trauma of what Fanon describes as the "slow composition of my *self* as a body in the middle of a spatial and temporal world" (Fanon 1967: 111). The sigh for Rankine is the slow denaturalizing of the black-body-in-pain. Rankine makes the sigh signal a partially unconscious letting out of that which one never wanted to take in. She describes the black body becoming a "cupboard" and then makes the sigh the black bodily response that creates discomfort because it has an opacity that differs from expressions of pure pain. The sigh is ambiguous. Rankine muses, "You sit down, you sigh. You stand up, you sigh. The sighing is a worrying exhale of an ache. You wouldn't call it an illness; still it is not the iteration of a free being" (Rankine 2014: 60). The sigh and the repression of the sigh, for Rankine, signal the heaviness of black flesh becoming a "cupboard" of the past and the disorientation a black subject feels as she is always hesitating, always on the edge of "moving on" (63, 66). Rankine makes the Black Lives Matter mantra "I can't breathe" morph into "I can't sigh": "Sometimes you sigh. The world says stop that. Another sigh. Another stop that" (59). The involuntary sigh, for Rankine, becomes a way of understanding the horror of all of the forces that make it so difficult to breathe while black. Rankine also makes the sigh a way of understanding the horror of the spectacle that keeps naturalizing black pain and erasing the possibility of release from that pain. She knows that the sigh is usually associated with sadness, but she makes the sigh signal a release of tension that cannot be pinned down as simply sadness. The sigh, in *Citizen*, signals the black emotional release that is shut down by the everyday performance of white privilege that makes it so hard to breathe while black. When Rankine makes it clear that the sigh is the "pathway to breath" and "allows breathing" (the release that would be necessary before one can breathe deeply), we feel the urgency of "I can't sigh" as the refusal of the idea that black people are *always already* having trouble breathing (60). Rankine writes, "Do you remember when you sighed?" (63).

Even as she centralizes the murder of Trayvon Martin and inveighs against the violence of an anti-black police structure that began during slavery, she also troubles the naturalizing of a culture of black pain. Rankine refuses to reproduce a culture of black pain even as she shows how steady the everyday enactments of white supremacy are. She creates space for an understanding of the "self-preservation" that is seized even as the anti-blackness continues to injure (60). After describing a couple's pain as they sit in the car hearing the news of Trayvon Martin's murderer being declared not guilty, she writes, "A breeze touches your cheek. / As something should" (151). The breeze on the cheek is a sign of what is not legible in the discourse that continues to imagine the black body as a collective, public place of pain. Rankine foregrounds the idea of black bodies as "public places" when she depicts the rhythm of "lay[ing] your body in the body." The full passage is:

> When you lay your body in the body
> entered as if skin and bone were public places,
> when you lay your body in the body
> entered as if you're the ground you walk on,
> you know no memory should live in these memories
> becoming the body of you. (144)

The feeling expressed in the words "entered as if skin and bone were public places" is often the feeling of *entered as if skin and bone were the public places of the black past*. Rankine expresses the horror of one's skin and bone becoming a public repository of the black past.

In the play *The White Card*, Rankine dramatizes the practice of "laying your body in the body" (2019: 61–62). The character Charlotte puts her body alongside the sculpture art (placed on the ground) that is an autopsy outline of Michael Brown's body after he was murdered by the white policeman. The scene is in the living room of the white collectors of black art (and black pain). Charlotte, when she lies on the floor and fills in the autopsy outline with her body, is trying to find a way to fight the violence of the white collectors' treatment of the black body as a public place where black pain can be aestheticized and owned and exhibited as art. As Charlotte lies on the floor, the white people who have invited her to this dinner party in their house continue to talk. Charlotte lies in silence as they argue. As this silent protest is performed on the theater stage, time slows down. The rush of the dialogue cannot move with the same frenzy as we look at Charlotte's body next to the artistic rendering of the autopsy of Michael Brown. Charlotte is shocked when Charles (the white art collector and investor in the building of prisons) unveils this art that gestures to Kenneth Goldsmith's 2015 reading of Michael Brown's autopsy report as a poem (Goldsmith's conceptual art performance "The Body of Michael Brown").

Charlotte is a black artist whose practice of reenactment (with photography) aims to make people see what they could not see in the "original" representations of acts of anti-black violence. After witnessing Charles's way of talking about this "artistic autopsy" that he has bought, Charlotte abandons her interest in reenactment and begins a new art project that aims to make whiteness visible. As Charles, in scene 2, looks at an excessive number of photographs of his skin, Rankine creates a sense of the slow composition of the *white self* as a *white body* in the middle of a spatial and temporal world. Rankine reshapes Fanon's "slow composition of my *self* as a body in the middle of a spatial and temporal world" into a focus on the white "burdens of epidermal inscription" (Cheng 2011: 13). In *Second Skin*, Anne Cheng describes the dream of a second skin as, for blackened subjects, the desire to "escape the burdens of epidermal inscription" (13). When Charlotte makes Charles the object of her photographic lens, she refuses to allow Charles to "escape the burden of epidermal inscription." When Charles sees the photographs that Charlotte has taken of him as she followed him without his being aware of her camera's gaze, he feels so much disorientation and frustration that he eventually removes his shirt, puts his hands in the air, and asks her to shoot him. The slow composition of his white self as a white body in the middle of a spatial and temporal world overwhelms him. Rankine, in scene one of this play, makes Rauschenberg's *White Painting* one of the works of art that Charles owns and displays in his living room. Charlotte's photographs of Charles's whiteness beg to be compared to Rauschenberg's *White Painting*. Rankine seems to be asking us to see the racialized and not racialized dimensions of Rauschenberg's painting as we also learn to see the marking and possible unmarking of whiteness and blackness on the bodies of Charles and Charlotte.

The White Card ends with the click and flash of a camera. Rankine ends with the sense of a photograph being taken (a photograph that, unlike Charlotte's photographs, will not be seen by the audience, a photograph that is not yet here). This final sound in this play is the ephemeral click and flash that disrupts the thick time that makes skin a receptacle of race (the time that shapes the earlier parts of scene 2 that make Charlotte's black body and Charles's white body the *matter* of race). After Charlotte rages against white power by making Charles's whiteness visible, Charles finally begins to discover (finally begins to realize) the white privilege imprinted on his skin and then muses about the everyday shedding of skin. The final sound of the click and flash of the camera is the temporal and spatial world of the shedding (the unmarking) of race. The play must end with this click and flash of the unmarking; we cannot fully experience this unmarking but we imagine the unimaginable. We almost feel the unmarking; the unmarking seems so close. It is *finna* happen. Within this click and flash, we stop believing what we see and begin to learn to see (or feel) what Toni Morrison, in *Paradise* (1997), hails as the "open body."

Morrison introduces the idea of the open body as she imagines, in *Paradise*, a type of art therapy that would allow women to mark and decorate templates of their bodies drawn on a cellar floor and learn, through this marking of the outlines of their bodies, how to shed some of the heaviness of the marks on their actual bodies. The open body emerges, in *Paradise*, as a women-centered alternative to the racial inscription that overdetermines the "8-rock" ideology of the depth of unadulterated blackness, the ideology that shapes the sensibility of the all-black, patriarchal town named Ruby that is set apart from the Convent where the women discover the "open body" (Morrison 1997: 265). The character Seneca "when she had the hunger to slice her inner thigh, . . . chose instead to mark the open body lying on the cellar floor" (265). Morrison makes the open body seem like the women's process of rediscovering the flesh that has been distorted and sculpted into the closed body.

What language can express what black flesh feels like during the fleeting moments of the "open body," when all of the forces of anti-blackness lose their ability to explain black life and we rehear the famous Sam Cooke lyric "change is gonna come" as a description of a radical black present, not an optimistic view of black futures? The lived experience of *finna* (of "gonna come") is not black optimism. It is the radical, impossible practice of black refusal of white power.

The Time of the Open Body

In Antoinette Nwandu's *Pass Over* (2018), the time of the open body is dramatized when Moses proclaims, "against my body / black and free / these weapons that you wield / have no more strength," as his words arrest the power of Ossifer (the white police officer who is attempting to capture him) (95). The words "against my body" express the pushing out of the forces that attempt to claim his body. The stage directions are "The space changes" (95). This time and space of feeling what is "against" the body is the vestibularity of flesh. This is the time and space of what R. A. Judy (2020: 184), in *Sentient Flesh*, describes as the simultaneity of being outside and inside the enclosures that make black subjects become the "enslaved captive body." Judy rethinks Spillers's hieroglyphics of flesh as Spillers's move from the architecture of the vestibule to the abstraction of "vestibularity." For Judy, this vestibularity is the "disciplining action of culture on the flesh" (184–85). When Judy thinks about the vestibule as the space where the "traces of being outside, such as shoes and outerwear, are left," the vestibularity of flesh becomes the in-between space when and where one is becoming the "enslaved captive body" even as the traces of being outside of that pure and total captivity remain (184).

The traces of being outside of the epidermalization of blackness are felt by blackened subjects in ways that remain opaque and illegible (in ways that are too opaque and illegible to continue to be visualized as some sort of double consciousness). In *Five Poems* (2002), a text with poems written by

Toni Morrison and silhouettes created by Kara Walker, the state of feeling the traces of being outside even as one is situated inside is figured, in Morrison's poem "The Perfect Ease of Grain," as "Welcome doors held open / When goodbye is 'So long'" (Morrison 2002: n.p.). Morrison captures the suspended time of what Judy describes as the "boundless exterior" and the "enclosed interior." Morrison's images in this poem are an apt way of rethinking the time of the open black body as the suspended state of the taking off of shoes and outerwear (in Judy's image of the vestibule) and also the suspended state of the holding on to underwear, the suspended state of the undergarments of flesh that race has touched but not removed. Racial epidermalization is the outer clothing that covers but does not remove the undergarments of flesh. In this poem "The Perfect Ease of Grain," the time of flesh is depicted as "Time enough to spill." Morrison makes time of the black open body feel like liquid. The liquid blackness flows through what Judy describes as the "boundless exterior" of flesh that is in the same space and time (the space and time of vestibularity) of what he describes as the "enclosed interior" of the "enslaved captive body." What time is it when you are black? It is, as Morrison teaches us in this poem, the time of liquid spaces that make us feel that which Fanon describes as the "congealed black blood" as actually still congealing (Fanon 1967: 92). In *Five Poems*, Morrison imagines five scenes of the open body, the black embodiment of the not yet here.

The first poem, "Eve Remembering," is the scene of the "undoing of the eyes" and the move to black abandon. As Morrison builds on her images of "bodacious black Eves" in *Paradise* (1997), she makes the black Eve in this poem gain a new way of seeing once she tastes "sweet power." The speaker proclaims, "The taste undid my eyes." Blackness becomes a structure of feeling, not a way of being seen, when we stop seeing what the racial epidermalization of blackness continues to naturalize. When our eyes are "undone," we can feel the freedom of the black abandon that Kara Walker captures in her non-illustration of this poem.

What time is it when you're black? For Walker, in this image, the visual non-answer is: Time for the withdrawal and release and refusal that becomes the space-clearing gesture of the outstretched hand and the taut arm of a black woman torquing and letting go of the eating (or wearing) of the banana given to black Eves who never had access to the forbidden apple given to white Eves.

The second poem, "The Perfect Ease of Grain," makes black abandon feel ecstatic as "red cherries become jam." Morrison writes, "Ecstasy becomes us all." This part of the poetic sequence shapes black abandon into the Ellisonian different experience of time. The "time enough to spill" is, for Morrison, the space of black love where trauma does not define black life. Time that does not spill (time that is contained) cannot explain the excessiveness of black abandon (the lived experiences of being possessed by dispossession). In the third poem, "Someone Leans Near," black abandon is shaped into the "breath" that is "on your skin": "Then on your skin a breath caresses / The salt your eyes have shed." These lines decenter the racial epidermalization of blackness as Morrison makes us imagine the imprint on the skin that the lightness of breath can create. The preposition "on" ("on your skin") signals Morrison's desire to make touched skin an alternative to the racial marking of skin. The fourth poem in this sequence is a move from "touched skin" to the "unadorned," the time of flesh that "comes naked into the world." Morrison, in each poem, moves closer and closer to the impossible unmarking of the black body. The final poem makes it clear that the Middle Passage has made the open body constantly fight to not be an "enslaved captive body": "Look how the fish mistake my hair for home."

When Morrison moves in this poetic sequence, from the "touched skin" to the "unadorned," she signals that there is a layer of ornamentalism embedded in the flesh that is called a black body. The ornamental personhood that Anne Cheng analyzes in *Ornamentalism* is not entirely different from the epidermalization of blackness. Cheng makes *ornamentalism* mean the objecthood that creates personhood (as opposed to the objecthood of blackened subjects who are rendered "parahuman") (Cheng 2019: 3). She poses the question, "What about bodies not undone by objectness but enduring *as* objects?" (22). Morrison's move to the open body is the illegible black ornamentalism (the hieroglyphics of the flesh) that is constantly being misread as the "enslaved captive body" with no access to the objecthood that creates personhood (the ornamental personhood of the yellow woman that Cheng analyzes).

Cheng muses, "Where black femininity is *vestibular,* Asiatic femininity is *ornamental*" (6). The flesh-always-in-the-process-of-becoming-the-black-body is vestibular, but Cheng herself, at the end of *Ornamentalism*, grants that black femininity is both vestibular and ornamental. Cheng draws on Morrison's image of the chokecherry tree on Sethe's back, Spillers's hieroglyphics of the flesh, and Lacan's focus on the tension between petrification and animation as she ends *Ornamentalism* with gestures to the connections between the ornamental personhood of the figure of the yellow woman and the ornamental vestibularity of the figure of the black woman. Cheng does not use this term *ornamental vestibularity,* but she *almost* arrives at this idea as she reveals the connections between the Asiatic femininity that gains life through objecthood and the black femininity that is crushed and undone when rendered an object. The amorphous flesh/body vestibularity of blackness gains the human/object tension of ornamentalism when blackness becomes tied to what Cheng calls "sartorial excess" and the "dream of a second skin" (Cheng 2011: 13).

Black Anticipation of Second Skin

The desire to not be burdened by epidermal inscription makes blackened subjects imagine other ways of being covered. Cheng, at the end of *Ornamentalism*, as she brings "black flesh and yellow ornament" together, proposes, "The flesh that passes through objecthood needs 'ornament' as a way back to itself" (154). She revisits Baby Suggs's sermon on flesh, in *Beloved*, as a means of crystallizing how ornamentalism is a medium that allows black flesh to continue to move through objecthood as black subjects live. I am interested in the conceptual turn that Cheng makes when she implies, at the end of *Ornamentalism* in this theory of passing through objecthood, that her earlier idea of black flesh being undone by objecthood is not entirely true, or if it is true, we must rethink what it means to be "undone." To be undone by objecthood might mean that one is living the undoing of the imagined boundaries between person and thing, and embodying the anticipated, not-yet-here space where blackness is vibrant matter. Cheng cites Paul D's words in *Beloved*: "you are your own best thing." To be undone by objecthood might mean that you are living the already here of the anticipated state of being "your own best thing." Cheng uses Lacan's petrification/animation tension to think about the difference between total crushing objecthood and the state of enduring as an object and developing a personhood that is animated through one's being touched by objects. The animation of "petrified pain" emerges as a way of rethinking the meaning of Spillers's words "hieroglyphics of flesh." Cheng allows us to rethink the hieroglyphics as both a state of opacity (this flesh we might call a black body) and a state of "articulate flesh" (Faulkner's words in *Absalom, Absalom!*). Blackened subjects live with the hieroglyphics of flesh touching and animating their enslaved captive bodies. Ornamental personhood surrounds and animates the petrified objecthood of blackened subjects.

Kara Walker's silhouette images that accompany Morrison's poems in *Five Poems* gesture to the undoing of petrified pain through animation. The silhouettes give shape to black flesh becoming and not becoming the enslaved captive body. Walker created these non-illustrations of Morrison's poems after she received the poems; Morrison wrote the poems before Walker created the silhouettes. The time of these silhouettes is literally the "time enough to spill" that Morrison hails in the second poem in *Five Poems*. Walker's silhouettes "spill" out of the non-container of Morrison's words. Since Gwendolyn DuBois Shaw's (2004) first book-length study of Kara Walker's art, the iconic black-and-white silhouetted figures created by Walker have been analyzed through many lenses, such as "seeing the unspeakable," as satire, and as a simultaneous representation and erasure of scenes of subjection. In *Five Poems*, as Walker's silhouettes speak alongside Morrison's words, they gain a scale that is strikingly different from the life-size images on gallery walls. In *Five Poems*, Walker's silhouettes are not arranged as scenes (as they are when viewed on gallery walls). As Walker responds to Morrison's words and moves to the smaller scale, the silhouettes lose the aura of a life-size narrative and gain the aura of abstract shapes in the process of gaining a recognizable, legible form. Without the life-size narrative (even when it is a blurred narrative) of slavery and the afterlife of slavery that shapes the iconic Walker silhouettes that have appeared on gallery walls, the Walker images in *Five Poems* pivot on the suspension of the body (not the suspension of time that we feel in the cinematic gallery wall images). This suspension of the body, in these images, produces a tension between forces that petrify the black subject and forces that allow her to keep moving. The most powerful connection between Morrison's words in the poems and Walker's images may be the feeling of the "unadorned," the time of flesh that "comes naked into the world." As Walker responds to these words written by Morrison, she captures the form of form-lessness that Morrison conveys. In Walker's images, Morrison's sense of the "unadorned" nakedness is transfigured into the adornment of nakedness as the silhouettes make clothing look like skin. The inseparability of nakedness and adornment saturates Walker's images. The edges of the cut-out silhouettes evoke the precarious edge between seeing arrested objects (enslaved captive bodies), signaled in Walker's images as naked primitivized black bodies, and seeing the motion of ornamental personhood, signaled in Walker's images as post-black body, fleshy shapes of black futurity.

Morrison, in *Tar Baby*, helps us feel the temporal dimension of this black ornamental personhood. She makes potentiality the tempo of this impulse to decorate as a way to escape the racial epidermalization. When Son in *Tar Baby* "just" needs Alma Estée to stand still in order to restore order to his sense of natural black beauty, it becomes clear that black ornamentalism is the kinetic energy, the movement of *finna*, that disrupts the stasis of racial epidermalization. Morrison writes,

Figure 1. Toni Morrison, *Five Poems*, illustrated by Kara Walker (Las Vegas: Rainmaker Editions, 2002), n.p.

> So he [Son] had changed, given up fraternity, or believed he had, until he
> saw Alma Estée in a wig the color of dried blood. Her sweet face, her mid-
> night skin mocked and destroyed by the pile of synthetic dried blood on her
> head. It was all mixed up. But he could have sorted it out if she had just stood
> there like a bougainvillea in a girdle, like a baby jaguar with lipstick on, like
> an avocado with earrings, and let him remove it. (Morrison 1981: 299)

This passage is a signature image of the difference between Fanon's idea of
"crushing objecthood" and Cheng's idea of ornamental personhood (the
idea that people can endure as objects and not be undone as objects). Son
cannot understand that Alma Estée is living in a state of potentiality as she
makes her body an assemblage that is "all mixed up."

Toni Morrison, in *God Help the Child*, her final novel and only novel set
in the twenty-first century, directly focuses on the theme of black ornamental personhood. The novel stages the difference between the temporal and
spatial dimensions of *enduring* through objecthood in a manner that contrasts greatly with the images of being shattered through objecthood in her
first novel, *The Bluest Eye*. Images of the interaction of people and objects
abound in *God Help the Child*: Bride's smile interacting with the lipstick
imprint of a smile on a wine glass, the image of Bride and Booker's spines
interacting with the car seats' "soft hide of cattle," and repeated images of
Booker's shaving brush rubbing against and being rubbed against Bride's
skin (Morrison 2015). Morrison makes the friction between people and surfaces matter as the tension between surface and depth becomes the prime
theme of the novel. Bride's mother cannot bear to touch Bride when she is a
child because she recoils from what seems to have always already marked
her as bound to have a hard, thick life of black trauma. Bride's ongoing fasci-
nation with the aliveness of objects that retain the touch of Booker occurs
alongside images of Bride's body literally becoming less marked by thick-
ness as she loses weight and gains a strange surface smoothness as her ear
piercings close and her pubic hair disappears with a total erasure different
from any waxing or shaving. Bride wears white clothing every day in order to
accentuate her dark skin and shape it into a glowing ornament. As Bride
becomes a well-paid executive in the beauty industry, her ornamental personhood (the everyday wearing of white clothes that make her dark skin
glow) makes her feel that she is no longer crushed by the colorism, performed by her mother, that made her childhood years so painful. In *God
Help the Child*, the white clothes (the seeming counterpart to Alma Estée's
red wig in *Tar Baby*) are Bride's dream of a second skin.

Cheng, in *Second Skin*, quickly but powerfully moves from white modernist fantasies of this second skin to black dreams of escaping the naturalized idea that the black body is eternally marked by the anti-black gaze. Morrison, in her images of Bride, shapes the black dream of a second skin into the actual lived experience of ornamentalized, exoticized dark skin as a covering and (as Bride's *black-in-white-clothing* daily performance makes her wealthy) a literal overcompensation for racial epidermalization. The all-white clothing is a prime example of the sartorial excess of the ornamental personhood that Cheng analyzes in *Ornamentalism*. Cheng begins and ends this study of the figure of the "yellow woman" with a focus on black flesh and a return to her analysis, in *Second Skin*, of the turning of Josephine Baker's skin into a complex surface and site where the binaries of essence and covering collapse. Cheng's use of the term "yellow woman" opens up other dimensions of her final move to the black layers of ornamental personhood. The once popular and now outdated phrase "high yellow," in the colorism discourse of African American communities, was used as black people internalized anti-black racism and imagined light-skinned black people (usually light-skinned black women) as hovering above "unredeemed" darker-skinned blackness. Within the colorism script of anti-blackness, the access to ornamental personhood that "high yellow" black women have as they live and "endure" as objects on the pedestal of being closer to whiteness differs greatly from the "crushing objecthood" that darker-skinned black women battle.

There is a temporal dimension to the difference between the ornamental personhood of the figure of the "high yellow" woman and the figure of the "enslaved captive" darker-skinned black body. There is, of course, a long history of images of the "high yellow" bodies as the "new people" emerging after the "older" darker-skinned black body. This image making is most striking when William Faulkner, in *Absalom, Absalom!*, describes the octoroon "butterfly . . . carrying nothing of what was into what is, leaving nothing of what is behind but eliding complete and intact," as opposed to his images of the "coal black and ape-like woman . . . dragged . . . out of whatever two dimensional backwater" (Faulkner 1936: 196, 205). This projection of a different time and space onto lighter-skinned and darker-skinned blackness has not entirely dissipated. What time is it when you are black in the twenty-first century? Beyoncé's darkening of her skin in a 2011 French fashion magazine tribute to Fela Kuti offers one way of understanding the way that colorism continues to limit the potentiality of black ornamental personhood (black ornamentalism's ability to continue to push back against the steady forces of racial epidermalization).

Figure 2. Beyoncé, 2011, *L'Officiel Paris* magazine.

In this 2011 photo shoot for *L'Officiel Paris*, Beyoncé's darkened face either looks like blackface or like the dream of a second skin that should not be automatically read as blackface. Not seeing Beyoncé as always already an embodiment of "high yellow" privilege is the only way one can see her darkened face, in these images, as a play with ornamental excess that does not need to be reduced to blackface. These images reveal the connections between Rankine's time of the sigh and Morrison's time of the open black body and anticipation of second skin. The sigh of exhaustion might be the most appropriate response to the very impulse of the Paris fashion magazine photographers to make darker skin on the light-skinned African American celebrity signal her connection to Fela Kuti and Nigerian culture at large. The sigh, for Rankine in *Citizen*, is also figured as the non-expression of what has become inaudible as the black subject refuses to react to an ongoing everyday performance of structural anti-blackness. The images of Beyoncé in the "second skin" of darker-skinned blackness may produce this other type of sigh, the inaudible one that signals, as Rankine shows in *Citizen*, that it is time for more black flesh work that reminds us that racial epidermalization itself continues to be as violent as blackface.

The responses to Beyoncé's wearing of this second skin included a significant amount of outrage over the photographers' inability to understand how offensive the images were to Nigerians (and all black Africans) who tire of the assumption that dark-skinned blackness signals "African." Dodai Stewart, a deputy editor of *Jezebel*, an online media platform, critiqued the photographers' treatment of Beyoncé as a "white model, i.e. a blank-palette object on which to place concepts" (HuffPost 2011). This language crystallizes what is at stake when Morrison creates the new grammar of the open black body. Given that the very idea of anyone being a "blank-palette object" is a sham, Morrison calls for a recognition of black people's right to make this fantasy of the open body an experience of black possibility and black futurity. The blankness of the "white model" continues to be reproduced, and the racial inscriptions on the black body continue to be naturalized. If we allow the waywardness of the *L'Officiel Paris* images to remain wayward, we might feel a sense of anticipation in these images as we wonder when blackened subjects might feel free enough to let go of any need to police what we do with our flesh and let the solidarity of *black flesh in motion* matter more than the *historicity* of the black body (Fanon 1967: 112).

The Flesh of *Finna*

Black flesh in motion is a marked body that feels marked and unmarked. The most resonant part of Spillers's theory of flesh is the idea that we need to find language that begins to capture what it means to "negotiate between the tenses" of "Let's face it. I am a marked woman" and the speculative wonder of the proposition of the "hieroglyphics of the flesh" (McDowell 1989: 144). The speculative tense of a hieroglyphics that has not yet become a recognizable language is embedded in Spillers's turn to the opacity of the hieroglyphic after beginning "Mama's Baby, Papa's Maybe" with the resonant declaration "Let's face it. I am a marked woman . . ." (Spillers [1987] 2003: 203). Deborah McDowell's lucid phrase "negotiating between tenses" opens up space to think about the lived experience of black temporality as such a profound undoing of the boundaries between past, present, and future that even naming the tenses "past, present, future" stops making sense. "Negotiating between tenses" captures the practice of new grammar embedded in any attempt to create space for black flesh and the open body within discourses that keep hailing the historicity of the black body and erasing the Ellisonian "outside history" offbeat of black flesh. The lived tension of tenses created by the afterlife of slavery is embedded in what Achille Mbembe describes as the "time of entanglement" (2001: 1). Mbembe, in *On the Postcolony*, inveighs against the constant rendering of Africa as a static place and proposes the "time of entanglement" as a way of feeling "time on the move" (66, 71, 73). The key move in all of these critics' rethinking of "what time is it when you are black" is the *simultaneous* emphasis on the marked black body and on what is moving as if it is not always already marked. As black people live their lives of *finna-tude*, they live the simultaneity of the afterlife of slavery and an always emerging *afterlife of the afterlife* of slavery (when one is no longer the captive).

This time of *finna*-tude is a state of disorientation. The "hey you" of interpellation does not always produce the turn of recognition. As Terry Eagleton (1994: 217) argues, "What if we fail to recognize and respond to the call of the Subject? What if we return the reply: 'Sorry, you've got the wrong person'? . . . There are, after all, many different ways in which we can be 'hailed,' and some cheery cries, whoops, and whistles may strike us as more appealing than some others." The cacophony of sounds that Eagleton imagines (the sonic refusal to respond properly) creates what Fred Moten calls "cut interpellation" (2003: 69). In *In the Break*, cut interpellation is presented as "incomplete christening" (69). This sense that we are not entirely what we are becoming (that we are turning in response to the ongoing hailing and caught in the torque that makes the turning itself the shape of our being) rethinks Louis Althusser's image of the turn of the individual as she becomes a subject. Althusser (1970: 131) writes, "The hailed individual will turn round. By this mere one-hundred-and-eighty-degree physical conversion, he becomes a *subject*." The turning force, the twisting force, of blackness might be the incomplete christening that makes the one-hundred-and-eighty-degree turn more of a state of suspension than an act of subjection. The cut interpellation is the cut act of subjection that makes black flesh a kind of torque, a kind of ontology that can only be felt in the torque.

This state of suspension is a space where the tenses of the black present are negotiated. Toni Morrison muses, "It is terrible to think that a child with five different present tenses comes to school to be faced with those books that are less than his own language" (Taylor-Guthrie 1994: 123–24). Morrison may be thinking about the uninflected "be" in African American Vernacular English (AAVE). Phrases such as "she do be late" are the black vernacular hailing of a present tense that can sound like it contains multitudes. The multitudinous present tense that destroys any need for a distinct past or future tense is the type of new grammar that can hold on to an awareness of everything that keeps making black people into captives and, also, hail everything that could somehow, some way, set the captives free. The flesh of *finna* is what Fanon discovers in the last pages of *Black Skin, White Masks* as he famously declares, "The Negro is not. Any more than the white man" (1967: 231). Homi Bhabha and others have read this *new grammar* as Fanon's move to the obsolescence of alterity, but this new grammar of the incomplete sentence is also the seizure of black is-ness even if that is-ness is an escape from legibility (a refusal of the "fact of blackness," Charles Markmann's provocative mistranslation of "L'expérience vécue du Noir," the title of chapter five in the French original of *Black Skin, White Masks*). The most direct translation of the French original would be "the lived experience of the Negro." Fanon's analysis of his case studies as a psychiatrist could never contain his anticipation of the lived experience of black flesh.

We feel most acutely Fanon's turn from the historicity of the black body to the anticipation of the offbeat of black flesh when we remember his image of the "tight smile" (in chapter five) and let this image speak alongside his explicit refusal of the "body of history" in the final chapter.

> "Look, a Negro!" It was an external stimulus that flicked over me as I passed by. I made a tight smile.
>
> The body of history does not determine a single one of my actions.
>
> (111, 231)

The black "tight smile" is formed as the speaker moves. The words "Look, a Negro" try to name and arrest the black flesh in motion. This passage complicates Fanon's assertion, in this same chapter, that the "black man has no ontological resistance in the eyes of the white man" (110). If we think the "eyes of the white man" is the only way of seeing, we understand this claim. But, in the image of the objectifying words that "flick over" but cannot "stick," Fanon makes us feel a black movement that the "eyes of the white man" cannot contain. The emphasis on the white gaze that cannot mark the black flesh in motion is strikingly different from Fanon's image of the "hemorrhage that spattered my whole body with black blood" (112). As opposed to the heaviness of the white gaze in some of Fanon's images of the "spatial and temporal world" of the black body, the image of the "tight smile" *pivots* on the lightness of what "flicks" over black flesh (111). The tension of being captive and being free holds that "tight smile" in place. What will happen when the tightness is released? What time is it when black release happens? What we *finna* do?

References

Althusser, Louis. 1970. "Ideology and Ideological State Apparatuses (Notes towards an Investigation)." In *Mapping Ideology*, edited by Slavoj Žižek, 100–140. New York: Verso.

Cheng, Anne Anlin. 2011. *Second Skin: Josephine Baker and the Modern Surface*. New York: Oxford University Press.

Cheng, Anne Anlin. 2019. *Ornamentalism*. New York: Oxford University Press.

Eagleton, Terry. 1994. "Ideology and Its Vicissitudes in Western Marxism." In *Mapping Ideology*, edited by Slavoj Žižek, 179–226. New York: Verso.

Fanon, Frantz. 1967. *Black Skin, White Masks*. Translated by Charles Markmann. New York: Grove Press.

Faulkner, William. 1936. *Absalom, Absalom!* New York: Modern Library.

HuffPost. 2011. "Beyoncé's Skin Darkened for *L'Officiel* Magazine: Offensive or Artistic?" February 11. www.huffpost.com/entry/beyonce-skin-darkened- blackface_n_826530.

Judy, R. A. 2020. *Sentient Flesh: Thinking in Disorder, Poiesis in Black.* Durham, NC: Duke University Press.

Marshall, Nate. 2020. *Finna: Poems.* New York: One World.

Mbembe, Achille. 2001. *On the Postcolony.* Berkeley: University of California Press.

McDowell, Deborah E. 1989. "Negotiating between Tenses: Witnessing Slavery after Freedom—*Dessa Rose.*" In *Slavery and the Literary Imagination,* edited by Deborah E. McDowell and Arnold Rampersad, 144–70. Baltimore, MD: Johns Hopkins Press.

Morrison, Toni. 1981. *Tar Baby.* New York: Plume/Penguin.

Morrison, Toni. 1997. *Paradise.* New York: Knopf.

Morrison, Toni. 2002. *Five Poems.* Las Vegas: Rainmaker Editions.

Morrison, Toni. 2008. *A Mercy.* New York: Vintage.

Morrison, Toni. 2015. *God Help the Child.* New York: Knopf.

Morrison, Toni. 2019. *The Source of Self-Regard: Selected Essays, Speeches, and Meditations.* New York: Knopf.

Moten, Fred. 2003. *In the Break: The Aesthetics of the Black Radical Tradition.* Minneapolis: University of Minnesota Press.

Moten, Fred. 2017. *Black and Blur (Consent Not to Be a Single Being).* Durham, NC: Duke University Press.

Muñoz, José. 2009. *Cruising Utopia: The Then and There of Queer Futurity.* New York: New York University Press.

Muñoz, José. 2020. *The Sense of Brown.* Durham, NC: Duke University Press.

Nwandu, Antoinette. 2018. *Pass Over.* New York: Grove Press.

Rankine, Claudia. 2014. *Citizen: An American Lyric.* Minneapolis: Graywolf Press.

Rankine, Claudia. 2019. *The White Card.* Minneapolis: Graywolf Press.

Sawyer, Michael E. 2018. *An Africana Philosophy of Temporality: Homo Liminalis.* Cham, Switzerland: Springer Nature.

Spellman, A. B. 1998. "Big Bushy Afros." *International Review of African American Art* 15, no. 1: 52–53.

Spillers, Hortense. (1987) 2003. "Mama's Baby, Papa's Maybe." In *Black, White, and in Color: Essays on American Literature and Culture.* Chicago: University of Chicago Press.

Spillers, Hortense. 2010. Pers. comm., April 9, in response to Harvey Young's conference presentation at Dartmouth's "Black Theatricality" conference.

Taylor-Guthrie, Danille. 1994. *Conversations with Toni Morrison.* Jackson: University Press of Mississippi.

Zanuttini, Raffaella, Jim Wood, Jason Zentz, and Laurence Horn. 2018. "The Yale Grammatical Diversity Project: Morphosyntactic Variation in North American English." *Linguistics Vanguard* 4, no. 1: 20160070. doi.org/10.1515/lingvan-2016-0070.

Universities as New Battlegrounds

Zeynep Gambetti and Saygun Gökarıksel, Editors

Zeynep Gambetti and Saygun Gökarıksel

Introduction: Universities as New Battlegrounds

A midnight decree on January 1, 2021, signed by Turkish president Recep Tayyip Erdoğan, leader of the conservative Justice and Development Party (AKP), appointed a political crony and entrepreneur as the new rector (university president) to Boğaziçi University. Boğaziçi is among the top three universities in Turkey. Established on the legacy of Robert College, the first American university to be founded outside of the United States, Boğaziçi continued to thrive and accumulate national and international prestige after being nationalized in 1971. Erdoğan's appointment violated existing principles of university autonomy and democracy, revered and jealously safeguarded by Boğaziçi faculty for decades.

Like twenty other university presidents in Turkey, the new rector was affiliated with the ruling party and did not go through elections or regular screening procedures for hiring faculty. In February, a law school and a school of communications were created at the university by another decree, blatantly contravening legal provisions that stipulate that the National Assembly must vote such units in. Several other illegal and illegitimate maneuvers were employed to open the way for hiring loyalists and changing the balance of forces within the university. For a year now, students, academics, and administrative staff have been protesting this illegitimate move to authoritatively seize and domesticate the university. The top-down imposition of a new rector was backed and reinforced by a heavy police siege of the campus and the securitization of the Istanbul neighborhood in which it is located. To the government's surprise, however, student and faculty protests gained nationwide and international attention and were hailed as harboring the seeds of organized resistance against the neoliberal authoritarian offensive in the academic sphere as well as in other social fields.

The South Atlantic Quarterly 121:1, January 2022
DOI 10.1215/00382876-9561615 © 2022 Duke University Press

This offensive certainly did not start with Boğaziçi, nor will it end there. Together with the ensuing protests, it registers a part of the global trend of offensives against educational institutions. From India, Greece, Hungary, and Poland to France, Brazil, and the United States, universities have come under increasing pressure and at times frontal assault. Invoking the sanctity of the Hindu nation, Indian prime minister Narendra Modi's neoliberal authoritarian government seeks to crack down on dissident academic institutions and forms of life. In Greece, with a new police law, the right-wing government seeks to demobilize and suffocate university campuses that have historically been the epicenter of antifascist and democratic struggles waged by students and academics. Viktor Orbạn of Hungary deploys punitive fiscal instruments to make universities redundant and expose them to the vagaries of the market through privatization and the criminalization of allegedly anti-Hungarian notions such as gender. In the same vein, the new minister of education in Poland seeks to punish disobedient academics and students who defend civil rights and freedoms against recent homophobic and anti-abortion policies and laws. In Brazil, Bolsonaro tries to meddle with the election of rectors and severely defunds universities. In France, the Macron administration demonizes anticolonial and gender studies by framing them as imported as well as complicit with Islamic terrorism. Denmark follows suit. In the United States, critical race studies are being accused of left-wing indoctrination, and in South Africa, struggles are being waged against privatization and the colonial culture of universities. Examples can be multiplied, and so can the range of instruments right-wing governments use to repress, control, and repurpose universities.

What is it about the current political conjuncture that makes universities a particularly important target for right-wing politics, not only by so-called Eastern despots, but also by the supposedly democratic governments of the West? What forms of power and domination intersect in such offensives against universities? What do the protests and their particular forms and language reveal about the current state of universities? What kind of future do academic struggles harbor? This special section of *SAQ* centers on the ongoing Boğaziçi protests to explore these and related questions, which, in our view, highlight some of the fundamental dimensions of the current moment of neoliberal authoritarian forms of power and the social struggles waged against new regimes of (post-)truth, homophobia, nationalist sovereignist body politics, and academic purges and expulsions.

The Turkish government's offensive against Boğaziçi is not an exception or anomaly in contemporary Turkey. The modern university in Turkey is integral to the historical constitution of the body politic of the nation-state.

As such, it has been shaped by the violent making of minorities and majorities, the fantasies of national unification and purification, the institutionalization of heteropatriarchal normativity and of the capitalist ideology of development that involves the theft, plunder, and appropriation of land, property, and labor. Added to this is the neoliberal authoritarian moment that the ruling AKP epitomizes. The party's power owes to both the processes of neoliberalization of society and the growing authoritarianization of the state. The AKP has been effectuating a form of *Gleichschaltung* (bringing into line) by hollowing out every institution in the country to make it subservient to its own aims. State violence is combined with biopolitical governmental strategies and neoliberal tactics of dispossession, resulting in the amplification of unpredictability and the constant production of equivocation.

For instance, the criminalization en masse of academics in 2016 was couched in political invectives portraying them as *would-be intellectuals* collaborating with terrorist organizations to undermine the capacity of the government to protect the country's territorial integrity. Prosecutors followed suit to concoct terrorist propaganda charges against more than a thousand signatories of a Peace Petition penned in reaction to the brutal antiterror operations in Kurdish towns. Within that same year, a failed coup attempt gave the AKP government the perfect excuse to devastate higher education by mass evacuations, administrative or judiciary action against professors, and the incarceration of scholars, students, and intellectuals. Many academics have fled the country and are now in exile in Europe and the United States. Also during this period, the government banished internal elections at universities and reintroduced the top-down method of nominating rectors.

Most public universities in the country are now but facades. Self-censorship is rampant, not because there is any strict control of curricula or research activity, but because of the loss of compass as to what would lead scholars into trouble. Universities are compelled to accept the neoliberal developmental roles they are asked to assume—among them, becoming startup factories, setting up techno-parks, and collaborating with the industrial-military complex. Any research that defies the ever-changing objectives and networks of the establishment is conveniently labeled subversive and banned by deploying a diversity of ruses.

Boğaziçi University is the last among public universities to resist the AKP's *Gleichshaltung*. Its endurance largely stems from the university's relative insulation from the forces of commercialization and its insistence on democratic governance. While its prestige might have partly served as a shield against outright political and economic encroachment, it is important to underscore that it is the student and academic struggles against commercialization and state control that helped the exercise of (relative) freedom. While many purged and expelled signatories of the Peace Petition experimented with new forms of education, praxis, and commoning, what one strikingly observes in the Boğaziçi protests is the rethinking of the university from *within* the site of university. The labor put into these protests revitalizes the university as a critical institutional space of autonomy and self-government, a site of engagement with democratic life, praxis, and poiesis. As such, it is not merely an academic struggle, but one that promises to strike at the neoliberal authoritarian enterprise at its heart.

As an outcome of the resistance at Boğaziçi Melih Bulu was removed from his position by yet another midnight executive degree on July 15. The essays in this special section evoke the period before the removal. They haven't lost any of their vigor, however, since the struggle continues. The vice-rector, who proved to be more royalist than the king, has temporarily replaced Bulu and has been applying even more coercive pressure and inflicting more reckless damage on the university. In any case, the problem was not the person of Bulu, but the conditions and forms of power that make such antidemocratic appointments possible. We hope that this "Against the Day" dossier will help highlight the connections between the ongoing struggle at Boğaziçi University and the other struggles against neoliberal and right-wing authoritarianism across the globe.

Zeynep Gambetti

The Struggle for Academic Freedom in an Age of Post-truth

Prelude

"**B**oğaziçi is *at last* doing science!" This interjection came from the new vice-rector, a professor at the Industrial Engineering Department who spent over eighteen years teaching and researching at Boğaziçi University. The "at last" resounded across networks of resistance as both pathetic and alarming. It was pathetic, since the vice-rector was deriding the only remaining center of excellence in the Turkish academic landscape, the university whose extensive research partnerships and top-quality education system allow it to acquire renown across the globe. It was alarming, since this "at last" announced the new game of post-truth politics that would snare the university from then on.

Boğaziçi professors and students had been resisting state interference into the university's governance structures by protesting on a daily basis and organizing on-site as well as virtual events since January 2021, but they were rather ill prepared to handle huge doses of untruth being flung at them by compromised colleagues in addition to state officials. Academics, by virtue of their (subjectively and normatively presumed) social role as producers and disseminators of reliable knowledge, are wont to believe in *living in truth*. It turns out, however, that academics in many countries around the world will now have to endure the alienating circumstances that Vaclav Havel calls "living the lie" (1990). The inversion of conventional syntax, the reversal of victimhood status, and the concoction of ad hominem arguments based on dubious causalities are not confined to the field of electoral or populist politics alone.

The South Atlantic Quarterly 121:1, January 2022
DOI 10.1215/00382876-9561629 © 2022 Duke University Press

Academic regimes of authentication are as vulnerable to the effects of post-truth as are other discursive norms. The struggle for scholarly freedom, as the Boğaziçi resistance amply shows, is simultaneously a tug-of-war between novel *dispositifs* of subjection and a demand to reinstate the power of knowledge.

An authoritarian context like the Turkish one reveals, however, that the war cannot be waged by relying on bygone laurels. It took Boğaziçi professors several months to realize this. Outraged by the poisonous interjection "*at last doing science*," they embarked on a parrhesiastic campaign of shouting truth to power in intra-university email forums and on social media. Untouched by the clamor, the vice-rector brazenly turned his "at last" into a hashtag on Twitter. What he meant by "science" was to be subsequently revealed, not in words but in deeds. First came the convoy of Mercedes-Benzes with tinted windows, bringing state officials to the rectorate. Then came the television satellite van. Men in dark suits were escorted into the conference hall to inaugurate a partnership with the Ministry of Transport. The vice-rector promised more contracts with the military-industrial complex. In turn, the new rector, appointed by midnight decree by President Erdoğan, prophesied that Boğaziçi University would become an "entrepreneurship factory" under his good guidance. Another newly appointed university administrator, the dean of the as-yet-inexistent School of Law, went on TV shows to boast the merits of a gigantic infrastructural project to construct an artificial canal between the Black Sea and the Marmara, parallel to the Bosporus, the already existing natural waterway. Billions of dollars and invaluable scientific expertise would be invested in that project, which has neither utility nor feasibility according to environmentalists and city planners. The dean, a law professor, also advocated the abrogation of the 1936 Montreux Convention Regarding the Regime of the Straits that guarantees free access to the Black Sea through the Bosphorus. With the convention out of the way, the new canal would become a hen that lays golden eggs, since transit fees could then be applied.

"At last doing science," hence, meant serving either capital or the state. Or rather, it meant serving both, given the corporatization of the state in the neoliberal era. This utilitarian redefinition of science might not sound new—the corporatization of academic knowledge and its subservience to the developmental or securitarian concerns of the state are already among our concerns (Giroux 2014; Brown 2015; Scott 2019). What was new, however, is the way in which the game was now being played. This was no longer chess, but Go, the Japanese board game in which no position is assigned at the outset and the number of possible moves is quasi infinite. In the post-truth Go contest, there are no moral, legal, or logical limits to the strategies that can be employed. Power outmaneuvers truth, since truth no longer procures power. As Nükhet Sirman and Feyza Akınerdem (2019: 136) succinctly put it, "Post-truth presents us with a way of operating in which the gap that separates the signifier and the signified in any act of representation is stretched beyond acceptable limits."

The result was the following: when faculty members evoked the principles of democratic governance that made Boğaziçi University unique in Turkey (and perhaps the world), the new team of administrators accused them of mobbing the "silent majority." The latter was purportedly intimidated and discouraged from collaborating with the new administration by "not more than 20 vocal academics" who cited participatory governance principles in order to wreak havoc (*Duvar English* 2021). Professors then reacted by assembling by the hundreds at the main campus square, each professor carrying a placard with a number inscribed on it to prove that they are not but a handful. As in Trump's inauguration ceremony, however, counting heads did not shatter the belief in "alternative facts" (Zerilli 2020). Pro-government media raised the stakes: the resistance was organized by thirty-three academics who were undercover "militants affiliated with terrorist organizations" (Ahval 2021). When the effects of that tactic wore out, a new set of invectives poured down from the mouths of politicians, pro-government journalists, and social-media trolls. Boğaziçi professors were labeled elitist, out of sync with the real values of the people. They had grown foreign to what was "homegrown and national" (Alemdaroğlu and Babül 2021). Boğaziçi must be domesticated in the double sense of the word: disciplined and nationalized. A public university should honor the state that feeds it. The interior minister even deemed it "fascistic" to oppose the will of the president.

Whether contesting a rector appointed by midnight decree on January 1 by President Erdoğan to Turkey's best university without any consultation whatsoever with faculty members is fascistic or not did not incite debate in the conformist media. In fiercely polarized public spheres, the inversion of meanings ceases to provoke cognitive dissonance. Looking for a hidden agenda, a hidden mastermind behind every word and deed, becomes something of a second nature. Everything that appears is met with suspicion. This generalized suspicion undermines trust in those regimes of truth that have so far regulated the production of valid statements concerning factual evidence and scientific verification.

"Organized lying," as Hannah Arendt somewhat naively formulated, does not produce disbelief but rather cynicism: "The result of a consistent and total substitution of lies for factual truth is not that the lies will now be accepted as truth, and the truth be defamed as lies, but that the sense by which we take our bearings in the world—and the category of truth vs. falsehood is among the mental means to this end—is being destroyed" (Arendt 1993: 257). This loss of direction is what I shall turn to now, to delineate the obstacles facing academic freedom and university autonomy in the era of post-truth.

Disorientation

If, in Sara Ahmed's (2006: 11) words, being oriented, having a home, or feeling at home in the world requires the transformation of the unfamiliar into the familiar, then post-truth involves the conversion of the familiar into the unfamiliar, the strange, and the alien.

The Boğaziçi experience shows that there are two ways of thinking about disorientation: (1) Familiar roads and lines are effaced, and signposts go missing. This involves not only the loss of direction but also that of familiar objects and recognizable places, and consequently results in a form of dispossession. Ahmed tells us that the investment made in lines, roads, places, and objects provides for "direction toward specific goals, aims and aspirations" (Ahmed 2006: 17). Being "knocked off course" can be considered a positive experience: it can open up new worlds, new orientations. It shakes our certainties, expands us, and allows us to rebuild our place in the world to accommodate more diversity. But when we are *constantly* knocked off course, when roads keep changing and the signposts too, we can no longer turn around to start reorienting ourselves. We are rather caught up in an endless turning around, an unremitting process of reversals and vacillations that does not allow for resettlement. When, for instance, in one single week, a part-time professor is banned from teaching at the university because of his advocacy for students, a person from an ultra-right-wing background is appointed secretary general of the university, and the elected dean of the Engineering Faculty is replaced overnight by the vice-rector, the procedural and customary practices of Boğaziçi are undone in countless ways. *Rehoming* would require accepting the new power game and relinquishing the principles of democratic governance, which is what the Boğaziçi resistance refuses to do.

(2) A second way to think about disorientation is to imagine that guidelines are drawn too thickly rather than made to disappear. When riot police put up barriers all around the neighborhood in which Boğaziçi is located, bodies and vehicle flows get constricted to narrow spaces. Alternative routes are preemptively foreclosed and so are desires. The habitual roads that lead

up to the university gates are transformed into uncanny spaces associated with alien images: warfare, state of emergency, open-air prison, metal piercing flesh. The familiar landscape is violated; home is desecrated.

There are two different but interrelated patterns of disorientation at work here. One involves the erasure of known paths and lines, leading to a state of schizophrenia where everything can turn into something else. The other involves rigid molding, compartmentalization, and stratification. The difference, as expressed by Gilles Deleuze (1992), would be that between the mold and modulation. Molds capture and paralyze. Modulations vacillate, are put in permanent motion, and reduce stability. In ways probably unforeseen by Deleuze, the post-truth game of Go is modulatory, as the Boğaziçi experience illustrates. Every word we utter returns to us in reverse: we say democracy, they say mobbing; we say freedom, they say terrorism; we say difference, they say deviance. Home becomes unrecognizable. The desire and labor invested in it is squandered. Hence the exclamation of an emeritus professor during one of the protests: "I spent sixty-five years of my life here. We cultivated this university like a rare flower, paying attention to every detail, every principle, every moral, and humanitarian value. . . . I do not consent to its getting wasted in this way! I do not consent to having this beautiful, rare and wonderful flower be plucked and thrown away!" (Boğaziçi Memories 2021).

As such, post-truth designates a disinvestment from long-established norms regulating what counts as true, without, however, introducing new criteria in their place. It implies a crisis whereby whether something is considered true or not ceases to matter, since utterances previously sanctified as "true" are dispossessed of their capacity to produce truth effects. Or rather, truth is valued only as long as it procures power. When the vice-rector declares that the university is "at last doing science," we professors take this as an obvious untruth: Boğaziçi has always done science. But the effect of landing state officials and industrialists onto the campus makes the question of whether Boğaziçi has done science before irrelevant. After all, who cares? The "at last" tells us how the game will be played: Boğaziçi will be "truly" doing science from now on since academic practices will be reorganized in such a way that past scientific norms will appear anachronistic and irresponsible.

To put it more sharply, it is my contention that molds have become modular in neoliberal societies. We are being deprived of a place in the world because of the conditions of precarity, virtuality, and polarization instigated by neoliberalism, information technologies, and populism, respectively. Power is modular: its endless vacillations point to nothing but itself. Power no longer constructs worlds but tends to dismember and disarticulate, without allowing for stable points of anchorage. This novel paradigm of power is productive as well, but it would not be wrong to suggest that the lines of desire that it produces summon endless disinvestment and reinvestment, such that power itself remains the only constant.

So the conundrum becomes, How is it possible to defend academic freedom and university autonomy given this state of affairs? What can academic freedom signify—to what concrete practice may it point—in a world governed by the imperatives of efficiency, impermanence, and antagonism? And what are the chances of reinstituting academic freedom as a right in an era of post-truth?

Law as Tactic

The dethroning of the academic as producer of reliable knowledge, in Turkey as well as elsewhere, unmistakably followed in the footsteps of the suicidal submersion of the liberal political system into the quicksand of capitalism. Former principles such as the rule of law, human rights, or participatory governance, and former sources of authoritative validation of knowledge such as the university or the judiciary, became largely incongruent and impotent in rationalizing what we could call, after Karl Polanyi (2001), the "great neoliberal transformation."

To my mind, neoconservatism and the rise of the new right should be inscribed within the lineage of the market-driven transvaluation of values across the globe. Again, in Turkey as well as elsewhere, the New Right emerged as the most appropriate ideological project with which to stitch back the layers of social tissue torn to shreds by the neoliberal assault on rights, social security, public services, and class cohesion. The so-called war on terror proved to be an incredibly efficient *dispositif* for criminalizing noncompliant portions of the population and inhibiting popular uprisings. The governmental regulation of everyday life is now being achieved without even having to modify constitutional provisions upholding fundamental rights. Governments are tactically deploying laws and leaving law enforcement agents the discretion to use them according to stated or presumed security objectives (Foucault 1991; Butler 2004).

It is not that sovereign power suspends the law to declare a state of emergency (though that, too, may be the case, as in 2016–18 in Turkey). But it is rather that the operations of governmentality expand the field of extralegality in which discretionary power and the tactical evocation of law meddle with the universality and temporality conventionally (and erroneously) attributed to rule of law. States of exception become both banal (Gökarıksel and Türem 2019) and mobile (Arslanalp and Erkmen 2020). To be sure, neither the state of exception nor the tactical deployment of legal *dispositifs* is new. The novelty lies in the fact that the law is not deferred; it simply ceases to take effect. Under contemporary conditions, not illegality but suspicion determines both the "crime" and the punishment to be meted out. Preventive policing becomes ontologically constitutive of both law and its transgression. Being deemed suspicious serves as a mandate for detention and trial. And, as Judith Butler (2004: 63) notes, the "indefinite extension of the war on terrorism" derealizes the binding nature of constitutional rights and by consequence the idea of the citizen as a rights-bearing individual. We might indeed be faced with a shift in the definition of the criminal from a legal one to a biopolitical and securitarian one (Gambetti 2020: 21). The responsibilization of the individual and the moralization of the capacity to adjust to the new game indicate how neoliberalism and the New Right are imbricated in each other. Put bluntly, legality is replaced by a form of regulatory power that functions through buzzwords such as *efficiency, risk control*, and the *well-being of the population* and that is prone to generating an accusatory and divisive politics.

Boğaziçi students, for instance, were subjected to an irrational and unjustified chain of detentions. Law was invoked on a biopolitical and partial basis ("the Covid-19 ban on open-air gatherings is to be applied to *this* city district but not to others") so as to concoct prohibited spaces in the name of public health. This allowed the police to take students under custody. The logic worked like this: if they are taken under custody, then they *must be* bogus students, that is, public hazards posing as students. Contesting the police by citing fundamental rights itself became a source of suspicion.

Given this new social order, which is more chaotic than orderly, it doesn't come as a surprise that universities are the new battleground. Universities are discouraged from harboring nonconformist approaches to knowledge production and fostering critical debate and political contestation. What we summarily call anti-intellectualism consists in accusatory practices that stigmatize academic knowledge production as militant when research challenges the doctrinaire identities fostered by the New Right to better perpetuate neoliberal processes of fragmentation. The criminalization of postcolonial and critical race studies in France under the infamous label *islamo-gauchisme*, the targeting of academics carrying out research on "nationally sensitive issues" such as the Holocaust in Poland and the Armenian genocide in Turkey, and assaults on gender studies programs in many parts of the world are all examples of inversion of the categories of victim and aggressor. The New Right follows in the footsteps of its predecessors in circulating discourses of victimization grounded in existential threats (Löwenthal and Guterman 1949; Yılmaz 2017; Samuels 2016). Violence and partiality are purported attributes of the Other, while respectability and neutrality are characteristic of the collective identities forged to authoritatively prearrange the distribution of precariousness.

Citing law or rights to defend academic freedom today thus becomes somewhat of a vain endeavor. To be sure, lawsuits may be (and are) opened against malpractices that are constitutionally and procedurally condemnable (*Bianet* 2021b). But these would barely be expected to withstand a whole assemblage of tactics that hollow out laws and institutions as well as truth. As in the case of Denmark, moreover, bills may be promulgated to curb what is termed "excessive militancy" in academia (Hivert 2021). Legal provisions alone will not suffice in saving it from assault. As Joan Scott (2019) has forcefully remarked, academic freedom is a collective freedom that requires institutional as well as practical support systems. Recognizing the political nature of critique seems therefore crucial in the struggle for academic freedom.

What Next?

The Mobius strip that entraps the debate around critical scholarship can be schematized as follows: critical scholars are accused of militancy (in shades that shift from partiality to support for terrorist organizations) by those in dominant positions in today's power matrices. The latter suppose that they are making the case for the depoliticization of knowledge production. At the same time, however, they fuel the polarization that they single-handedly attribute to critical scholars. Paradoxically, this amounts to restricting knowledge production to only those fields and epistemic paradigms that conform to the existing game of power. This is indeed a paradox, because any depoliticization thus achieved would be partial rather than impartial. It would functionalize the university and thereby reproduce the proscriptions determined by those who happen to be the game makers at some particular juncture.

Accusations that those who struggle for academic freedom are politicizing science actually reveal how politically significant critical research is— how it can have the power to offer reorientation despite and potentially against the toxic practices of the post-truth era. It is because we have become vulnerable as scholars that we understand how the institutional arrangements that support academic freedom are both extremely vital and extremely fragile. It is because we are criminalized that we understand how interconnected our fate is with those struggling for a more just, egalitarian, and plural society. This should prompt us to rethink the role of intellectuals in dark times. The ivory tower has collapsed. We can no longer claim to be outside the political field. Avowing that our research is linked to struggles against racism, sexism, neoliberal exploitation, and fascistic tendencies does not imply a move away from impartiality. On the contrary, such an avowal acknowledges that resisting encroachments on academic freedom will not be a purely academic matter or a struggle concerning only academia. Given the material and structural conditions of post-truth, constituting a new regime of truth, one that is inclusive and collective, calls for the labor of commoning. It requires prefiguring a model of politics other than the one that blurs the lines between critique, resistance, and terrorism. The Boğaziçi University resistance beckons such an alternative—this, I believe, is the reason that it summoned up so much solidarity as an embodied as well as intellectual promise of rehoming.

References

Ahmed, Sara. 2006. *Queer Phenomenology: Orientations, Objects, Others.* Durham: Duke University Press.

Ahval. 2021. "Turkey's Pro-gov't Circles Going All-In to Defend Boğaziçi University Intervention." February 4. ahvalnews.com/bogazici-protests/turkeys-pro-govt -circles-going-all-defend-bogazici-university-intervention.

Alemdaroğlu, Ayça, and Elif Babül. 2021. "Boğaziçi Resists Authoritarian Control of the Academy in Turkey." *Middle East Research and Information Project,* February 23. merip.org /2021/02/bogazici-resists-authoritarian-control-of-the-academy-in-turkey/.

Arendt, Hannah. 1993. *Between Past and Future.* New York: Penguin.

Arslanalp, Mert, and T. Deniz Erkmen. 2020. "Mobile Emergency Rule in Turkey: Legal Repression of Protests during Authoritarian Transformation." *Democratization* 27, no. 6. doi.org/10.1080/13510347.2020.1753701.

Bianet. 2021a. "Soylu Finds It 'Fascistic' to Say, 'You Have Appointed a Trustee Rector.'" February 3. bianet.org/bianet/politics/238607–soylu-finds-it-fascistic-to-say-you-have -appointed-a-trustee-rector.

Bianet. 2021b. "Three New Lawsuits by Academics of Boğaziçi University." May 28. bianet.org/ english/law/244786–three-new-lawsuits-by-academics-of-bogazici-university.

Boğaziçi Memories (@bounmemories). 2021. "Bugün hocalarımızın basın açıklamasından sonra çok uzun bir süre Boğaziçi'nde ders vermiş olan Emeritus hocalarımızdan Oya Başak kısa bir konuşma yaptı" ("Following the press statement made by our professors today, Oya Başak, an Emeritus Professor who taught for many years at Boğaziçi, gave a short speech"). Twitter, February 5, 6:14 a.m. twitter.com/i/status/1357648811204 706307.

Brown, Wendy. 2015. *Undoing the Demos: Neoliberalism's Stealth Revolution.* New York: Zone.

Butler, Judith. 2004. *Precarious Life: The Powers of Mourning and Violence.* New York: Verso.

Deleuze, Gilles. 1992. "Postscript on the Societies of Control." *October* 59 (winter): 3–7.

Duvar English. 2021. "Hundreds of Boğaziçi University Academics Teach Erdoğan-Appointed Rector 'How to Count.'" February 5. www.duvarenglish.com/hundreds-of-bogazici-university-academics-teach-erdogans-rector-melih-bulu-how-to-count-news-56149.

Foucault, Michel. 1991. "Governmentality," translated by Rosi Braidotti and Colin Gordon. In *The Foucault Effect: Studies m Governmentality,* edited by Graham Burchell, Colin Gordon, and Peter Miller, 87–104. Chicago: University of Chicago Press.

Gambetti, Zeynep. 2020. "Exploratory Notes on the Origins of New Fascisms." *Critical Times* 3, no. 1: 1–32

Giroux, Henry. 2014. *Neoliberalism's War on Higher Education.* Chicago: Haymarket.

Gökarıksel, Saygun, and Z. Umut Türem. 2019. "The Banality of Exception? Law and Politics in 'Post-coup' Turkey." *South Atlantic Quarterly* 118, no. 1: 175–87.

Havel, Vaclav. 1990. *Living in Truth.* London: Faber and Faber.

Hivert, Anne-Françoise. 2021. "Le débat sur 'le militantisme excessif' dans la recherche académique gagne le Danemark" ("The Debate on 'Excessive Militancy' in Academic Research Spreads to Denmark"). *Le Monde,* June 8. www.lemonde.fr/international/article/2021/06/08/la-liberte-academique-en-danger-selon-les-chercheurs-danois_6083281_3210.html.

Löwenthal, Leo, and Norbert Guterman. 1949. *Prophets of Deceit: A Study of the Techniques of the American Agitator.* New York: Harper.

Polanyi, Karl. 2001. *The Great Transformation: The Political and Economic Origins of Our Time.* Boston: Beacon Press.

Samuels, Robert. 2016. *Psychoanalyzing the Left and Right after Donald Trump: Conservatism, Liberalism, and Neoliberal Populisms.* Cham, Switzerland: Palgrave-Macmillan.

Scott, Joan Wallach. 2019. *Knowledge, Power, and Academic Freedom.* New York: Columbia University Press.

Sirman, Nükhet, and Feyza Akınerdem. 2019. "From Seekers of Truth to Masters of Power: Televised Stories in a Post-truth World." *South Atlantic Quarterly* 118, no. 1: 129–44.

Yılmaz, Zafer. 2017. "The AKP and the Spirit of the 'New' Turkey: Imagined Victim, Reactionary Mood, and Resentful Sovereign." *Turkish Studies* 18, no. 3: 482–513.

Zerilli, Linda M. G. 2020. "Fact-Checking and Truth-Telling in an Age of Alternative Facts." *Le foucaldien* 6, no. 1: 2–22.

Saygun Gökarıksel

University Embodied:
The Struggle for Autonomy and Democracy

The university is a critical institution or it is nothing.
—Stuart Hall

Üniversite direnişte vardır.
—Serdar Tekin

At noon on an ordinary workday, we silently stand still in our academic gowns, our backs turned to the Rector's Office for half an hour, facing the group of students who likewise stand still and broadcast our vigil. Behind the students appears a group of undercover police who anxiously observe the people attending the protest and take their photos. The famous dogs and cats of the campus join us, casually lying on the lawn in front of us. At about 12:30 p.m. we start clapping with the students, which goes on for a full minute. The sound of clapping travels across the campus, echoing from the buildings and seeping into the Rector's Office. Excited, the dogs start barking.

Since Ankara's top-down, illegitimate appointment of the new rector to Boğaziçi University on January 1, 2021, this scene has more or less repeated itself daily. It quickly has become the iconic image of Boğaziçi faculty protests, gaining nationwide and international traction. Many of us have received support messages from different people who saw the vigils. The appointed rector (and the one that recently replaced him) made no secret that he has been deeply disturbed by these daily protests. He even started to build a new office in another Boğaziçi campus on the other side of the Bosporus, where he would not see the faculty turning their backs to him. How to make

The South Atlantic Quarterly 121:1, January 2022
DOI 10.1215/00382876-9561643 © 2022 Duke University Press

sense of the popular traction of these protests? What might explain the appointed rector's particularly aggravated reaction to the embodied performances? What is it about the current condition of dissident or oppositional politics that has enabled Boğaziçi protests to resonate so widely?

To be sure, the popular force and valor of Boğaziçi protests cannot be understood without the general political context of the authoritarian offensive against higher education institutions in Turkey and, indeed, across the world, as Zeynep Gambetti and I have suggested in our introductory essay to this dossier. But what those protests, particularly the faculty vigils, highlight are the embodied forms of power and labor of resistance, especially the bodily dimension of public collective action. Indeed, Boğaziçi protests, I would argue, could be seen as part of the making of a counter or dissident body politic, which seeks to rethink and invigorate, at this conjuncture of neoliberal authoritarianism, the university as a critical social institution and as an arena of democratic struggle interconnected to other social struggles for equality and liberty in the country and beyond. Drawing on the collective history of struggles and different forms and scales of action, this making of the dissident body politic weaves together embodied public performances; mediatized communicative labor, including online forums, commissions, media commentaries, and productions; and formal institutional resistance and legal action such as litigation. Altogether, Boğaziçi protests highlight, or, better, seek to *flesh out*, the importance of university autonomy and democracy, reposing the question, What is a university? at this critical moment when public life and institutions have been violently targeted by the apparatuses of the state and capital. While Boğaziçi protests are certainly not free of internal tensions and conflicts, and the challenges they face are enormous, their real contribution, perhaps, might be better understood not so much within the conventional terms of defeat or victory as within the social groundwork they perform, the dissident body politic they might help thrive and multiply, and the hope they might harbor for the future struggles to come.

"Ben devletim" (I Am the State)

The modern university in Turkey is integral to the violent making of the body politic of the nation-state. As a key ideological apparatus and a site for social reproduction, universities have been tasked to nationalize education and knowledge and cultivate the bodies and souls of citizen-subjects. While universities have been the hotbed of purges of "dangerous" or dissident academics and students from the body politic in the past, especially during the military coups and repressions, they also have played a central role in many social struggles, as in the student movements of the 1960s and 1970s.[1] Since the termination of the peace process between the Turkish state and the Kurdistan Workers' Party (PKK) in 2015, the universities, like other public institutions and realms of democratic life, have become increasingly hollowed out and targeted by the Justice and Development Party (AKP) government. The Turkish state's dirty war in the Kurdish provinces and the failed coup attempt of July 2016, which inaugurated the era of normalized state of exception and the rise of ultra-nationalist, neoliberal conservative populism, have muscled the political repression and control in the academic world. The ever expanding, incessant so-called war on terror has not only diminished the exercise of democratic rights and freedoms—whatever was left of them— but it has also opened up a space of accumulation of capital and redistribution, through which the AKP government has aimed to produce consent and complicity, and cement its ruling bloc. Indeed, the neoliberalizing state, as often noted, has increasingly taken the model of corporation, endorsing a number of private business-state alliances to govern economy and politics. In this configuration, the leading sectors of capital have become construction, energy, and armament, which arguably underpin the government's current domestic and international policies (Madra and Yılmaz 2019).

The current offensive against Boğaziçi University has brought these processes together. The Turkish government's illegitimate appointment of Melih Bulu has perfectly aligned with the by-now normalized trend of anti-democratic appointments to many elected positions, especially in the Kurdish provinces, referred to as *kayyım* ("trustee") appointments. Not surprisingly, the Boğaziçi protests have widely used that term to qualify the political context of the offensive against the university and relate Boğaziçi to other institutions that faced a similar attack on their autonomy. Moreover, the kind of neoliberal university advocated by Melih Bulu in his public statements has reflected well the new composition of capital, the extractionist "military-energy-construction complex" endorsed by the government (Madra and Yılmaz 2019: 42). The two new schools—law and communication—that the appointed rector endeavors to establish focus on techno-politics, especially the energy sector, corporate law, and the law of war and sea. It would not be wrong to say that with this offensive, the government mainly seeks to turn Boğaziçi into its think tank and capitalize on the national and international reputation of this prestigious institution to increase the credibility and legitimacy of its geopolitical and economic policies (İdil 2021).

No less important are the micro practices through which this authoritarian neoliberal offensive against Boğaziçi has been conducted. They reveal much about the AKP government's phantasmic investment in nationalist sovereignist body politic. Boğaziçi University's campus has been under heavy police siege since early January 2021. The security forces have aspired to institute their own regime of sensibility. On the way to the main campus in the neighborhood of Rumelihisarüstü, one has had to pass under the suspicious eyes of the police forces, equipped with heavy machine guns, antiriot gear, and armed vehicles, some of which had been used in the Kurdish provinces. In the first four months of the protest, the police forces used tall iron bars to fence the entire neighborhood. The constant presence of hundreds of uniformed and undercover police aims to divide and control the space and time of neighborhood life, which might as well pave the way for an urban renewal project targeting Rumelihisarüstü. The police supervision not only seeks to name and fix one in the symbolic order but also works by the infamous police instruction, "Move along! There's nothing to see here!" (Rancière 2010: 37). The iron bars and heavily armed police forces in Rumelihisarüstü aim to ensure that no one could *stand still* and look at the people embodying the state in the eye. As I describe below, standing still, disrupting this regime of sensibility, and refiguring it is precisely what the Boğaziçi protests have tried to do.

Technologies of control, Begona Aretxaga (2001) writes, work through phantasmic investments of power, which become manifest in the excess of rational purposive action. The security measures deployed against Boğaziçi that I discussed above have materialized a part of the fantasy invested by the state agents in their approach to the university. Let me give two examples to further illustrate this point. The first one concerns a solidarity protest organized by students from different universities in front of the main Boğaziçi campus, which has been closed to all except current Boğaziçi students and faculty under the pretext of Covid-19 pandemic emergency. When students coming to Boğaziçi left the nearby subway station to join the protest, the police forces shouted at them to "look down" (aşağı bak) and "move along" (devam et). There were snipers on the rooftops of the houses near the campus and an intense show of armed antiriot and special antiterror forces. The message was clear. And so was the government's phantasmic investment in security and control. As some media commentators noted, this notorious police instruction, "look down," ordering the subject to bow down and not see, captured viscerally the history of state oppression of Kurdish and leftist protests, thus linking Boğaziçi protests with other historical protests (Topuz 2021). What lurked in the police instruction was the longstanding nationalist sovereignist fantasy to subjugate and control the bodies of the enemies of the state (Üstündağ 2019).

It is thus not by chance that at one moment during the student protests in front of the Rector's Office—and this is my second example—the university's special security officers shouted angrily at the students, "I am the state," a statement that the appointed rector himself invoked in his public commentaries.[2] In this way, the protests against the appointed rector have been accused of engaging in an illegal, antistate activity, which is indeed part of the well-known authoritarian populist strategy of the government to demonize its opponents. The media criminalization of students and academics as quasi terrorists or perverts, especially LGBTI+ students, has also worked to that effect, using the tired conspiratorial vocabulary to pit the protesters against the sovereign heteropatriarchal body of the state. Yet, despite its efforts and its control of the mass media, the government has largely failed to diminish the popular support for the Boğaziçi protests.

This context helps make sense of the specific mode and popular force or valor of the faculty and student protests. The struggle for university autonomy and democracy has had the potential to resonate widely in the public, partly because of the form of the offensive against Boğaziçi and partly because of the social struggle against that offensive. The operation to control space and time recalls the well-established protest bans based on temporal and spatial exceptions (Arslanalp and Erkmen 2020). The phantasmic investment in the technologies of security and control, the criminalization of protests, and the use of executive decrees and shock-and-awe tactics to accelerate time and disorganize the opposition are well-known tactics of the AKP government (Küçük and Özselçuk 2019). But the university-based struggle for plural and egalitarian democracy and academic freedom has also signaled the interconnection between different struggles.[3] The interconnection between struggles became particularly visible in the solidarity meetings outside the campus, which brought together labor unions, feminist and LGBTI+ groups, and environmental activists. In the protests, the bodily action has played a key role, which is at once symbolic-material and strategic-practical. It has materialized and indeed enacted the possibility of resistance-in-alliance and of a counter–body politic against the neoliberal authoritarian politics of sovereignty.

The Space between Bodies

For politics to take place, the body must appear. I appear to others and they appear to me, which means that some space between us allows us each to appear.
—Judith Butler

Judith Butler offers insight into the bodily dimension of public protests, especially the assemblies and occupations that took place in the 2010s in the USA, Egypt, and Turkey, among other countries. In conversation with Hannah Arendt's work, Butler points to the way bodies constitute the "space of appearance," where one becomes visible to another and produces a sense of the common world. The space between bodies refers to the social, relational, embodied space collectively formed in the course of bodies acting together (2015: 75–77). That space has a multilayered social-material dimension that registers a history of power and struggle and shapes the specific form and force of protests. Indeed, popular protests, as often noted, tend to be articulated within the dominant ideological and institutional framework of power. For instance, the process of neoliberalization, which endorses flexible forms of labor and diminishes the capacity of organized labor by dismantling unions and valorizing private interests and entrepreneurship, also fragments the field of social struggles, thus contributing to the dominance of issue-based, isolated, and short-term struggles (Greenberg 2014).

The embodied world of Boğaziçi protests, especially the faculty vigils, can be usefully understood in this context. In the face of the offensive that aims to accelerate time and almost literally push students and faculty off campus, the protests have aimed to inhabit the space and stand still to say, "we are here" and "we are the university." Against the police that say there is nothing to see and do, but "move along," to use again Rancière's words, the protests have sought to occupy and refigure the space of the university for the "appearance of the subject." Since the beginning of the protests, two key slogans have organized the horizon of collective action: "we don't accept" and "we don't give up." These slogans have expressed the will of the protests, their act of *refusal* and *perseverance* in the face of the offensive. Boğaziçi resistance, by repeating these slogans, has sought to constantly regenerate itself, on the one hand, and, on the other, hold the ground against the destructive and co-optative efforts of the appointed administration. Student and faculty protests in different ways have claimed the public space of the university and attempted to make visible and material through bodily action the stakes of the protests, that is, the abstract principles of university autonomy and democracy including academic freedoms.

Beyond the terms of the offensive, Boğaziçi protests also need to be understood with respect to the accumulated experience of organized action in the university, which has offered the "infrastructure" that "supported" the ongoing protests, to use Butler's (2015) terms. In one of the Boğaziçi solidarity online meetings, Nazan Üstündağ put it nicely: "We [Boğaziçi faculty] are not just innocent victims of state violence. For years, we have been actively criticizing and opposing the government's authoritarian actions."[4] The agentive power of Boğaziçi protests, indeed, must not be underestimated. The collective experience of past struggles has significantly contributed to a collective ethos, which constituted, at least partly, the social infrastructure of the current protests. Among these struggles, one can mention the mid-2000s student and faculty protests for the education rights of veiled Muslim students, who had been denied access to classrooms; the anticapitalist Starbucks occupation in December 2011 led by students against the commercialization of the campus space, which then paved the way to faculty and student forums and, eventually, to the articulation of the principles of university autonomy and academic freedom by the University Senate that the protests today invoke; and, more recently, the social struggle concerning the judicial and media criminalization of the academics who signed the Peace Petition to condemn the war crimes and human rights violations perpetrated by the Turkish state in the Kurdish provinces in 2015. Moreover, the university campus life, which offered, relatively speaking, a pluralistic environment of free speech and critical thinking, was another key source for the current protests. The already existing social bonds of intimacy and friendship and the new ones born out of acting together contributed crucially to the social infrastructure of Boğaziçi resistance.

Similarly, some of the forms of protest have rested on past experiences of university protests in Turkey. With respect to the vigils, the idea of wearing the academic gown was certainly readily available. In that, there is perhaps little novelty, as the professorate, in many parts of the world, has been one of the few occupations, next to judges and priests, entitled to wear a gown in modern public life. The gown signifies their special autonomous position vis-à-vis the secular power of the state and capital, giving those occupations a sense of independent responsibility, historical tradition, and vocation (Kantorowicz 1949). The faculty from other Turkish universities also recently wore their gowns to protest the government's offensive against academic freedom, particularly the recent purges of dissident academics from the universities; but that certainly did not deter the police violence. At Boğaziçi, since at least 2016, there have been different occasions where academics in their gowns stood together on campus and read statements to condemn the government's antidemocratic actions. Thus, the gown, instead of producing the effect of elitist privilege or exclusion, has been used to create a relatively autonomous aesthetic space to express a public and institutional critique of the authoritarian repression of universities and democratic life in the country.

Moreover, while symbolizing the university, the gown has also created the effect of depersonalization and anonymity, highlighting that what is at issue is not one or another individual person's discontent, but a collective democratic critique. Standing together in that gown generates a symbolic, aesthetic space, which does not belong to any single body, but to *everybody* inhabiting that space. In this sense, this embodied performance hints at the "empty place of power," to use Claude Lefort's (1986) formulation for democracy, and has been an important factor contributing to the popular force of the vigils. Further, by denoting an autonomous institutional space and tradition, the gowned performances have countered the narrative constructed by the authoritarian offensive. They have enabled the faculty to uphold the university's principles and reframe and integrate the offensive into the long history of the university. In this sense, the vigils highlight the fact that the struggle against the offensive also involves the struggle over writing the history and future of the university.

Certainly, the faculty vigils—embodied protests—have not functioned in isolation but have been supported by a number of other activities, which help articulate the meaning of the university. While seemingly forming a closed, carefully ritualized and choreographed aesthetic space, the vigils are at the same time open to improvisation. In response to particular events, the vigils have integrated signs that condemn, for instance, the police violence against the students (the slogan of "look down") or they have expressed support for LGBTI+ students by displaying rainbow umbrellas. Every Friday, academics, as part of the vigil, read a weekly digest to report on the developments in the campus, which has been secluded from the rest of Istanbul. In brief, the vigils have become an important occasion to embody and communicate the will of Boğaziçi protests.

Yet, the full meaning of the kind of autonomous and democratic university aspired to by Boğaziçi protests could be articulated only in tandem with the other activities such as online faculty forums, the work of commissions, cultural events, and solidarity panels inside and outside Turkey. These activities have been essential to the work of framing and scaling up the stakes of the protests. On different platforms, the faculty and students have discussed the importance of the institutional autonomy of university with respect to academic, financial, and social matters, and the way a department- and commission-based, participatory democratic government is indispensable to the practice of academic freedom and to the pluralistic, egalitarian campus life. As often noted, the university struggle has been at once for Boğaziçi, for the notion of public university, and for the universal principles of academic freedom tied to the principles of equality and liberty.

Seen this way, bodily occupations could not to be limited to the vigils. Occupying the commissions and formal institutional structures such as the Senate is of great importance. In fact, resistance in the institutional space of the university has been profoundly important in the practical organization of the protests. Holding the ground also means keeping the seats and amplifying the voices in the commissions that deal with the daily administration of

Boğaziçi. Yet, that also at times creates important tensions concerning, for instance, the questions of where to draw the line in terms of participating in university administration when it is led by the illegitimate rector, and how not to normalize the offensive while taking care of the daily problems. There were also other tensions among Boğaziçi faculty resulting from the unequal distribution of vulnerabilities and the classed and gendered inequalities integral to the society at large. Besides, the issue of tenure and the particular job contract one had with the university has also shaped the kind of risk one embodies in the act of protesting and exposing oneself to the state authorities.

All this organizing and communicative labor, with its tensions and dilemmas, has been indispensable to the making of the body politic, which manifests itself in the vigils. Zeynep Gambetti (see this issue) suggests that the vigils could be seen as a "show of force" to the state authorities and the general public. We can also conceive them as a site for the social production of the subjectivity of the protesters. From the beginning, the vigils have been part of the everyday labor of protest, without which no perseverance could be possible. While "stillness" enacted by the vigils might seem like the rupture of the continuous flow of daily life (Seremetakis 1994), here it also means the reconstitution of the daily life of protest. Reflecting on women activists in Northern Ireland, Begona Aretxaga has suggested that "political agency— the capacity of people to become historical subjects deliberately intervening in the making and changing of their worlds... presupposes a degree of consciousness and intentionality... but it is anchored in a cultural repository of largely unconscious discourses and images, modes of thinking and feeling" (Aretxaga 1997: 8). The vigils could be seen as part of the making of that agency, not just by standing still and clapping as a collective body, but also through the quotidian practices following the vigils such as the exchange of information, gossiping, eating and drinking together, and interacting with the students and administrative workers.

Thus, in Spinozist terms, the vigils, one might say, could be seen to enact the power to affect and to be affected. They have been essential not only to communicate with the onlookers and the general public but also to create a social, affective, relational bond of solidarity and friendship among the members of the university. Perhaps one valuable, concrete achievement of the ongoing struggle against the government's offensive will be precisely this engendering of a dissident body politic, a social subjectivity, which would reproduce the memory of the struggle and might serve one day as the infrastructure of the future struggles to come in Boğaziçi and beyond.

Notes

This essay would not be possible without the Boğaziçi resistance and the numerous discussions that I have had with students, colleagues, and friends from Boğaziçi University, especially Seda Altuğ, Mert Arslanalp, and Zeynep Gambetti, and from international solidarity networks.

1   There are, of course, many different, important turning points in the historical development of universities in Turkey, which I cannot discuss here. For an overview, see Erdem and Akın 2019.

2   See, e.g., *Cumhuriyet* 2021 for the news from February 2, 2021.

3   For instance, this year's Ayşenur Zarakolu Freedom of Thought and Expression Award, recently given to Boğaziçi constituencies by the Human Rights Association (Istanbul), publicly acknowledged that point: see *English Bianet* 2021.

4   See LSE Sociology 2021 for the solidarity meeting organized by the London School of Economics and Political Science on April 28, 2021.

References

Aretxaga, Begona. 1997. *Shattering Silence: Women, Nationalism and Political Subjectivity in Northern Ireland*. Princeton, NJ: Princeton University Press.

Aretxaga, Begona. 2001. "The Sexual Games of the Body Politic: Fantasy and State Violence in Northern Ireland." *Culture, Medicine, and Psychiatry*, no. 25: 1–27.

Arslanalp, Mert, and Deniz Erkmen. 2020. "Mobile Emergency Rule in Turkey: Legal Repression of Protests during Authoritarian Transformation." *Democratization* 27, no. 6: 947–69.

Butler, Judith. 2015. *Notes toward a Performative Theory of Assembly*. Cambridge, MA: Harvard University Press.

Cumhuriyet. 2021. "BÜMED Başkanı Şahin, Bulu ile görüşmesini anlattı: Öğrencilerle bu yüzden görüşmedi!" February 2 (2 Şubat). www.cumhuriyet.com.tr/haber/bumed-baskani-sahin-bulu-ile-gorusmesini-anlatti-ogrencilerle-bu-yuzden-gorusmedi-1810732

English Bianet. 2021. "Boğaziçi Constituencies, HDP's Gergerlioğlu Granted Freedom of Expression Award." June 14. bianet.org/english/human-rights/245619-bogazici-constituencies-hdp-s-gergerlioglu-granted-freedom-of-expression-award.

Erdem, Esra, and Kamuran Akın. 2019. "Emergent Repertoires of Resistance and Commoning in Higher Education: The Solidarity Academies Movement in Turkey." *South Atlantic Quarterly* 118, no. 1: 145–63.

Greenberg, Jessica. 2014. *After the Revolution: Youth, Democracy, and the Politics of Disappointment in Serbia*. Stanford, CA: Stanford University Press.

İdil, Neşe. 2021. "'Neoliberal Authoritarianism at Its Best': Boğaziçi University Academics Defy Erdoğan's Rector Appointment." *Duvar English*, January 7. www.duvarenglish.com/neoliberal-authoritarianism-at-its-best-bogazici-university-academics-defy-erdogans-rector-appointment-news-55763.

Kantorowicz, Ernst H. 1949. *The Fundamental Issue Documents and Marginal Notes on the University of California Loyalty Oath*. www.lib.berkeley.edu/uchistory/archives_exhibits/loyaltyoath/symposium/kantorowicz.html (accessed June 21, 2021).

Küçük, Bülent, and Ceren Özselçuk. 2019. "Fragments of the Emerging Regime in Turkey: Limits of Knowledge, Transgression of Law, and Failed Imaginaries." *South Atlantic Quarterly* 118, no. 1: 1–21.

Lefort, Claude. 1986. *The Political Forms of Modern Society: Bureaucracy, Democracy, Totalitarianism.* Cambridge, MA: MIT Press.

LSE Sociolgy. 2021. "Defending Academic Autonomy in Turkey." Facebook, April 28. www.facebook.com/watch/live/?v=2867959660084935&ref=watch_permalink.

Madra, Yahya, and Sedat Yılmaz. 2019. "Turkey's Decline into (Civil) War Economy: From Neoliberal Populism to Corporate Nationalism." *South Atlantic Quarterly* 118, no. 1: 41–59.

Rancière, Jacques. 2010. *Dissensus: On Politics and Aesthetics.* London: Continuum.

Ross, Fiona C. 2002. *Bearing Witness: Women and the Truth and Reconciliation Commission in South Africa.* London: Pluto Press.

Seremetakis, Nadia. 1994. *The Senses Still: Perception and Memory as Material Culture in Modernity.* Chicago: University of Chicago Press.

Topuz, Ali Duran. 2021. "Aşağı bak komutunun kısa tarihi" ("The Short History of the Instruction of Look Down"). *Duvar,* 2 Şubat. www.gazeteduvar.com.tr/asagi-bak-komutunun-kisa-tarihi-makale-1512085

Üstündağ, Nazan. 2019. "Pornographic State and Erotic Resistance." *South Atlantic Quarterly* 118, no. 1: 95–110.

Cenk Özbay

State Homophobia, Sexual Politics, and Queering the Boğaziçi Resistance

On April 13, 2021, private security officers blocked me from passing through the main entrance to the Boğaziçi University campus, although I am an alumnus and a former professor. It was the hundredth day of what has been termed the Boğaziçi resistance against the top-down appointment of the rector Melih Bulu. As a response to the exuberant spirit of the hundredth day of protests, the appointed rector ordered the security personnel to close the gates to visitors in order to prevent them from participating in demonstrations against his contested position.

While I, alongside several other guests deemed unwanted, was trying to convince the security guards that the purpose of my visit was academic, a queer student showed up and started to yell at the security personnel: the campus belonged to scholars and students, the new rector and his oppressive policies were unacceptable, and we (the visitors) should not listen to or comply with what the security personnel had to say to stop us. When the officers responded angrily with assaults and indecent language about his gender display and sexual identity, the student did not get intimidated or back down as I would have expected. Instead, the student persisted, swore back at them, and said buoyantly, "We're here to fight with you; we aren't going to leave this place to you." This encounter made me recognize the organized countermovement in the Boğaziçi habitat as a form of resistance to the emergent state homophobia in Turkey. The queered public of Boğaziçi is a prism to comprehend the changing sexual politics in the country.

The appointment of Bulu by the president of Turkey, Tayyip Erdoğan, ignited a wave of reaction, criticism, and disdain from the public. Academics

The South Atlantic Quarterly 121:1, January 2022
DOI 10.1215/00382876-9561657 © 2022 Duke University Press

and students at Boğaziçi started protests and called for elections straight away. The unprecedented strong retort to and vociferous rejection of his decision pushed Erdoğan to take the issue as a personal affront, and an affront to the nature of his sovereignty. He stated in a self-absorbed manner that he "had found Bulu as suitable, worthy of becoming the new Boğaziçi rector," and declared that the students who were protesting were "terrorists" (*Bianet* 2021a). The stigmatization of the students as terrorists materialized when police raided the on-campus office that was used jointly by the Women's Studies Club (BUKAK) and the LGBTI+ Studies Club (BULGBTI+). Police confiscated rainbow flags and a book that recounts the history of PKK (Kurdistan Workers' Party) as what they called evidence of an assumed connection to terrorist organizations and activities.[1]

The conundrum I will be addressing in this essay is the following: What made the queer students' actions and position within the university so central to this particular academic and governmental crisis? What were the conditions that made them so vulnerable and, from the point of view of the state, so illegitimate and threatening?

In this essay, I argue that the LGBTI+ and queer students at Boğaziçi showcase to a certain extent the recent queering of sexualities in Turkey (Özbay 2017) with their destabilizing and nonbinary gender/sexual identities, political struggles against heteronormativity and homonormativity, and recalcitrant demands for creating safe public spaces of performative, intimate, and challenging visibility. State homophobia emerges as a response to the students' demands and to the institutional culture that enables the making of a queer public through activism and resistance. Beyond aiming to strengthen the gap between straights and queers, state homophobia draws a distinction between acceptable and abject queers. However, as it unfolds in the case of the Boğaziçi resistance, heterosexuals are convinced that if the state is allowed to intrude into the LGBTI+ lives, theirs will be exposed to threats as well. In other words, straights are free only as much as queers are. Hence, the resistance against the appointed rector is queered as the university is queered through the resistance.

Queers on Campus

The recent troubling confrontation between the LGBTI+ people at Boğaziçi and state homophobia is not the first incident of this kind at Boğaziçi. For instance, a conference titled "Queer, Turkey, Identity" to be held at the rectorate building in 2004 had also caused trouble. The president of the Council of

Higher Education (YÖK, the national bureaucratic authority that supervises universities in Turkey) called the then rector and inquired about the event that was publicized by the press. Embarrassed and angry, the rector went to the conference room and strove to interrupt the presentations about sexualities and intimacies. The professors who organized the conference resisted, and the rector had to leave without being able to cancel the event. In 2015, the Boston Gay Men Chorus performed at Boğaziçi University after their Istanbul concert was canceled at the last minute as a result of political pressure. In 2019, a student from BULGBTI+ adapted the Turkish national anthem's lyrics to queer slang in a humorous way in an email sent to club members. When the email came out publicly, the club was accused by the Islamist, pro-government press of ridiculing and disrespecting national values. The student faced a minor disciplinary penalty, and the rectorate demanded that the student club apologize and keep a low profile. The then rector (also selected by the president) prevented the Boğaziçi Pride Parade from marching between the two campuses on the street and confined the event to the university premises. After a while, the university administration asked the queer students not to shout sexually explicit (indeed playful and mocking) slogans, such as *faşizme karşı bacak omza*—meaning, "leg to shoulder [the piledriver] against fascism."

There have been many other examples of the perturbing relation between queer students and the previous university administration, especially since the former emerged as an active and visible group in Turkey in the last two decades. However, the situation has never been so bleak as in the days following Bulu's appointment. Bulu and his associates attacked the visibility and culture of LGBTI+ students to reinforce and legitimize his contested post. Meanwhile, the rector canceled BULGBTI+'s "candidate student club" status, which implies its formal closure. The closure was announced by the president's office—which added to the unending series of procedural flaws and malpractices to the process.

Indeed, Bulu might not be acting alone. Following Erdoğan, the Islamist press was claiming that the BULGBTI+ were "sympathetic to terrorists." The Istanbul Governorship released a press statement claiming that among students detained at the protests were members of the "LGBT-I." By using this hyphenated spelling, the governor's office was metamorphosing the struggle for sexual freedom into an illegal or antistate organization (most underground leftist or Islamic group acronyms have a hyphen, as in DHKP-C or IBDA-C). The interior minister declared that "four LGBT deviants that disrespected religion at Boğaziçi University were captured."[2] During the students' pretrial hearing for the accusation of disparaging religious (Islamic) symbols on campus, the judge asked them if they were "members of the LGBT," suggesting that it was an insurgent organization. Inspectors from the Interior Ministry went to municipalities governed by opposition parties to ask if they had any "LGBT activities" to report. The minister of Family and Social Services posted a tweet saying, "There is a global movement that wants to normalize homosexuality and make it a norm." The dismissed imam of Hagia Sophia,[3] who happens to be a theology scholar, made a public call for the founding of a "national social media platform," in which people "could exercise the freedom to criticize Israel and LGBT"—Israel being the traditional enemy of the Islamists, and LGBT being the new, emerging one to be apprehensive about.

President Erdoğan also retorted that "Turkey's youth" was loyal to national and moral values and were consequently not LGBTI+ (*Bianet* 2021b). After Erdoğan's vilification, state and government organs, official spokesmen, and their so-called troll accounts on social media reiterated his hostile attitude. One direction that these discursive attacks took was to frame the students and demonstrations as an LGBTI+ insurgence and describe the issue as a moral crisis. This frame aimed at stigmatizing the protestors as abject and the protests as illegitimate, criminal, and unlawful, while simultaneously serving to consolidate an imagined, pro-government moral majority that is assumed to be positioned automatically against the LGBTI+ rights and sociability.

Boğaziçi University is often seen as a liberal and empowering place for minorities. The multiplicity of active student clubs is a very important aspect of this environment. Thus, the closure of BULGBTI+ had a huge impact on the inclusive and pro-diversity philosophy and reputation of the university.

I talked to four Boğaziçi students (whom I will quote from farther below) from a variety of backgrounds, majors, political views, and gender and sexual identities in order to learn about their experiences and feelings. They emphasized how BULGBTI+ meant possibilities for meeting, socialization, networking, self-confidence, and *gullüm* (joyous fun time). They said the club is their "home at Boğaziçi," it provides a "safe space" on campus, and it is crucial for the formation of political consciousness, identity, and activism. BULGBTI+ gives "a *queer* education, not just gay, but strange" (Bollen 2020: 260; emphasis original), for the students who strive to live in a relatively less homophobic and more embracing environment. The closure of the club thus reveals the desire to silence queer students and erase the accumulated knowledge and affective experiences.[4] In this sense, Boğaziçi University is intentionally turned into a target of state homophobia enforced by the appointed rector with the support of the state—including its ideological apparatuses and law enforcement units.

State Homophobia

The state in Turkey has merged with the consecutive AKP (Justice and Development Party) governments in the last two decades and produced a compound, seemingly inseparable end product. What is experienced at Boğaziçi reminds me of Katherine Verdery's (2018: 21) formulation of the state, which "has organizational, territorial, and ideological aspects. On the one hand, it has a very material existence. . . . On the other, extensive ideological work by groups within it goes into creating the impression that a state is a real actor, which 'does' things." The party-state in the liminal and polarized context has evolved into a *real actor* embodied in security officers, rectors, ministers, imams, judges, governorships, the police, social media trolls, and all others who echo them. What we have witnessed at Boğaziçi University and the statements made by *state actors* are both an intensification and stabilization of state homophobia in Turkey.

The early conceptualization of homophobia was problematized as individualizing and psychologizing the circumstances instead of underscoring the systematic "sexual oppression in general" (Plummer 1981: 62) and hiding that it was a "political problem rooted in social institutions and organizations" (Kitzinger 1987: 154). Recently, homophobia was retheorized (sometimes as *political* or *official* homophobia) through the constellation of social and political structures and complex cultural logics that undergird violent and abusive practices and expressions that target queers across different social situations (Mendos 2019; Murray 2009; Weiss and Bosia 2013).

I argue that state homophobia refers to a series of articulated hatred, fear, disgust, and dehumanization discourses regarding LGBTI+ and queer identities, communities, movements, and politics by various organs of the state and representatives of the government in an organized manner. Rooted in a secular policy and modernizing orientation, the Turkish Republic has never officially made queer individuals illegal or imposed punitive measures on their same-sex sexual acts despite its unquestionably heteronormative tendencies (Özbay and Öktem 2021; Savcı 2021). But public authorities have repeatedly rejected, marginalized, and condemned queer bodies, visibilities, and actions via religious, nationalist, fundamentalist, traditionalist, and statist grounds despite the fact that discrimination among citizens is forbidden by the constitution in Turkey.

The recent increase and systematization of homophobic assaults (depicting them as sinners, terrorists, or deviants) and the denial of the existence of queer citizens by state officials point to dangerous and daunting circumstances that may legitimize and cause in-person attacks, risk, and harm as well as a possible rollback of democratic gains, rights, and mechanisms that must be secured in an inclusive and diverse society. In this sense, recent positive examples may provide a more balanced and even optimistic understanding that is flourishing in society against state homophobia. The Republican People's Party (CHP) and People's Democratic Party (HDP), for instance, put forward LGBTI+ candidates in national and local elections; some municipalities celebrated Pride Week on their official Twitter and Facebook accounts with the now-banned rainbow flags; many queer student clubs, formal associations, and NGOs have been legal and active for almost two decades; the popular hashtag "#LGBTIhaklariinsanhaklaridir" (#LGBTIrightsarehumanrights) has been shared on social media by many intellectuals, public figures, and opinion leaders, including even some right-wing politicians. And despite the recent state-led wave of homophobic criminalization and demonization at Boğaziçi University, neither students (irrespective of political stance) nor most of the student clubs rejected or condemned queer students.

Respected Citizens versus Terrorist Queers

The encounter between the Boğaziçi University protests and state homophobia transmuted into a symbolic opposition between the state's "desirable" (heterosexual) citizens and the "rebellious," "unruly," "immoral," and "terrorist" queers. The underlying state logic in this opposition is that one cannot choose to be queer but can choose not to be aligned with social and political others of the state. Supporting this logic, President Erdoğan had once declared, "Those *marginals*, who appear in the streets of Beyoglu, can stay in this country as one of its colors if they remain *within moral boundaries*" (*Cumhuriyet* 2018; emphasis mine). The Beyoglu district Erdoğan referred to is home to Gezi Park and Taksim Square, where queers wanted to celebrate the LGBTI Pride Parade as they were able to do before it was banned in 2015. Although Erdoğan didn't explicitly say so, it is possible to interpret the president's words as a warning against queers who demand equal rights and public visibility through challenging, destabilizing, and unapologetically performing their identity against the compulsory heteronormative matrix. Thus, this was a tacit threat to the queers to remain within the limits of acceptability, respect, and tolerance.

Such an interpretation would encourage queers in Turkey to be homonormative subjects, who don't provoke or disrupt heteronormativity, who accept being a mere color within diversity, and who respect the boundaries of an imagined public morality: a group whose existence is condoned as long as they act "unassertively and accommodatingly" (Özbay 2021: 15). Consequently, the Turkish case would substantiate the claim that "the nation not only allows for homosexual bodies, but also actually disciplines and normalizes them; the nation is not only heteronormative, but also homonormative," in Jaspir Puar's words (2007: 50).

Through the queering of sexualities in Turkey in the last decade, gay orientation and identification shifted toward a more destabilizing, unapologetic disposition with the celebration of gender fluidity, sexual diversity, unfixed identities, and disobedient bodily performances in both intimate and communal spaces. BULGBTI+ has exemplified and even led this trend. By self-identifying as LGBTI+ and queer, these (mostly younger) people were politicized against both the gender and sexual mainstream of heteronormativity as well as the desired proper gay men (and to a lesser extent, women) of homonormative precepts. The "self-responsibilized" homonormative subject is supposed to be complicit with hegemonic structures that legitimize the multilayered social inequality. Reclaiming the heteronormative public space for queer public visibility, performance, sexuality, and safety becomes a significant aspect of sexual politics—which is what the state in Turkey is deliberately against, as evident in the prohibition of the pride parade, the state interventions to the scripts of television series in order to censor gay characters, and the security guards' (another state actor) homophobic assaults on the queer visitors in urban parks (Tanis 2020).

Local and National Queers

In Turkey, the citizens' right and capacity not to be devout, conservative, nationalist/patriotic, or traditionalist, ergo the right to inhabit somewhere outside the discursive justification of the state, has been seemingly on hold in the last decade. The state organs reiterate and exalt the value of being, feeling, or acting on phantasmagoric "local and national values." It is almost a mundane matter to be called a terrorist or a traitor because of the choices one is supposed to have a right to make freely.

As one of the four Boğaziçi students I interviewed, Canburak, puts it, for example, "They [the statesmen, the Islamist press] didn't directly say that we should shut BULGBTI+ down. That's why they planted the book and called us terrorists. Actually, they don't accept *lubunya* [queers] who are not local and national."

Another, Derya, says that there were no hostile reactions against *lubunya* people at Boğaziçi if they did not go beyond what was allowed: "They call it the threshold of provocation. If you'll provoke us, you'll suffer the consequences. And when it happens, you have to say I'm Muslim, I'm with my state, to save yourself. Know your place and don't transgress. The state retaliates when it thinks that you're not standing with it." What has happened recently at Boğaziçi, with the precursors and the backlash, is the harsh response to the active refusal of homonormative prescriptions by this group of students around BULGBTI+. It is also a response to the institutional milieu and cultural-political context that facilitates the formation of a queer public. This is not a form of simple homophobia generated and disseminated by the state. Going beyond that, it is simultaneously a warning to young citizens who reject being homonormative (respectable, decent, normalized) and instead choose to come out and come together, get organized, turn to activism, get politicized, criticize, and resist. The state in Turkey, with all its power and state actors, does not only communicate the message "don't be queer" in toto; it also conveys the message "don't be queer in the way that we dislike and forbid." Thus, state homophobia emerges not only in the differentiation between gay and straight identities but also in the homonormative hierarchization among queers (Benedicto 2014; Özbay 2021).

Queering and Resisting

The four students I talked to (Derya, Canburak, Berk, and Ogun) and their friends from the BULGBTI+ network felt terrified and mesmerized when they unexpectedly came up against state homophobia, the rebuke on social media, being labeled as deviant by the minister of interior and terrorist by the president, and police incursions into students' homes. They said they stayed somewhere else instead of their homes for a while during the police attacks, and it was unsustainable to be constantly too scared to sleep in their beds at night. However, these extreme psychological conditions and material hardships did not make them change their minds and move away either from the Boğaziçi resistance or BULGBTI+. They deem themselves at the center of the resistance, the club as a *catalyst*. Berk notes that they have been active since the beginning of the protests with their rainbow flags, hence they are the most visible, most shunned, and most attacked group. Ogun observes that they "were on top of the public agenda because of the art piece that brings together the Kaaba with the flags of sexual minorities," although BULGBTI+ declared that the contested artwork was not their production and that they did not know about it until the state-led Islamic circles accused the club members of disrespecting religion.

So far, BULGBTI+ has been stigmatized with scorning national values (by queering the national anthem's lyrics) and religion (by exhibiting that particular work of art) as well as accused of being related to terrorism because of the PKK book. It has been presented as the perfect other to what is assumed to be national and local (and moral). Still, the now-forbidden rainbow flag is transmogrified into the symbol of resistance as it ubiquitously emerges everywhere, including in the hands of the professors, who stand with their backs to the rectorate building every day to protest. Canburak says that "most of the academics weren't always so welcoming toward queer politics, they didn't pronounce the word LGBTI in the past. The resistance made them understand the contours of the struggle and incorporate us."

Derya underscores a significant point regarding the dynamics between the sexual minority and the heterosexual majority within the university community:

> Queers and straights share the same anxieties about what sort of a life we'll have, how will we be able to use our bodies. The state tried to instrumentalize queers to alienate straights from us and stop the resistance. However, it had the opposite effect: everybody saw that when the state intervenes into queer activity, it signals and justifies that it can intervene in straights' lives as well. Straight students and professors saw that freeing us means freeing themselves from the state's bullying.

In Turkey, the rainbow flag was appropriated and used as a symbol for LGBTI+ liberation in tune with global cultural trends in the late 1990s. State organs and actors have recently redefined it as a sign of impropriety and delinquency and hence transformed it into a symbol that belongs to contradictory social imaginations and cultural uses through the "shared significance" (Griswold 2013: 20) that it gathers from both sides. The rainbow flags demonstrated to the public that not everyone in the Boğaziçi resistance was heterosexual and queers were also present. When the state forcefully bans the rainbow flag and takes students under custody—by presuming or presenting them as queers—heterosexual students face homophobic treatment. Derya emphasizes that "this is the formation of a new subjectivity and the queering of Boğaziçi and the resistance." What Derya means was crystallized in a challenging and transformative event, when several cisgender and heterosexual students shouted the slogan "We are all trans" ("Hepimiz dönmeyiz") in front of the rectorate building.

As I am writing this essay, the Boğaziçi resistance is still going on and the university community continues to reject the administration. The resistance has been spectacularly queered by the state's decision to shut down BULGBTI+ and the queer students' unfailing tenacity. More importantly, the university is queered through the resistance, as BULGBTI+ and the rainbow flags turned into the symbols of resistance that virtually everyone knows, accepts, and shares.

Notes

1   The club members I talked to claimed that the book did not belong to them and that police planted it during the search to blame the BULGBTI+.
2   The club members I talked to said that the contested artwork that put together an image of the Kaaba with the flags of sexual minorities wasn't related to them. They could not identify the four distinct flags on the image during our conversations. They said they did not like the art piece, but they would defend the right to produce and exhibit art freely.
3   Built in 537 as a church by the Eastern Roman Empire, Hagia Sophia was converted into a mosque by Ottomans in 1453. The modern-secular Turkish Republic transformed Hagia Sophia into a museum. Erdogan reconverted it into a mosque in 2020 in order to satisfy the demands of the Islamist minority and demonstrate his counterrevolutionary predispositions. The imam of the new Hagia Sophia Mosque was symbolically the most important imam in the country.
4   Homosexual and queer students at Boğaziçi University got organized around the idea of a social club some twenty years ago (Firat 2001).

References

Benedicto, Bobby. 2014. *Under Bright Lights*. Minneapolis: University of Minnesota Press.
Bianet. 2021a. "Erdoğan Says Bulu Suitable for Rectorship." January 8. bianet.org/english/politics/237275–Erdoğan-calls-bogazici-university-protesters-terrorists-as-15–more-people-detained.
Bianet. 2021b. "LGBT Youth Statement by Erdoğan." February 1. bianet.org/english/politics/238511–lgbt-youth-statement-by-president-Erdoğan.
Bollen, Christopher. 2020. *A Beautiful Crime*. New York: Harper.
Cumhuriyet. 2018. "Erdogan: Beyoglu'ndaki marjinaller" ("Erdogan: Those Marginals in Beyoglu"). March 23. www.cumhuriyet.com.tr/haber/erdogan-beyoglundaki-marjinaller-rahat-durmazlarsa-kulaklarindan-tutar-firlatiriz-947611.
Firat, Gulay. 2001. "Bogazici'nde bin escinsel var" ("There Are a Thousand Homosexuals at Bogazici"). *Milliyet*, January 22. www.milliyet.com.tr/pembenar/bogazici-nde-bin-escinsel-var-5292782.
Griswold, Wendy. 2013. *Cultures and Societies in a Changing World*. London: Sage.
Kitzinger, Celia. 1987. *The Social Construction of Lesbianism*. London: Sage.

Mendos, Lucas Ramon. 2019. *State-Sponsored Homophobia*. Geneva: ILGA.

Murray, David. 2009. *Homophobias*. Durham, NC: Duke University Press.

Özbay, Cenk. 2017. *Queering Sexualities in Turkey*. London: I. B. Tauris.

Özbay, Cenk. 2021. "Living Like a Hetero: Southern Homonormativity in Istanbul." *Sexualities*, OnlineFirst, doi.org/10.1177/13634607211014477.

Özbay, Cenk, and Kerem Öktem. 2021. "Turkey's Queer Times." *New Perspectives on Turkey* 64: 117–30.

Plummer, Ken. 1981. *The Making of Modern Homosexual*. London: Hutchinson.

Puar, Jasbir. 2007. *Terrorist Assemblages*. Durham, NC: Duke University Press.

Savcı, Evren. 2021. *Queer in Translation*. Durham, NC: Duke University Press.

Tanis, Edanur. 2020. "Macka Parki'nda homofobik saldiri" ("The Homophobic Attack in Macka Park"). *Medyascope*, June 17. medyascope.tv/2020/06/17/macka-parkinda -homofobik-saldiriya-ugrayan-turgay-yildirim-ile-soylesi-bu-ulkede-can-guvenligim-yok/.

Verdery, Katherine. 2018. *My Life as a Spy*. Durham, NC: Duke University Press.

Weiss, Meredith L., and Michael Bosia. 2013. *Global Homophobia*. Urbana: University of Illinois Press.

Cihan Tekay

#AşağıBakmayacağız ("We Will Not Look Down"): International Solidarity with Boğaziçi University Protests and the Struggle for University Autonomy under Authoritarian Neoliberalism

Shortly after a new rector close to the ruling Justice and Development Party (AKP) was appointed by Turkey's president to its flagship Boğaziçi University on January 1, 2021, faculty and students started protesting this top-down decision daily with all their might. For a university that had been electing its own rectors by faculty votes, the appointment was a direct, albeit not entirely unprecedented, incursion on its autonomy. Solidarity protests spread outside the campus quickly, reaching across Istanbul and then other cities in Turkey. This struggle for democracy and university autonomy resonated almost simultaneously across the world: protests were organized in Berlin, New York, Paris, Brussels, Cologne, Düsseldorf, Amsterdam, and Barcelona, as well as other cities in Europe, Asia, and North America, ranging from only a dozen to more than a hundred people participating. In London, where pandemic measures prevented large gatherings at the time, supporters met in pairs to respond to the call from groups of Boğaziçi alumni to document international support by taking photos of the protesters' main slogan, #AşağıBakmayacağız ("We will not look down"), next to the landmark buildings of the cities (*5Harfliler* 2021).

Of course, in the age of the internet and pandemic measures urging people to stay at home as much as possible, the reverberations of on-the-ground protests extended to a multitude of online spaces. Panels sprung up featuring Boğaziçi students and faculty, academics exiled from Turkish

The South Atlantic Quarterly 121:1, January 2022
DOI 10.1215/00382876-9561671 © 2022 Duke University Press

universities in the past five years, as well as their international supporters, organized by colleagues working in Greece, Italy, the UK, Germany, the United States, and Canada, to name a few. In addition to the Middle East Studies Association of North America (MESA), which has been consistently documenting the erosion of academic freedom at Turkish universities for the past several years, and Scholars at Risk, which has been founded expressly for this purpose, universities such as Bremen and Central European University, student and higher education unions, human rights organizations, professional associations, and even academic programs and departments signed petitions supporting the struggle at Boğaziçi. These statements declared their solidarity with Boğaziçi students and faculty, decried the government attempts to undermine the autonomy of universities and civic organizations in the country, condemned the police violence against students, and called for reinstating academic freedom. As the protests grew and continued during the months following January, they also gained some news coverage and sympathy outside the higher education community, being featured in German, British, US, and Spanish media, among others. They reported the protests' resonance beyond the campus and cited the concerns of young people across the country who are facing unemployment, uncertain futures following a drawn-out economic crisis, obstacles to their freedom of expression, an eroded meritocracy, and a hunger for political change among this population.

For the purposes of this article, I will focus on the question of why Boğaziçi has become a point of traction for international solidarity, drawing on my own experience in and knowledge of Turkey's diaspora in Europe and North America, as well as short interviews with people who have participated in solidarity actions internationally. In this respect, the increasing migration of university graduates and academics from Turkey during the past decade is important, as is the resonance of demands for university autonomy and democratically run public institutions across publics from Europe, North America, and the global South under conditions of neoliberal authoritarianism. A discussion of the broad reverberations of the struggle of younger generations, together with their older counterparts, for a less economically and politically precarious future will help the reader understand that the case of Boğaziçi should not be considered an Orientalized exception. Rather, the demands for academic freedom, university autonomy, and democratically organized public institutions resonate across the globe, while populist right-wing movements are on the rise, and neoliberalism and privatization have created politically and economically precarious conditions for both faculty and students.

Sociological Underpinnings: The New Generation Abroad

One of the major conditions for the persistent and extensive support for the Boğaziçi resistance is the ubiquity of the university's alumni, as well as other university graduates from Turkey, across the globe. While this older generation, of which I am a member, is not the first to be exiled from Turkey due to political and economic developments, this is a new type of diaspora, and with different qualities than those of the generations preceding them. This population has especially grown during the past decade, as the latest round of political and economic changes in Turkey have not only displaced those who have been politically active, as was the case in the aftermath of the 1971 and 1980 coups. There is a much bigger section of society, chiefly among millennials, who have left Turkey in the hope of living in more liberal political climates and better economic conditions. Many of these people reside in Europe, especially in Germany, where there is already a significant Turkish and Kurdish population. Differently from their counterparts in the previous generations, who were peasants turned factory workers, they arrive as university graduates with some work experience in white-collar jobs, already speaking English, with some working proficiency in the languages of their adopted countries. Some have already participated in Erasmus exchange programs in Europe, and some arrive to pursue graduate degrees and stay thereafter. Although their reasons for migration are not necessarily active political membership in an organization, they might still have political reasons for migrating. They cite the inability to work in the areas in which they were trained, because of the ubiquity of nepotism in the country. They cite the difficulties of being women or LGBTI+ people in a society where the government has increasingly openly enforced conservative ideas of morality. As well, they cite the deteriorating, increasingly unregulated working conditions in neoliberal Turkey, where long working hours, including weekends, and abusive supervisors are rampant not only in the factories but also in office buildings.[1]

Because of the sociological reasons that I cited, this new generation tends to be quite involved in the ongoing political issues in Turkey, as oftentimes their leaving is not necessarily a form of refusal to engage, but rather stems from a difficulty of finding a place for themselves in the current social, political, and economic climate in Turkey. Unlike the previous generations of migrants from Turkey, who, save for the minorities and dissidents such as Kurds, Alevis, and socialists, have largely been co-opted by AKP's propaganda machine in Europe during the past few decades, the new generation overwhelmingly sympathizes with various sectors of the political opposition in Turkey, if they are not actively supporting it. Many are university graduates, or alumni of Boğaziçi itself, which they credit for teaching them liberal and left values like coexistence, critical thinking, collectivization of resources, appreciation of diversity, and a distrust of those forcefully holding on to power. Furthermore, unlike Germany, where students tend to stay in their general region for university education, and unlike the United States, where students either stay in their state for higher education where they pay lower tuition for public universities or take on debt to study in private colleges and universities across the United States, Turkey still has a socialized education system that also provides some mobility to the high-scoring test takers. When these students arrive in the best universities of the country, their education, already free of tuition, is often further subsidized with scholarships. Although the test system that affords access to higher education has often been rightfully criticized and has also been at the center of political controversy in Turkey, it seems to still engender enough regional and class mobility to provide a diverse campus environment in every way, albeit skewed toward the most prestigious public universities in Western cities like Istanbul, Ankara, İzmir, and Eskişehir, along with the metropolitan cities of other regions, such as Diyarbakır and Van.[2] Together with programs like Erasmus that fund semesters in other European campuses, a university education like this not only opens the door to learn from others who might be speaking different languages at home, or worshipping in different ways, or not believing in major religions at all in one's own country; it also familiarizes students with people and cultures beyond what they consider their homeland. And one of the key aspects of this system, I believe, is that although the upper-class families can always bolster their children's chances by hiring more tutors, the access to quality public education remains almost completely free in Turkey, and therefore reachable by young people across the country.

From the early 2010s on, when these same young people graduated from universities like Boğaziçi and faced difficulties in living in their homeland with the values they learned on campus, not only in the classes taught by faculty but also within the collective life among each other in the dorms, student clubs, and student houses, they went to look for it elsewhere, while always having one foot back in their homeland. During the past decade, I listened to many versions of this story of displacement from people born from the mid-1970s through the 1990s. To update my understanding of what draws them to organize solidarity actions with Boğaziçi's resistance now, I talked to some of these alumni across the world as well as read their accounts online. Some themes emerged consistently: the alumni of Boğaziçi as well as other comparable public universities in Turkey have experienced the university as the first place in which they participated in a pluralist collective life, after feeling isolated by the competitive process of preparing for the university exams for several years. They refer to the campus as a place of safety, an oasis, a utopia, a place of belonging that feels like family. When they get together in protests in squares across the world, being in this solidaristic community makes them feel like they are at the South Square (Güney Meydan) again, the main gathering place of the campus where the current resistance for university autonomy is also taking place. While the government, in a populist move, tried to delegitimize these types of experiences as reserved for the privileged, portraying those concerned for Boğaziçi as elites detached from the country's reality, the wide support that the Boğaziçi resistance gained across students and other young people within and outside the country tells a different story. A Turkish doctoral student who studies in New York, who is not herself a Boğaziçi alumna, told me that Boğaziçi is a space of possibility for many, for those who hope to be able to find a place for themselves in society when they can finally return home from abroad, for instance. This is echoed in the account of an engineer who is an alumna of Yıldız Technical University and works in Spain. She says she participated in the protests because she wants to be able to return to a country that respects human rights (*5Harfliler* 2021). Another supporter in Paris, who took part in organizing the solidarity actions there, says that the Boğaziçi resistance has become the voice of those who had to leave their countries, and not just of the constituents of Boğaziçi (*5Harfliler* 2021). A former faculty member who now lives and works in New York confirmed this sense that Boğaziçi symbolizes a space of hope and possibility for many in Turkey—people tend to project their aspirations to it—and witnessing the last remaining institution that had managed to stay relatively autonomous from the regime now being brought under political control affected many who felt this way. As opposed to being elites, he explains, many alumni who are organizing solidarity protests with their alma mater across the world come from humble backgrounds: it is high-quality public universities in Turkey like Boğaziçi that afforded them the opportunities they got in life, and they wish for the country to be able to provide the same for future generations as well.

The status of Boğaziçi as a symbol of something larger than itself also rang true for the exiled academic with whom I discussed his impressions of the Berlin protests: he informed me that the Boğaziçi solidarity protests engendered new connections between the different generations of migrants and exiles from Turkey, erasing the much talked about divide between the so-called new wave and the old-timers in the city, the reasons for which I have explained above. According to him, people as young as twenty, mostly recent arrivals working on their graduate degrees, and older generations, some of whom are as old as eighty and had taken part in Turkey's iteration of 1968 in the universities and factories, resolved their differences in language and politics during the weekly gatherings that featured Turkish and Kurdish folk songs and dances, live performances by musicians, and open classes/lectures by exiled academics. Greek students and members of German left parties such as Die Linke and Die Grünen also participated in these actions. Although the protests included activists from the full spectrum of Turkey's left and social democratic political parties, the collective solidarity with Boğaziçi was at the forefront, and the only flag featured was that of the LGBTI+, whose struggle is at the center of the resistance at Boğaziçi itself (Busi 2021). In this vein, he described it as a "miniature Gezi [uprising]" where decision making was horizontal, and differences among groups were patiently and respectfully negotiated. Arguably the biggest international solidarity group with recent and direct connections to Boğaziçi and other universities in Turkey, the Berlin protests even featured a replica of an art exhibit that was on display on the Boğaziçi campus before it was removed by the police. The collective in Berlin went on to organize actions in solidarity with the imprisoned members of parliament from the pro-Kurdish People's Democratic Party (HDP), and they participated in May Day actions and protested femicides in Turkey. As such, it seems like the protests in solidarity with Boğaziçi in Berlin were an extension of those within Turkey, as the struggle for the university's autonomy turned into a focal point for the resistance against various ongoing antidemocratic practices in Turkey, encroaching on increasingly more numerous aspects of life from the political to the social and private.

In Turkey, many of us who were around Boğaziçi and other universities that afforded similar opportunities learned a form of collective life that we carried with us to the places to which we emigrated. The practice of organizing among ourselves rapidly and democratically around a cause, whether it be political, such as the student occupation of a space rented out to Starbucks on campus in the 2010s, which was then replaced by a student lounge, or about student life issues, such as the displacement of club rooms, stayed with many of us for longer than we had anticipated. Abroad, we created collective living spaces like the student apartments on campus, where we read, discussed ideas, lived together with our differences, learned each other's languages, and supported each other's political, professional, and academic endeavors by collectivizing our resources. Our insistence in holding on to each other, and to others similarly exiled from their homes in Southern Europe, the Middle East, Africa, Asia, the Caribbean, and Latin America under neoliberal political and economic conditions, continues to create new geographies of solidarity.

Academic Freedom, Democracy, and International Solidarity under Authoritarian Neoliberalism

There is a second reason the Boğaziçi resistance resonated internationally and beyond the groups that have migrated from Turkey. During the neoliberal era in the United States and in Europe, higher education has increasingly been privatized and academic work has become precarious.[3] Despite the questionable conditions of academic freedom within North America itself, where women, people of color, and politically engaged scholars face some pressure from academic institutions,[4] where public education is increasingly under pressure from right-wing populists (Illing 2021), and where university administrators are not elected, the resonance of Boğaziçi protests for university autonomy and in defense of democratic structures have been somewhat limited. And since the town/gown divide in the United States is already quite stark, the resonance of Boğaziçi protests remained within academic circles who are already in constant dialogue with the Boğaziçi faculty and alumni, at the universities where many former students and current faculty have received their graduate degrees or are currently studying or employed. In addition to the Boğaziçi alumni, those organizing the panels and discussions were groups like Academics for Peace–North America and Research Institute on Turkey, the two remaining organizations including people who have been the locus of international solidarity with Turkey's dissidents in North America during the past five to ten years. A surprisingly large protest in New York was organized and attended by a mix of Boğaziçi alumni in New York / New Jersey and a subset of the intellectual, cultural, and art worker milieu that has been displaced from Turkey. One exception to these somewhat insular circles might be the larger Middle East scholars' community in North America, where we have an opportunity to become more familiar with issues in other Middle Eastern countries, for example through channels like the ezine *Jadaliyya* or the Middle East Studies Association (MESA). A member of MESA told me that she thinks the prestigious position of Boğaziçi in the international academic community has played a role in the visibility of the struggle for the university's autonomy. This idea was confirmed in published interviews with Boğaziçi faculty, who add that the Boğaziçi resistance has afforded a renewed visibility to the ongoing authoritarian conditions in Turkey overall (Altuğ and Gökarıksel 2021). Many of the academics I have spoken to underlined that it is rare to see faculty resisting together with students, and that given the authoritarian attacks on the university and other social institutions in Brazil, France, and India, as well as the United States, it can resonate with more people than before.

Both insights were shared by another faculty member I spoke to, who is an Academic for Peace exiled from Turkey and now living and working in a small university town in Germany. Residing outside the major cities in Germany where far-right movements like AfD and the Querdenken are thriving, and where some of these groups are even organized among the senior faculty, she observes the right-wing populist threats against students and academic life in Germany more closely, as well as the students' reactions. Coupled with the neoliberal erosion of universities in Germany at an unprecedented scale, she relates that the students and the younger, precarious academic staff at the universities in the German periphery are looking for ways to resist this double encroachment. For this group of students and precarious academic staff, some of whom have arrived in Germany from war zones or are from migrant families, she says, the Boğaziçi resistance has been inspiring, especially because of the collaboration between the students and faculty, as it points to possibilities for changing things at the universities in Germany. The students and academics have been following the resistance to authoritarian conditions in Turkey and India, and in this instance student collectives in Germany organized a solidarity debate together with students from the UK and Boğaziçi, with faculty acting as facilitators, learning more about each other's contexts and resistance practices (Mueller 2021). Academics and students from Germany, the UK, Turkey, India, Lebanon, Italy, and Greece participated in these solidarity debates. More critical approaches to German solidarity practices, for example, one account from Cologne, and others I have spoken to, cite a disconnection between native and migrant dissidents, where the latter can feel like they are being spoken for or that the "native" left is unable to see the current similarities between the authoritarian regime in Turkey and the political problems of Germany, displacing the former to a backward past that they assume Germany has overcome, which feels disingenuous while fascism has been rising globally (*5Harfliler* 2021).

At times, I have felt the same discomfort working with our colleagues in the United States on these issues, although in the post-Trump era, the liberal-left bloc in the United States had to abandon some of its illusions regarding American democracy, owing to the mishaps that have come to the surface during the former presidency. Furthermore, one of the best remedies for this is to organize in solidarity across various struggles where possible, as in the current example of Black-Palestinian solidarity in the United States (Ziauddin 2021), which has been forged in both political and academic circles (Seikaly et al. 2017).

While the conditions of rising authoritarianism and right-wing populism, coupled with the devastating effects of decades of neoliberal rule, has displaced many of us across the world, it has also created conditions for us to learn from each other's struggles and to collaborate. Students and increasingly precarious academic workers spread across the world during the last decade's wars, and conditions of instability are an important part of the struggle against continued neoliberal and authoritarian assaults on public and academic life. The international mobilization in solidarity with Boğaziçi shows us some of the fault lines that emerged during the past decade both at home and abroad, which I tried to sketch above. Increasing collaboration within and across borders, as well as among faculty, students, and those outside the universities, might be the catalyst for change globally toward more democratic universities and, hopefully, publics.

Notes

1   To clarify, I am not arguing that these problems do not exist in Europe. However, these are the existing conditions of Turkey that people currently seek to escape from. While they might find some respite from these problems in the West/North, many also encounter racism after migrating.

2   For more on what could have been in the universities in the majority-Kurdish cities, and what went wrong, see Özok Gündoğan 2020.

3   For neoliberalization of higher education in the United States, see Brown 2017; for Europe, see Vatansever 2020.

4   For an overview of this issue regarding Middle East politics, see Deeb and Winegar 2016 and Petersen-Overton 2011. For academic freedom issues across disciplines, see Associated Press in New York 2021, Eltagouri 2017, American Association of University Professors et al. 2017.

References

5Harfliler. 2021. "Dünya'dan Boğaziçi'ne Dayanışmayla." February 11. www.5harfliler.com/dunyadan-bogazicine-dayanismayla/?fbclid=IwAR1BxUN5DYgtaa6IgDS_OZInpri-J8k1lT_FoZUWjo1WAwyTRBEGbm9T5oXQ.

Altuğ, Seda, and Saygun Gökarıksel. 2021. "An Interview with Boğaziçi Faculty on Contemporary Protests." *Jadaliyya*, March 5. www.jadaliyya.com/Details/42457/An-Interview-with-Bo%C4%9Fazi%C3%A7i-University-Students-on-Contemporary-Protests-42457.

American Association of University Professors, American Federation of Teachers, and Association of American Colleges and Universities. 2017. "Taking a Stand against Harassment, Part of the Broader Threat to Higher Education." September 7. www.aaup.org/sites /default/files/Statement%20on%20Harassment.pdf.

Associated Press in New York. 2021. "US Scholars form Academic Freedom Alliance to Defend Free Expression." *Guardian*, March 8. www.theguardian.com/us-news/2021/mar/08 academic-freedom-alliance-college-university-free-speech.

Brown, Wendy. 2017. *Undoing the Demos: Neoliberalism's Stealth Revolution*. New York: Zone.

Busi, Alessia. 2021. "Boğaziçi University under Attack: Resistance against the Violence of Heterosexualism." *Security Praxis*, March 23. securitypraxis.eu/bogazici-university-under -attack-resistance-against-the-violence-of-heterosexualism/.

Deeb, Lara, and Jessica Winegar. 2016. *Anthropology's Politics: Disciplining the Middle East*. Stanford, CA: Stanford University Press.

Eltagouri, Marwa. 2017. "Professor Who Tweeted, 'All I Want for Christmas Is White Genocide,' Resigns after Year of Threats." *Washington Post*, December 29. www.washington post.com/news/grade-point/wp/2017/12/29/professor-who-tweeted-all-i-want -for-christmas-is-white-genocide-resigns-after-year-of-threats/.

Illing, Sean. 2021. "Is There an Uncontroversial Way to Teach America's Racist History?" *Vox*, June 11. www.vox.com/policy-and-politics/22464746/critical-race-theory-anti-racism -jarvis-givens.

Özok Gündoğan, Nilay. 2020. "Kurdology in Turkey: Barometer of the Peace Process." *Jadali-yya*, November 2. www.jadaliyya.com/Details/41947/Kurdology-in-Turkey-Barometer -of-the-%E2%80%9CPeace-Process%E2%80%9D.

Petersen-Overton, Kristofer J. 2011. "Academic Freedom and Palestine: A Personal Account." *Arab Studies Quarterly* 33, nos. 3–4: 256–67.

Seikaly, Sherene, Noura Erakat, Judith Butler, Samera Esmeir, and Angela Davis. 2017. "Thinking Palestine Intersectionally." *Status* (podcast), November 19. www.statushour .com/en/Interview/1290.

Telli, Asli. 2021. "Whither Universitas?—A Solidarity Debate among Students Across Borders." *Wissenschaftler*innen für den Frieden*, April 23. academicsforpeace-germany.org /2021/04/23/a-brief-review-from-the-organizers/.

Vatansever, Aslı. 2020. *At the Margins of Academia: Exile, Precariousness, and Subjectivity*. Leiden: Brill.

Ziauddin, Sharmeen. 2021. "What Do Black Lives Matter and Palestine Solidarity Have in Common?" *Open Democracy*, May 25. www.opendemocracy.net/en/north-africa-west -asia/what-do-black-lives-matter-and-palestine-solidarity-have-common/.

Notes on Contributors

Badia Ahad is professor of English at Loyola University Chicago and author of *Freud Upside Down: African American Literature and Psychoanalytic Culture* (2010) and *Afro-Nostalgia: Feeling Good in Contemporary Black Culture* (2021).

Margo Natalie Crawford is the Edmund J. and Louise W. Kahn Professor of English at the University of Pennsylvania. She is author of *Dilution Anxiety and the Black Phallus* (2008), *Black Post-Blackness: The Black Arts Movement and Twenty-First Century Aesthetics* (2017), and *What Is African American Literature?* (2021).

Eve Dunbar is professor of English at Vassar College (NY). She is the author of *Black Regions of the Imagination: African American Writers Between the Nation and the World* (2012). Her work has been published in academic journals such as *American Literature, African American Review, American Literary History*, and various public venues.

Julius B. Fleming Jr. is an assistant professor in the Department of English at the University of Maryland, College Park, where he specializes in African American literary and cultural production and performance studies. He is currently completing his first book manuscript, titled "Black Patience: Performance, Civil Rights, and the Unfinished Project of Emancipation," which will be published in March 2022. His articles have appeared in journals like *American Literature, American Literary History*, and *Southern Quarterly*.

Zeynep Gambetti is an independent scholar who taught as associate professor of political theory at Boğaziçi University from 2000 to 2019. Her research interests include nineteenth- and twentieth-century continental thought, critical theory, and theories of collective agency and public space. Inspired primarily by Arendt, Marx, and Foucault, her theoretical work focuses on contemporary forms of violence and resistance. Among her publications are *Rhetorics of Insecurity: Belonging and Violence in the Neoliberal Era* (coedited with Marcial Godoy-Anativia; 2013) and *Vulnerability in Resistance: Politics, Feminism, Theory* (coedited with Judith Butler and Leticia Sabsay; 2016).

Tao Leigh Goffe is assistant professor of Africana studies and feminist, gender, and sexuality studies at Cornell University. She is the author of articles recently published in *Small Axe, Amerasia Journal* and *Women and Performance*. Her book "Black Capital, Chinese Debt" is forthcoming.

Saygun Gökarıksel is an assistant professor of anthropology at the Department of Sociology, Boğaziçi University. His writing and research interests concern the themes of law, history, and politics, particularly the critical Marxian and decolonial approaches to transitional justice, memory, violence, and international revolutionary and liberatory politics. His current research focuses on the judicial and ethical-political reckoning with the communist past in Eastern Europe in the post–Cold War context of neoliberal globalization and right-wing authoritarian populism. His writings have appeared in journals and blogs including *Comparative Studies in Society and History, South Atlantic Quarterly, Dialectical Anthropology, Jadaliyya*, and *LeftEast*. He is currently finishing a book manuscript tentatively titled "Moral Autopsy: A Critical Anthropology of Reckoning with the Communist Past in Poland's Neoliberal Democracy."

Habiba Ibrahim is associate professor of English at the University of Washington and author of *Troubling the Family: The Promise of Personhood and the Rise of Multiracialism* (2012) and *Black Age: Oceanic Lifespans and the Time of Black Life* (2021).

Shaun Myers is an assistant professor of English at the University of Pittsburgh. Her writings include articles in *American Literary History* (2019), *African American Literature in Transition, 1980–1990* (forthcoming), and *Los Angeles Review of Books* (2021). She is completing a book manuscript, "Black Anaesthetics: African American Narrative Beyond Man," and continuing work on a second book about the aesthetics of black transit.

Cenk Özbay (www.cenkozbay.com) is an associate professor of sociology and gender studies at Sabancı University, where he specializes in masculinities, sexualities, and urban culture. He is the author of *Queering Sexualities in Turkey: Gay Men, Male Prostitutes, and the City* (2017) and coeditor of *The Making of Neoliberal Turkey* (2016).

Kaneesha Cherelle Parsard writes about the legacies of slavery and emancipation in the Caribbean and broader Americas, with an emphasis on how gender and sexuality structure race, labor, and capital. She is working on a book project titled, "An Illicit Wage." She is assistant professor of English at the University of Chicago.

Frederick C. Staidum Jr. is an assistant professor of English at Loyola University Chicago. His research interrogates representations of race, gender, and sexuality alongside the symbiosis of liberalism and coloniality within late eighteenth- and nineteenth-century Atlantic literature and visual culture. His work has appeared in *The Black Scholar* and has been supported by the Institute for Citizens and Scholars, the National Endowment for the Humanities, and the Andrew W. Mellon Foundation. He is currently finishing a book project titled "Landscapes of Lack, Landscapes of Excess: New Orleans, Geographies of Difference, and Atlantic Liberalism."

Sarah Stefana Smith is a visual artist, scholar, and assistant professor of gender studies at Mount Holyoke College. Smith received a PhD from the University of Toronto and an MFA from Goddard College. Their research examines the intersections of visuality, queerness, and affect in Black art and culture. Smith has published in *The Black Scholar, Women and Performance,* and the *Palgrave Handbook on Race and the Arts in Education,* among others. Smith is currently working on their book project, "Poetics of Bafflement: Aesthetics of Frustration." For more information, visit www.sarahstefanasmith.com.

Cihan Tekay is a PhD candidate in anthropology at the Graduate Center, City University of New York. Her current research is a historical ethnography of imperialism and electrification between Europe and the Ottoman Empire. More broadly, she is interested in understanding the effects of capitalism on people's relationships to each other and to their environment. She teaches as second faculty at the Brooklyn Institute for Social Research, where she provides an anthropologist's perspective on economic systems. She has been writing and speaking publicly in Turkish and English on gender, war, protest, higher education, arts, and the environment. She is a coeditor of the Turkey page for *Jadaliyya.*

DOI 10.1215/00382876-9561685

Keep up to date on new scholarship

Issue alerts are a great way to stay current on all the cutting-edge scholarship from your favorite Duke University Press journals. This free service delivers tables of contents directly to your inbox, informing you of the latest groundbreaking work as soon as it is published.

To sign up for issue alerts:

1. Visit **dukeu.press/register** and register for an account. You do not need to provide a customer number.

2. After registering, visit **dukeu.press/alerts**.

3. Go to "Latest Issue Alerts" and click on "Add Alerts."

4. Select as many publications as you would like from the pop-up window and click "Add Alerts."

read.dukeupress.edu/journals

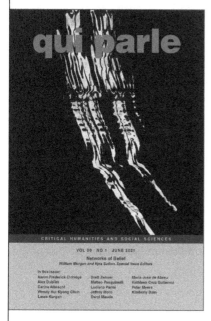

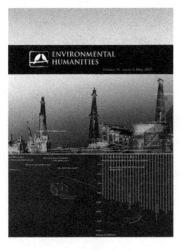